# Latin America in a New World

# Latin America
# in a
# New World

*edited by*
## Abraham F. Lowenthal
## Gregory F. Treverton

AN INTER-AMERICAN DIALOGUE BOOK

## Westview Press

BOULDER • SAN FRANCISCO • OXFORD

Copyright © 1994 by Westview Press, Inc.

Published in 1994 in the United States of America by Westview Press, Inc., 5500 Central Avenue, Boulder, Colorado 80301-2877, and in the United Kingdom by Westview Press, 36 Lonsdale Road, Summertown, Oxford OX2 7EW

Library of Congress Cataloging-in-Publication Data
Latin America in a New World / edited by Abraham F. Lowenthal, Gregory
F. Treverton.
    p.   cm. — (An Inter-American Dialogue book)
    Includes bibliographical references and index.
    ISBN 0-8133-8670-5 (hardcover). — ISBN 0-8133-8671-3
(pbk.)
    1. Latin America—Foreign relations—1980–  .  2. Latin America—
Relations—Foreign countries.   I. Lowenthal, Abraham F.
II. Treverton, Gregory F.   III. Series.
F1414.2.L3283   1994
327.8'009'045—dc20                                                      93-47321
                                                                          CIP

Printed and bound in the United States of America

The paper used in this publication meets the requirements
of the American National Standard for Permanence of Paper
for Printed Library Materials Z39.48-1984.

10     9     8     7     6     5     4     3     2

# Contents

## Part One
### Assessing the Impact of Global Change

## Part Two
### The Prospect for New Partners

# Acknowledgments

The contributions to this volume were commissioned by the Inter-American Dialogue as part of its ongoing effort to illuminate key issues in U.S.–Latin American relations and to develop constructive policy responses to regional problems. Founded in 1982, the Inter-American Dialogue is both a forum for sustained exchange among leaders of the Western Hemisphere and an independent, nonpartisan policy research center, focusing on Western Hemisphere political and economic relations. The Dialogue's 100 members—from the United States, Canada, and 16 Latin American and Caribbean countries—include 5 former presidents, as well as prominent political, business, labor, academic, media, military, professional, and religious leaders.

This book is the result of a special Dialogue project, for which we served as codirectors. On behalf of all participants in this collaborative exercise, we express our deep appreciation to the Pew Charitable Trusts and especially to Kevin F.F. Quigley, director of Pew's public policy programs. Pew's support made it possible for the authors to meet twice as a group and for us to commission background research, to conduct interviews in many capitals, and to exchange drafts and ideas with our colleagues over an extended period. We are also grateful to others who participated in the project's seminars: François Bourricaud, Michael Desch, the late Fernando Fajnzylber, Gary Gereffi, Wolf Grabendorff, Peter Hakim, Mark Katz, Luis Rubio, Ronaldo Sardenberg, John Stremlau, Viron P. Vaky, Elizabeth Valkenier, Raymond Vernon, Francisco Weffort, John Williamson, and Stephen Wollcock.

We also record here our great appreciation to Alberto Cimadamore, Gregory Corning, Jeffrey Hawkins, David Mefford, Carina Miller, Susan Smolko, and Carol Wise for research assistance; to those who provided logistic and staff support, especially Daniel Broxterman, Christopher Evans, Jennifer Ezell, Tina Gallop, Lorraine Morin, Andrew Oros, and Steven Spiegel; to Linda C. Lowenthal for superb editing of three chapters; to Elizabeth Knowlton of the University of Southern California's Center for International Studies for shepherding the final version through numerous obstacles; and to Barbara Ellington of Westview Press for her interest and patience.

*Abraham F. Lowenthal* & *Gregory F. Treverton*

# Introduction

## Abraham F. Lowenthal
## and Gregory F. Treverton

It is a commonplace—but no less true or important—that the world has been changing remarkably. It is hard to imagine, indeed, that only a few years ago, Europe was still starkly divided at the Berlin Wall, the Soviet Union was almost universally rated a superpower, Nelson Mandela was in jail, the Sandinistas governed Nicaragua, civil war raged in El Salvador, Yugoslavia was a nation at peace, and the notion of a North American Free Trade Area (NAFTA) lay beyond the bounds of realistic policy options.

This volume attempts to analyze how Latin America and its world role have been reshaped by the stunning international developments of the past few years and by the underlying transformations that, in turn, gave rise to such global sea changes. Eighteen contributors—from Latin America, Europe, China, Japan, Russia, and the United States—have worked together to examine the specific meanings for Latin America of the end of the Cold War and the breakup of the former Soviet Union, the expansion of the European Community (EC) and its progress toward enhanced integration, the widespread validation of democratic governance and market economies, the revision of global commercial and financial regimes, the incipient tendency toward regional economic blocs, and the fundamental changes in the world economy, driven by technological innovation.

The book is divided into three parts: broad overviews on inter-American relations after the Cold War; chapters on Latin America's relations with major extrahemispheric regions; and essays on the policy responses by the nations of the Western Hemisphere, individually and collectively, to the challenges posed by the new world, with all its disorder and variety. These last include briefer comments from the practitioner's perspective by four distinguished

1

Latin American political leaders: Senator José Octavio Bordón of Argentina; Osvaldo Hurtado, former president of Ecuador; Jesús Silva Herzog, Mexico's former finance minister and now its minister of tourism; and Celso Lafer, the former foreign minister of Brazil.

The arguments and emphases of the book's authors differ; some opinions flatly contradict others. We have tried neither to resolve nor to avoid these conflicts but rather to let them stand as authentic expressions of differing takes, from diverse angles, on a moving target.

The target is, indeed, still a moving one; our book is thus necessarily a report of work in progress on a world in change. Nevertheless, several broad themes emerge in the chapters that follow, at least as hypotheses or provocations. Stated most grandly, if the first question is, How much difference has the end of the Cold War made to Latin America? the answer emerging from these chapters is, on the whole, perhaps less than meets the eye. In many respects, the world today reflects the main trends, political and economic, that were already evident before the Cold War's end.

Economically, those trends are striking: Although the variations across the region are significant, the United States is *more* important to almost all of Latin America, not less, than it was twenty years ago—but most of Latin America, Mexico prominently excepted, may be in some ways *less* important to the United States. Politically, if the security anxieties of the Cold War impelled the United States to pay most attention to the countries closest to it (those in Central America and the Caribbean), so, too, may some U.S. attention in the years ahead be focused there again, though for new reasons—immigration and drug trafficking, in particular.

In this context, the chapters of the book's second part primarily describe problems that have not yet materialized—dogs that have not yet barked. Europe's preoccupations with its own east and the capital requirements of the task of rebuilding it constrain its interest and ability to be more than a modestly increasing partner for Latin America. Japan, too, has limited interest in Latin America. It is now internally preoccupied, its external attentions are focused mainly on its own region, and its strategy for the Western Hemisphere continues to revolve around the United States and its market. Russia's internal turmoil makes it an uncertain international actor in general, and it has none of the former Soviet Union's ideological reasons for interest in Latin America. If China's boom continues, that may open some possibilities for expanded commerce with Latin America, but major business with China is a very long-term prospect.

The policy essays in the third part cluster around whether the circumstances of the years ahead bid fair for new—and genuine—partnerships between Latin America and the United States. A yes answer is suggested by the striking turn of Latin America toward democratic politics and more open economies; by the concerns Latin America now holds in common with the United States—especially the battle against narcotics and the quest to safeguard the environment; and by the absence of available interlocutors for any alternative Latin American strategy of international engagement.

But the conversion to U.S.-style free market economics is, as yet, ambiguous and insecure in many Latin American countries. Strong doubt remains about the willingness or ability of several nations, Brazil in particular, to emulate Mexico in seeking full economic integration with the United States. Moreover, even where values are shared, as with democratic governance, formulating policies designed to promote them may well be as contentious an undertaking in the future as it was in the past. And in the end, the economic stakes of the United States remain highly diversified, arguing against an exclusive partnership with Latin America.

## Assessing the Impact of Global Change

Which global changes are most relevant to Latin America, and how have they been affecting the region?

Richard H. Ullman argues that the Cold War's end is making the Latin American–U.S. relationship both less intense and less conflictive than it has been for many decades. U.S. military interventionism in Latin America will diminish in the 1990s because Washington's security and geopolitical preoccupations have declined and because the negative consequences of interventionism for the U.S. capacity to achieve other foreign policy objectives have become more obvious. In the Western Hemisphere, the United States is increasingly concerned with issues—such as immigration, narcotics, arms control, border conflicts, and the environment—that are not susceptible to unilateral action; these require greater inter-American cooperation and demand a strengthening of hemisphere-wide institutions.

Jorge G. Castañeda takes a much more pessimistic view of the impact on Latin America of the Cold War's end. Castañeda believes that U.S. interventionism in Latin America will continue, albeit for new reasons: promoting democracy, preserving the environment, and fighting drugs. He suggests, moreover, that Latin America will have less international leverage and more restricted autonomy than it enjoyed during the Cold War years. This is so, he argues, because Latin America will not be able to play the superpowers off against each other and because it will be disadvantaged in the international competition for capital. With the partial exception of Mexico, which seems to have finally captured the attention of the United States, Latin America in the 1990s may find itself in a sadly paradoxical bind, Castañeda suggests, with

greater geopolitical leeway than it had during the Cold War but with fewer resources and much tighter economic constraints.

Helio Jaguaribe recognizes that the new status of the United States as the
world's only remaining superpower inevitably restricts Latin America's international options. But Jaguaribe observes that the United States itself is no
longer an economic superpower, that it has recently felt able to project its military power only against very weak rivals, that it faces grave internal problems
of its own, and that it still lacks a coherent and strategic worldview appropriate
to the new world situation. Latin Americans should understand, therefore,
that the United States is by no means self-sufficient and that in the 1990s,
Washington will likely recognize a need for better relations with Latin America. This is particularly true because both the United States and Latin America
are now of less interest to the countries of Western Europe, which are fasci-
nated both by the European Community's future and by their new relations
with Russia and the nations of Central and Eastern Europe.

In these circumstances, both the United States and Latin America can gain
from progress toward regional integration, such as the Mercosur (Mercado
del Sur) arrangement among the Southern Cone countries. But difficult, concrete issues will have to be faced in order to reconcile expanded hemispheric
trade liberalization within Mercosur and other such areas with the temporary
protection needed to nurture technological advance and build domestic industry.

Albert Fishlow examines global and regional economic changes and focuses
on the as yet unresolved choices that will determine whether Latin America
will generally be included in an expanding world economy in the 1990s or
whether much of the region will decline. He stresses that Latin America's
structural adjustments and changes in policy during the past decade or so have
made it a different region economically and that its leaders are now better prepared to consider what strategy of international integration is most likely to
generate sustainable growth in the future: diversification of trade within the
framework of the General Agreement on Tariffs and Trade (GATT), combined with subregional commercial arrangements, or emphasis on a prospective Western Hemisphere free trade zone. Latin America's options, in turn,
are partially limited by U.S. policy, still being shaped as part of the Clinton administration's sharp focus on rejuvenating the U.S. economy and restoring international trade competitiveness.

Fishlow's prescription, a bit short of a confident prediction, is that both
Latin America and the United States should gain from a Western Hemisphere
free trade agreement, one that integrates Latin America into the world economy and revives capital formation while also beating back protectionist tendencies in the United States and boosting U.S. exports. Neither Latin America nor the United States would gain, however, by carrying a regional

approach too far; regionalism and globalism must be reconciled, and partners must be sought in other parts of the world.

## The Prospect for New Partners

With the Cold War rivalry no longer relevant and with a Soviet counterpoint to U.S. influence no longer available to Latin America, what are the prospects for Latin American efforts to dilute U.S. dominance by building new partnerships with countries outside the Western Hemisphere?

Alberto van Klaveren assesses European–Latin American relations in the light of Europe's moves toward a single market, the end of its Cold War division, and Latin America's own diverse paths. During the 1970s and 1980s, van Klaveren points out, Europe's economic presence in Latin America grew, but the region nevertheless did not rate much priority in European foreign policy; this asymmetry led Latin Americans to push, unsuccessfully for the most part, for greater political attention and economic assistance from Europe.

As van Klaveren notes, European economic involvement and political engagement in Latin America diminished during the 1980s, despite strenuous diplomatic efforts by Latin leaders. But during the past few years, although European interest in the Western Hemisphere was expected to wane, there has actually been a growing European commercial and investment involvement in Latin America—mainly by Spain, Italy, and the United Kingdom. Ultimately, the future of Latin American–European relations will depend more upon trends in Latin America than those in Europe. Ideological "special relationships" will no longer significantly affect these ties, but concrete opportunities for mutual gain could strengthen relations between the regions—or, more precisely, between specific countries in the two regions.

Barbara Stallings and Kotaro Horisaka collaborate in a detailed study of the changing patterns of Japanese–Latin American relations. Long linked to a few Latin American countries through commerce and migration, Japan became much more generally and deeply engaged in the Americas during the 1960s and 1970s. Japan became the second-largest trading partner (after the United States) for many Latin American countries, its banks became the largest holders of Latin American debt, its firms invested extensively in some Latin American countries and sectors, and its government became the most important lender to Latin America, both bilaterally and through contributions to international financial institutions. With the collapse of the Soviet bloc and Europe's self-absorption, Latin Americans naturally looked to Japan for a further expansion of this involvement, and their leaders began to visit Japan.

But the rising Latin interest in Japan during the 1980s was countered by a waning Japanese enthusiasm for Latin America. Japan found the region's economic growth disappointing and its political instability disconcerting; related doubts, reinforced by mounting economic and political difficulties at home, have contributed to a marked retrenchment in Japan's Latin American involvements, especially in Brazil, which was previously the prime focus of Japanese engagement. Trade with Latin America is no longer significant for Japan, Japanese investment has dropped, and banks have begun to sell their Latin American portfolios. Yet there is incipient and growing Japanese investment in Mexico, Chile, and Venezuela, as well as enlarged Japanese government assistance to several countries: Bolivia, Paraguay, Peru, and several Central American and Caribbean nations. As with Europe, Japan's future involvement will depend mainly on Latin American policies—when concrete reforms and incentives make a particular country or sector attractive to the Japanese, especially if it is clear to Japan's leaders that their involvement will be welcomed by the U.S. government. Japan thus remains a significant factor in contemporary Latin America, with the potential to play a still more important role in those countries that get their own houses in order and provide pragmatic economic opportunities for Japanese firms.

Sergo Mikoyan reviews the history of and prospects for Russia's relations with the countries of Latin America and the Caribbean. From 1917 to 1991, the Soviet Union had an ideological and political presence in Latin America—more in certain countries and times, less in others—and some limited economic activity, although the degree of Soviet influence was always far less than both U.S. policymakers and Soviet officials claimed and probably believed. Soviet aid to Cuba, Nicaragua, and other friendly states and movements was real and not negligible, but it was never crucial or decisive for any Latin American nation—not even for Cuba, much less others.

In the aftermath of 1989 and especially after 1991 and the disintegration of the former Soviet Union, Mikoyan argues, there has been a general tendency, both in the Western Hemisphere and in Russia, to minimize Russia's continuing involvements in the Americas and to underestimate its likely future role. Indeed, for a while, Russian officials were so desperately eager to ingratiate themselves with the United States that they retreated from Latin American engagements, especially in Cuba, with unseemly haste. But this attitude of "infantile accommodation" with Washington has already ended, Mikoyan contends. He projects a nontrivial future for Russian–Latin American relations: a still significant Russian engagement with Cuba, focused primarily on economic interests; increased commercial exchange and some continuing political involvement in Central America; expanding commercial ties and technological cooperation with Brazil; and growing trade with several Latin American countries that have economies that complement Russia's: Argentina, Colombia, Ecuador, Peru, Uruguay, and perhaps others.

Feng Xu argues that China's ties with Latin America are largely derivative, primarily determined by the respective relations of China, on the one hand, and the Latin American countries, on the other, with the industrial North. In the post–Cold War world, a few Latin American countries will be of somewhat greater interest to China than in the past because of their relatively advanced economic level and political stability, their growing international influence, and the marked complementarity of their economies with China's own. For their part, several Latin American countries—Argentina, Brazil, Chile, perhaps Mexico, and, for different reasons, Cuba—may also seek closer relations with China: as a potential market, as a source of capital, and as a possible ally on broad North-South issues related to the international economic and political order, especially matters like technology transfer, debt reduction, and trade regimes. Brazil and Cuba have the most to gain from closer ties with China for they are the least likely to benefit from current moves toward North American integration and a prospective regionwide free trade zone.

## Framing Policy Responses

Does the end of the Cold War really open the prospect of new partnerships between North America and Latin America?

Andrew Hurrell broadens the discussion of regionalism by analyzing the factors that explain the recent revival of Latin American interest in some form of an inter-American hemispheric bloc and those likely to limit the growth of inter-American regionalism in the long run. He emphasizes that Latin American countries have been pushed toward hemispheric cooperation by the worldwide turn to economic liberalism, by the evident costs of confrontation with the United States, and by the perceived absence of alternative partners. But there are disadvantages and dilemmas for many countries in turning to regionalist approaches on economic security, environmental, and political issues. Furthermore, it is by no means clear that the apparent current interest of the United States in Western Hemisphere regionalism will be long sustained for it contradicts U.S. interests in broader trade relations and the logic of economic globalization. Crosscutting and countervailing pressures are thus at work, pushing in contradictory fashion for subregional integration within Latin America, for an inter-American hemispheric bloc, and for heterogenous international linkages of many kinds. The dominant pattern for the 1990s is not yet established.

Heraldo Muñoz draws both on his academic background and on his diplomatic experience to assess the role of the Organization of American States (OAS) in a new era. Although the OAS was born during the Cold War and primarily as a response to it and although it became increasingly irrelevant during the 1980s, the end of the Cold War has not further weakened the organization, as might have been expected, but has actually given it a new lease on life. The countries of the Western Hemisphere are now redefining the organization's purposes and potential around a new regional agenda of shared concerns: trade, security, drugs, the environment, and the promotion of democratic governance.

This last issue—the defense and promotion of democracy—will determine the significance of the OAS in the 1990s. The end of the Cold War and the nearly hemisphere-wide consensus on democratic ideas has freed the organization to play a role in this field, but the tough cases of Haiti and Peru show how hard it will be to translate broad convergence into implemented, multilateral practice. It is too soon to tell, therefore, whether the member governments can seize this chance to build a strong and effective hemispheric institution.

Jorge I. Domínguez focuses sharply on the one Latin American nation most affected by the end of the Cold War and the former Soviet Union's collapse: Fidel Castro's Cuba. The fundamental premises of Havana's foreign policy and international relationships for more than thirty years have been shattered, for the Soviet Union's collapse has caused a drastic reduction in the economic resources and political support available for Cuba: economic aid subsidies, technical assistance, free weapons, and political solidarity. To adjust to this new world, Cuba has had to alter its foreign economic policy very significantly and rapidly: promoting tourism, welcoming foreign investment, accepting the withdrawal of the Russian military presence, and strengthening commercial and political relations with China. Except for residual arrangements with Russia and continuing hostility with the United States, Cuba's foreign policies in the 1990s are, by and large, like those of other Caribbean nations—subject to the same narrow constraints imposed by geography, economics, and history. What remains to be seen is whether Castro can and will take the next step toward normalizing Cuba's international situation by opening up his country's domestic politics—or whether Castro himself will be replaced. In either case, Havana's policies later in the 1990s are not likely to be too dramatically different from what they are today. Cuba's biggest adjustments to a new world situation have already been made, Dominguez suggests, and even a post-Castro Cuba will find its international options and possibilities extremely limited.

The four Latin American statesmen who have contributed to this volume all emphasize the striking changes in attitudes that have occurred in Latin America—not just the revival and perhaps surprising resilience of democracy but also the end of import-substituting development and the consonant turn toward more open economies. They also mention the hopeful signs that the "lost decade" of stagnation and debt is ending, with growth resuming.

Yet they also puzzle over certain issues. Renewed growth has come to only some countries of the region, and it could be snuffed out if, for instance, tightness in global capital markets drives interest rates upward again, putting debt front and center on Latin America's agenda once more. Democracy, though resilient, remains challenged by the need to produce tangible results for common citizens everywhere and by terrorists or drug traffickers in several countries. And few nations have followed the example of Mexico or Chile in reducing bloated state bureaucracies and opening their economies to international competition while maintaining a strong state. These authors argue that Latin America needs not just a smaller state but a more efficient one. It remains to be seen whether Latin America can transform the roles of its states without reproducing the inefficient protectionism of the past.

These Latin American leaders also emphasize a final theme: responsibility. In the past, they say, Latin Americans were tempted to blame their failures on external factors—the United States in particular or, more generally, the unfairness of prevailing interactions between the industrial North and the developing South. Now, though, most Latin American leaders accept the proposition that the nations of their region must assume the responsibility for progress in Latin America. And policies that reflect that responsibility must be implemented and sustained.

In a brief final chapter, commenting on the prospects for U.S.–Latin American relations in the 1990s, Abraham Lowenthal points out that these relations depend not only on Latin America's economic and political trajectory but also—and perhaps even more directly—on the fate of U.S. attempts to confront an accumulated agenda of domestic concerns. Many Latin American nations are now looking to Washington for partnerships, but it is still unclear whether the United States is ready for hemispheric accords, especially if they are exclusive or exclusionary. One of the many questions about the new world in which Latin America finds itself in the 1990s is whether the United States will lead a bold hemispheric adjustment to changed circumstances or whether it will revert, instead, to policies that are protectionist, restrictionist, punitive, and unilateral. The answer to that question will have great significance for the countries of Latin America and the Caribbean.

# PART ONE

*Assessing the Impact
of Global Change*

# 1

# The United States, Latin America, and the World After the Cold War

## *Richard H. Ullman*

For the relationship between the United States and Latin America, the Cold War was both a glue and a caustic: It served to bond the northern and southern parts of the hemisphere together, but it did so in a way that burned. The political transformation that began with the collapse of the Soviet Union's Eastern European empire during the summer and autumn of 1989 has begun to loosen the bonds and denature the caustic. The hemispheric relationship should therefore be more benign than it was during the years of the Cold War. It may, however, be a relationship of benign neglect.

Despite their protestations of concern for hemispheric solidarity, policy-makers in Washington have not seemed to regard Latin America as very important since the 1920s, certainly not by comparison with Europe, Asia, and the Middle East. In part, that attitude has been a reflection of economic realities. It has also reflected geopolitics: Like Africa, Latin America was more distant from the Soviet Union, the dark star at the center of the geopolitical cosmos of the administration of every U.S. president from Harry Truman through George Bush. Even more than the globe-circling capabilities of Soviet missiles, it was the Red Army's relative proximity to the territory of vital allies that made political leaders in the United States and elsewhere sit up and take notice.

Distance from direct Soviet military danger notwithstanding, as long as the Cold War lasted, Latin America nevertheless occupied a special place on U.S. presidents' lists of what could hurt them. The only development more calami-

tous than "losing" a Latin American country to communism was having it
then become a base for Soviet forces. With the exception of Cuba—and even
then, only on a most limited basis[1]—that never happened. But Guatemala, the
Dominican Republic, Chile, El Salvador, Nicaragua, and Grenada were all, at
one time or another, the objects of Washington's special anxiety and targets
for (mostly covert) action. Losing a country to communism or even to Communist influence had large domestic political costs. And because of the potential repercussions in U.S. domestic politics, the specter of communism haunt-
ing the hemisphere was credited with a potency far beyond its feeble
accomplishments. "When your Senators and Congressmen come down
here," a Nicaraguan journalist told North American visitors in 1983, "they
are interested in their own politics, not in ours."[2]

The end of the Cold War drains these images of their poisons. Third World
revolutionaries now find Washington and Moscow coordinating their policies
on issues where once they automatically chose opposite sides. Marxism-Leninism is now discredited in the polity that first proclaimed it to be official
state dogma. If any ideology is currently promoted by the former Soviet
Union, it is an anachronistic and exclusivist Russian nationalism—an expression of aspiration that a few Latin American nationalists might admire, but
scarcely one with transcendental appeal. Insurgents within the hemisphere no
doubt will continue to use the rhetoric of worldwide solidarity with workers
and peasants. Importantly, however, they will no longer have at their elbows
the promise of Soviet support that made so many officials in Washington so
nervous so often. And no longer will those same officials be able to plausibly
justify military assistance to repressive Latin American regimes by claiming
that a lack of aid would allow Moscow another foothold in the hemisphere.

## The Global Structure of Power

During the remainder of the 1990s, the effects of the changes in the international system in which the United States and the nations of Latin America
now find themselves should become plain, but their outlines are already evident. Academic analysts earn their pay by discerning, within complex phe-
nomena, underlying patterns of behavior that can be explained with simple
models. And through most of the forty-five years of the Cold War, the dominant analytical model of the international structure and the relationships of
power within it depicted a bipolar system organized around the United States
and the Soviet Union. These superpowers had at their disposal conventional
military forces whose overall capabilities were substantially greater than all
others. In addition, they possessed nuclear weapons stockpiles that were
larger by orders of magnitude than those of other nations. The United States,
of course, was the world's preeminent economy. During much of the
period—until the mid-1970s—the Soviet leaders also presided over a massive

(if insular and enormously inefficient) economy, one that could support a giant military establishment while at least a tolerable amount of attention was
directed toward domestic needs. As long as the Soviet economy continued to
function and as long as Moscow's domination of Eastern and Central Europe
continued to breathe life into the Warsaw Treaty Organization, the international system could aptly be called bipolar.

Today, the economic failure of the former Soviet Union and therefore the
fundamental weakness of Russia and the other succession states for the foreseeable future is amply apparent. No longer is Moscow a center of influence
and attraction. The often-heard appellation "Upper Volta with missiles" may
not be apt because Russia's universally literate, trained labor force (not to
mention its vast natural resources) assures it a place among the industrialized
powers, but the contradiction between its continuing military strength and its
economic weakness will exist for some time to come. So pervasive are the effects of Russia's economic collapse that many Western observers now believe
that the greater danger lies not in a Russian attack but in the dissipation into
unauthorized hands, perhaps even into private commerce, of former Soviet
nuclear warheads.[3]

In the aftermath of the Gulf War's demonstration of the effectiveness of
technology-based U.S. military power, some analysts proclaimed that the
once-bipolar international system has become unipolar, with the United States
now the only country able "to be a decisive player in any conflict in whatever
part of the world it chooses to involve itself."[4] This notion is simple, com-
manding, self-evident, and mostly beside the point.

In the international system of the next two decades, U.S. military power
will continue to be an important fact of geopolitics, one to be taken into account by governments around the globe. Yet over that period, military power
itself is likely to become increasingly irrelevant in determining outcomes in international politics. And for the United States in particular, military might
should provide solutions to very few, if any, of the serious problems that U.S.
society will face. Those problems—involving education, infrastructure, race
relations, drugs, and the like—are not dissimilar to problems faced by many
other industrialized states. But in their U.S. variant, many of them are more
severe. Moreover, they raise larger questions about the international competitiveness of the U.S. economy and therefore of the ability of the United States
to provide for the well-being of an increasingly complex society and frag-
mented domestic population. In the long run, if these questions are not addressed by the political system, they will erode the nation's ability to field effective military forces.[5]

If the evolving international system is currently unipolar militarily, it is mul-
tipolar with respect to other dimensions of national power. It has been more
than two decades since the United States wielded anything resembling com-
manding power in the international economy. And today, there are three

broad blocs of nations within that context. The countries of the European Community and the African and Caribbean states that have special monetary and trading connections with them form the largest and most clearly defined bloc. Second is the free trade area of the United States and Canada, to which Mexico will likely soon be added; eventually, Chile and other Latin American states may enter. Third is Japan, which is forging increasingly interdependent relationships with members of the Association of Southeast Asian Nations (ASEAN), around which other Asian and Pacific economies may cluster.

There is political multipolarity today, as well, but it is much more difficult to define. Some states are important in their regions. Russia and (to a lesser extent) China each span a number of regions; they are obviously powers to be reckoned with in their respective spheres. So, in their own regions, are India and Brazil and perhaps Nigeria. Today, the United States just might be able to get its way in south Asia against the opposition of India, in South America without the agreement of Brazil, in the Persian Gulf without that of Saudi Arabia—to specify only a few examples—but doing so would entail real political costs. And in the future, such dominance might not be possible at all.

Iraq's invasion of Kuwait in August 1990 gave rise to a demonstration of yet another kind of political multipolarity—the codification of great-power status in the Charter of the United Nations, whose drafters conferred permanent membership in the Security Council, with right of veto, on the United States, the Soviet Union, Britain, France, and China. The Gulf War and the crises in Yugoslavia and Somalia demonstrate that the council is likely to be a much more important forum for organizing political and military action in the future than it has been in the past. Further, the more the council is used, the higher the political costs one of the permanent five would incur by acting unilaterally in the absence of consensus. That is a consideration that will impinge with particular force upon the United States, the power most used to taking unilateral action.

## The Declining Probability of Major War

Whether or not the United Nations becomes a central forum for coordinating the policies of the major powers, the probability of an outbreak of war among them is lower than it has been at any time in modern history. This is not to say that the probability was ever high during the forty-five years of the Cold War. The bipolar confrontation of two blocs, each wielding formidable armed forces that included enormous quantities of nuclear weapons, assured a robust structure of deterrence that left little doubt as to what the consequences of war might be.

Two other characteristics of the Cold War international system should be noted here. First, although its wars were fought entirely on the periphery, the system was highly Eurocentric. Europe was where the line between the two blocs was most sharply drawn, and it was the site of the densest concentrations of their opposing military forces. That made for safety through an almost frozen stability. Yet it also introduced a potentially dangerous bias toward escalation: If a hot war in Europe had ever started, each side would have sought to strike early in an effort to destroy the other's nuclear weapons and command-and-control facilities, certainly those in Europe but perhaps those in the superpowers' homelands, as well. The result would thus have been a widening and deepening, rather than a damping, of the conflict.

Second, although this escalatory bias discouraged war in Europe—anywhere in Europe—there was no such bias in the rest of the world, and consequently, there were fewer disincentives for either the superpowers or their clients to risk military action. There, the U.S.-Soviet rivalry led both nations to acquire seemingly vital interests in the survival of Third World client regimes. Some wars in which the superpowers had substantial stakes raged for years—for example, those in Korea, Indochina, Angola, the horn of Africa, Afghanistan, and Central America. As long as U.S. and Soviet forces did not come directly into contact—a tacit rule of their engagement in the Third World—there was little danger of escalation. But neither were there incentives to dampen the conflicts. The United States was willing to continue hemorrhaging vast quantities of blood and treasure to avoid "losing" in Vietnam; so was the Soviet Union in Afghanistan. And in any conflict, each was willing to go to great lengths to see that its clients prevailed.

The end of the Cold War turned these processes of commitment and escalation upside down. The transformations of recent years promise to make violent conflict in Europe more likely than before, and if conflict in the rest of the world is not less likely, then at least it will be less protracted and less ferocious. These points deserve explanation.

In Europe, the liberation of Moscow's East European satellites and the reunification of Germany has reduced the probability of conflict virtually to zero along the one axis where a catastrophic war might have taken place, the line running from Germany to Russia; therefore, the probability of war among Europe's major states is also reduced.[6] No longer is there a link between the perceived legitimacy of the regimes of Eastern Europe and the regime that sits in Moscow. That means that Moscow no longer has any interest in using force to keep those client regimes in power. Similarly, reunification has transformed the Federal Republic of Germany from the only fundamentally revisionist state in Europe into a satisfied bulwark of the status quo. Thus, neither the German nor the Russian government now faces any question for which the expansionist use of military power might seem to be the answer. That is a profound change in international relations. Moreover, there is every reason to believe that the change is secular, not cyclical.

This does not mean, however, that there will be no more war in Europe. On the contrary, there is already much violence within and among the constituent parts of former multinational states like Yugoslavia and the Soviet Union. There may also be conflicts between some of the liberated countries of Eastern Europe, such as Hungary and Romania. But it is very unlikely that these conflicts would escalate into larger wars. Nor is it likely that they would drag in Europe's larger powers. The post–Cold War European system has a de-escalatory bias, as the major state (but not all the minor ones) have neither ideological nor nationalistic reasons for making wars larger or for expanding their own spheres of territorial control.

Now that Marxism-Leninism has been discredited, no comparable ideology will arise to take its place—within Europe, at least. And at the end of the twentieth century, it is widely understood within advanced industrialized states that territory—land as such—now has much less economic or even military importance than the scientific and technological know-how of the people who reside on it; moreover, most realize that there is nothing quite as likely to make such people nonproductive as a foreign occupation. The recent past has seen many demonstrations of just how difficult and unrewarding it is to instill any kind of legitimacy in a regime that is presiding over ethnically distinct peoples.[7]

## The United States and the Use of Force in the Third World

The end of the Cold War and, with it, the end of the superpowers' search for clients has radically changed the circumstances in which the United States might plausibly wish to use its military power within the Third World. Of all the sites of possible conflicts, only the Korean peninsula offers anything even remotely resembling the dangers of the past. That is not because of the few remaining links between North Korea and Russia but because the regime in Pyongyang seems untouched by the winds of change that have blown through nearly all the world's other Communist societies. North Korea's regime still poses a credible threat to a government to which the United States has an explicit commitment.

No other U.S. allies in Asia face comparable threats. It strains credibility, for example, to imagine a Russian or Chinese attack upon Japan or a Chinese attempt to invade Taiwan. The governments of the Philippines and (to a lesser extent) Thailand face challenges from internal revolutionary movements, but they are not menaced by their neighbors. And Vietnam is preoccupied with its own timid version of perestroika. Like many regimes that once were expansionist, it seems to be increasingly aware that attempting to maintain physical control over alien peoples is an enterprise whose costs exceed its benefits.

Regarding Africa, little need be said. U.S. involvements there, aside from economic assistance programs, have been motivated almost entirely by the rivalry with Moscow; their scale—even the many years of support to anti-Communist factions in Angola—has been minimal. No circumstances, other than an antiterrorist or hostage-rescue effort, could lead to the employment of U.S. military forces on that continent.

Much the same can probably be said about future U.S. military intervention in Latin America. There, it is worth noting, the Cold War imperatives all worked in one direction. Later in this volume, Jorge Castañeda observes that the prospect of Soviet retaliation elsewhere may have deterred U.S. administrations from giving free rein to their ambitions in Latin America. Undoubtedly, as Castañeda points out, this notion was "ever-present in many Latin American statesmen's minds" and now causes some of them to mourn the passing of the Cold War.[8] Such thoughts may have had some currency in Latin America, but there is no real evidence that the idea of the putative Soviet balancer ever had much resonance in Washington. Quite the contrary: The prospect of Soviet counterintervention never led U.S. administrations to feel constrained against intervening militarily in the hemisphere. That was probably true even regarding the case that would have been most provocative to the Soviet Union: a direct U.S. attack on Cuba. In that instance, Moscow would have responded with a ferocious propaganda barrage but little more. Its ability to project forces over long distance was never even remotely as great as Washington's. That ruled out Soviet counteraction in the hemisphere, and other regions had their own dynamics that were little affected by events elsewhere.

Indeed, the Cold War led administrations in Washington to perceive stakes in the political coloration of Latin American regimes that they would not otherwise have seen; thus, it increased, rather than diminished, the prospects of forcible U.S. intervention. That was a crucially important aspect of U.S.–Latin American relations.

Despite these perceived stakes, South America (as distinguished from Central America) never saw significant intervention by U.S. military forces, and the end of the Cold War means that the probability of such intervention is now even lower. Current U.S. support of local police and military organizations working to curtail narcotics production and traffic in Bolivia, Colombia, and especially Peru may presage a more extensive involvement. Yet here again, it is implausible to imagine U.S. forces fighting to replace a sitting government or, conversely, intervening to assure a client government's security to the extent of becoming embroiled in the factional fighting that accompanies civil war.

By contrast with South America, Central America and the Caribbean have seen repeated U.S. interventions. Moreover, the policies and practices of the Cold War years created dependent clients (e.g., in El Salvador or Guatemala) who will continue to press claims on Washington for support. Although only an optimist would predict that the days of unilateral U.S. intervention in the region are altogether over, it is also true that the Clinton administration will find it easier to resist those claims than a second Bush administration—with its own clients and those of the Reagan administrations that preceded it, not to mention its right-wing domestic constituencies—might have done. In any case, it is of surpassing importance that with anticommunism no longer a viable rationale for intervention, Central America will cease to be a contentious issue in U.S. domestic politics.

In the 1990s and beyond, different issues will call forth different responses. A fundamental difference between the likely contingencies of the 1990s and the U.S.-supported Third World counterinsurgency campaigns of the past is that when an operation like a narcotics interdiction is not working, the effort and the policy behind it can be abandoned with relative ease. The issue now is practical efficacy, not victory or defeat in a global struggle—as the stakes were so often perceived to be during the ideologically rooted conflicts of the Cold War. In the past, to have admitted that a policy was not working was tantamount to admitting defeat in a much larger contest. The result was seemingly endless wars like those in Central America, fueled by the USSR and Cuba, on one side, and the United States, on the other.[9] That era is now closed.

The new era has already seen one example of U.S. military intervention—the forcible removal of Manuel Antonio Noriega from Panama in December 1989 to stand trial in Florida for narcotics trafficking. To many in Latin America, regardless of their dislike of Noriega, it seemed that Washington was up to its old tricks again. Yet the tangled aftermath of the affair might have desirable effects. In the future, Central American dictators will undoubtedly be more cautious about flouting U.S. law. And it may not be too much to hope that U.S. administrations have learned that when they intervene as decisively as they did in Panama—first with financial sanctions, then with actual armed force—they cannot merely walk away from the economic and political wreckage they leave behind.

## Broadening the Security Agenda

To the extent that security will be an issue in U.S.–Latin American relations during the coming decades, it will be security defined broadly enough to include harms that are nonmilitary in nature. These are, for the most part, harms that will flow from south to north, preeminently people and drugs. The United States continues to be a magnet for Latin Americans in search of a better life, and U.S. absorptive capacity seems astonishingly high. Immigration is not yet and may never be a threat to the well-being of the communities where the migrants initially settle, but those communities nevertheless have real fears that their welfare and education systems will be overwhelmed. Such fears are felt most acutely during times of economic downturn, which exacerbate the problems of absorbing immigrants into the developed, industrialized states of the North and, at the same time, add to the pressures in the countries of the South that cause migrants to leave.[10]

Drugs, of course, are a vastly more serious harm, and the flow of narcotics has become the most significant issue between the United States and several Latin American countries. This is not the place to discuss the relationship between narcotics production, economic development, and the strength and resilience of Latin American political institutions. But it seems probable that the only kinds of programs likely to help curb international narcotics traffic are those that emphasize trade-and-development carrots at least as much as they do law-and-order sticks.

Another item on the U.S.–Latin American security agenda will be international trade in high-technology weapons. Both Argentina and Brazil have become exporters of such weapons to Third World states, and Brazil especially has developed a multifaceted and sophisticated arms industry. During the coming decades, it is likely that Brazil will substantially close the technology gap between it and its First World competitors. Although weapons produced by these suppliers may be purchased by other Latin American states, they would probably not be used in the hemisphere, where there is little danger of interstate war. Rather, they are intended for sale to more affluent buyers in more turbulent regions, such as the Middle East, and they may thus complicate international efforts to limit arms flows. Such efforts may well prompt well-founded complaints about a double standard that allows, for example, the United States to sell military aircraft to Israel and Egypt while seeking to prevent Brazil from selling missiles to Syria or (eventually) Iraq.

Efforts to induce Latin American states to eschew nuclear weapons production should be more successful. The agreement signed by the presidents of Argentina and Brazil at the Iguaçú Falls on November 28, 1990, renouncing the use and development of nuclear weapons and placing their nuclear power facilities under international inspection, marked at least a hiatus and possibly the end of their countries' efforts to develop nuclear forces. It appears that only a plausible threat from a nuclear-armed state could cause either government to depart from the agreement, and no such threat—other than the one each might pose against the other—seems remotely likely to arise. In an era when domestic needs press harder and harder upon their economies, devoting resources to acquiring nuclear weapons may well seem an irrelevant and possibly dangerous distraction that voters are not likely to appreciate.

## Interstate Conflict in Latin America

It is difficult to imagine circumstances in which any Latin American state might feel that its security would be enhanced by possession of nuclear weapons. That is because the probability of interstate war in Latin America is very low. As I argued earlier, land as such has declined in importance as a stake in the relations of advanced industrialized nations. The same process is at work among developing states, as well. And the more developed a country becomes, the more its wealth will depend upon the value that an educated population can add to that of resources acquired anywhere, rather than upon the possession of extractable resources themselves. The sole exception to this generalization seems to be oil. As the Gulf crisis demonstrated, wars might still be fought over rich oil fields; however, they are unlikely to be fought over copper deposits or farmland or even access to the sea, unless established routes through intervening territory are arbitrarily closed.

The situation is altogether different when the issue is ethnic irredentism or conflicts inflamed by perceived mistreatment of conationals living within other polities, such as Hungarians living in Romania or the many ethnic minorities spread across a Soviet Union increasingly divided along national lines. Things are also different when the territory in contention is claimed for what might be called symbolic reasons—to right historical wrongs—as is largely the case with Israeli claims to the West Bank of the Jordan River (the ancient Jewish lands of Judea and Samaria). Nearly all Latin American territorial disputes are of this sort—for example, Venezuela's claim to Guyana, Guatemala's to Belize, or Argentina's to the Falklands/Malvinas. But with the possible exception of the last, these claims are no longer asserted with the fervor that once characterized them.

By contrast with other geographic regions, Latin America is mercifully free of international disputes rooted in ethnic conflicts. That is not to say that no Latin American governments repress identifiable ethnic groups: Such repression, particularly of Indian peoples, still occurs, and it is a root cause of some insurgencies. But this repression takes place, for the most part, within states and rarely spills across borders.

There is no reason to think that these patterns will change significantly in coming years, which means that wars among Latin American states will continue to be very unlikely. But it does not mean that Latin America will be free from large-scale violence or that other Latin states will be inclined to follow the example of Costa Rica and abolish their armies. On the contrary, the recession-induced strains felt by all of the area's economies, most of them already weakened by the continuing debt crisis, are likely to exacerbate domestic tensions and fuel insurgent movements. It is probable, too, that they will further diminish the ability of some governments to deal with powerful forces, such as the drug cartels, that are daily undermining their authority. The result may be prolonged internal warfare in certain cases, perhaps not on the scale or of the vicious intensity of some of the army-guerrilla struggles of the 1970s but nevertheless amply violent and destructive.

These will be problems of nation-building, and the arena for their solutions will be primarily national. Weak linkages among Latin American economies mean that states will not be able to export their problems by inducing others to share the burden of adjustment. And unlike the situation in the 1970s and, indeed, the 1980s, governments will not be able to point to hypothetical or actual Soviet and Cuban threats as a means of prying military and economic support from the United States.

Meanwhile, the United States will be preoccupied with the problems of other regions, notably those of the former Soviet Union, Central and Eastern Europe, and the Middle East. Russia, especially, is already making sizable claims on U.S. resources. To the extent that it and other former Communist states succeed in solving their economic and political problems, their claims— and their ability to extract both assistance and investments—will grow even larger. That is why Washington's response to appeals from Latin America may seem to approach benign neglect.

## Institutionalizing Hemispheric Security

Precisely because Latin America's problems will be so internal to its nation-states, the next decade may be a propitious time for strengthening the network of regional institutions that comprise the so-called inter-American system. Those institutions, all which are under the umbrella of the Organization of American States, are the subject of Heraldo Muñoz's chapter in this volume, which points out that the inter-American system is already much more developed than all but close observers realize.[11]

Not surprisingly, the functional side of the OAS's structure of institutions—organizations dealing with issue areas such as public health, telecommunications, agriculture, and exchanges of technical and scientific data—is the most developed. After all, these functions are the least politicized. But Muñoz notes that in the promotion and protection of human rights, the record of the OAS and its subordinate institutions, the Inter-American Commission on Human Rights and the Inter-American Court, is unsurpassed by that of any other international organization.

It is in the realm of traditional security concerns that the OAS now has the greatest possibilities for further development. Until now, the organization has mainly been a sounding board for the Cold War agenda of the United States—a forum for legitimizing Washington's campaign against real or imagined Soviet influence in the hemisphere. Now, however, with the Cold War over, the OAS might learn from the example of Europe's Conference on Security and Cooperation (CSCE). First convened in the early 1970s, CSCE is a forum where members of the North Atlantic Treaty Organization (NATO) and the Warsaw Treaty Organization, as well as Europe's neutrals, can address common security concerns. One example involved the desire of all European states, especially the smaller ones, to be assured that no potential adversary was secretly preparing a surprise attack. This concern gave rise to a number of measures, all subsumed under the rubric of "confidence- and security-building measures" (CSBMs). Some might usefully be transplanted to the Western Hemisphere.

One important CSBM might resemble CSCE's requirement that long prior notice be given before important military maneuvers are conducted. That would ban sudden maneuvers by the forces of a member state near the frontiers of any other—a provision that would make Latin American governments eager to have the United States as a member of any hemispheric CSBM regiome. They would hope to write restrictions in a way that would rule out intimidating maneuvers like those the United States carried out in Honduras near the Nicaraguan border and in waters off Nicaragua, during the years of the U.S. campaign against the Sandinista government. To be sure, such measures, though popular in Latin America, would be resisted in Washington for they would, indeed, restrict U.S. freedom of action. But a U.S. administration would find it difficult to reject measures in its own backyard that its predecessors had negotiated in Europe.

Another useful CSBM would be a requirement that governments fully disclose the nature, size, and location of their military forces. They should also be required to justify the forces they possess. Coming at a time when the danger of interstate war in Latin America is minimal, a full disclosure of this type might be acceptable to governments. It would also make it possible for a regional security organization to begin to press the governments to justify maintaining more than constabulary armed forces and spending money on equipment better suited for attacking a neighbor rather than assuring domestic tranquility. CSCE has formally been assigned the task of carrying out the intrusive inspections required for monitoring compliance with the November 1989 treaty regulating conventional arms levels in Europe. The OAS might serve as both a negotiating forum and a monitoring agency for the same kind of arms limitation agreements in Latin America.

## The Problem of U.S. Exceptionalism

For the OAS to do so would bring the organization squarely up against the problem of U.S. exceptionalism. The armed forces maintained by the United States are probably greater in terms of aggregate personnel strength and certainly many times more capable than the combined forces of all the states of Latin America and the Caribbean. Even after Cold War peace dividends are realized, the disparity will still be great. There are obvious reasons—rooted in history, politics, and economics—why this has been the case. But Latin Americans may well ask why the United States should constantly avail itself of the latest and most potent products of military technology while at the same time it seeks to restrict its Latin American neighbors to outmoded weapons and downsized forces. And some will intend this as more than a rhetorical question.

The United States finds itself in a similar position in Europe. Its armed forces and those of the former USSR are much larger than those of any other members of CSCE, and no doubt they will stay that way for a long time. The Gulf crisis demonstrated that the evolving international order, such as it is, depends on the threat of forceful action by large powers to assure conformity with norms of behavior. Washington administrations will continue to size U.S. armed forces with one eye on those of the former Soviet Union and another on the very large and potent forces wielded by authoritarian Middle East states such as Syria or even a reconstructed Iraq.

Current and would-be U.S. allies in Europe seem to find that situation reassuring. By and large, they seek continued active engagement by the United States in the international politics of the Continent, including some sort of U.S. military presence. But history provides Latin Americans with fewer reasons to view U.S. military power as wholly benign. That makes it all the more important that U.S. leaders should publicly and repeatedly make known their intention to adhere to the norm, enshrined in the OAS charter and other hemispheric documents, that proscribes unilateral intervention.

Earlier, I argued that the end of the Cold War has made such military intervention much less likely. Indeed, the probability is that the course of policy may run in the opposite direction—toward neglect that may, in the long run, not seem so benign. In fact, the coming decade or so may see the impoverishment and outright disintegration of some Latin American states. Peru is the prime example of a nation where the forces of disorder threaten to overwhelm the capabilities of any governing authority, but there are other countries whose situations may, under worst-case conditions, become nearly as bleak.

Such circumstances cry out for humanitarian intervention, just as the plight of the Kurds in Iraq or the people of Somalia did. Intervention might need to combine forcible action (in the case of Peru, to provide security against both guerrilla groups and narcotics traffickers) and substantial economic assistance. It could scarcely take place unless requested by the recognized governing authority of the failing state or unless mandated by the OAS. Moreover, as things now stand, such intervention is not likely to occur unless the United States takes the lead in organizing it. Yet U.S. politicians have more pressing concerns on other agendas. The operations involved would be risky, and the cost of effective economic assistance could be very large. Thus, neglect—even at the cost of increasing chaos and misery in the affected state—would be a far more probable response than action.

A scenario of this sort would also conflict with the noninterventionary norm that has been so deeply ingrained in the thinking of Latin American politicians. That norm may erode in coming decades, however, as it becomes more apparent that harms originating in one Latin American state flow across the borders of others. This may even apply to acts of environmental degradation, like the annual burning of vast tracts of Brazil's rain forests that has a harmful effect upon the ecosystems of the entire planet, including those of Brazil's neighbors.

Similarly, narcotics production and trafficking has never recognized international frontiers. As long as the final markets are the United States and Western Europe, Latin American governments have not felt impelled to offer much more than rhetorical condemnation of their neighbors' inability to curtail the flow. Furthermore, as Jorge Castañeda points out later in this volume, the aggressive actions of the U.S. Drug Enforcement Agency (DEA) have been bitterly resented in Latin America.[12] But if, after the current recession ends, rising affluence among the middle and upper classes of countries like Brazil and Chile opens larger markets for drugs, the agents of the DEA may not feel quite so alienated.

Such a development would be enormously healthy for inter-American relations. The stereotypical view of relations among the states of the hemisphere posits Washington in the role of *demandeur* against the others. But in a number of issue areas, including the highly politicized area of human rights, Latin Americans now assert common values shared throughout the hemisphere. The inter-American system of the twenty-first century may well be increasingly regionalized, with neighboring states entering into cooperative arrangements that significantly depart from traditional notions of sovereignty.

The stronger these arrangements become and the more the entire system of inter-American relations is institutionalized, the less likely it would be for any administration in Washington to contemplate unilateral intervention. The end of the Cold War has significantly diminished the likelihood of any intervention by U.S. armed forces elsewhere in the hemisphere for reasons of security or great-power rivalry. The further development of regional and hemispheric institutions would go far toward eliminating the perception—and the fear—of a high-handed North American superpower intervening for its own narrow advantage on other grounds. A hemisphere of good neighbors may yet be possible.

## Notes

1. Soviet installations in Cuba were, of course, the cause of the 1962 U.S.-Soviet missile crisis. Later in the decade, when Moscow sought to use the Cuban port of Cienfuegos for nuclear-armed submarines, it bowed to the Nixon administration's insistence that establishing a base was unacceptable. Afterward, relatively small Soviet military units remained to train Cuban forces, and Soviet aircraft flew reconnaissance patrols from Cuban airfields but not on missions that seemed to threaten the United States.

2. See Richard H. Ullman, "At War with Nicaragua," *Foreign Affairs,* 62, no. 1 (Fall 1962), p. 47.

3. See Kurt M. Campbell et al., *Soviet Nuclear Fission: Control of the Nuclear Arsenal in a Disintegrating Soviet Union* (Cambridge, Mass.: Center for Science and International Affairs, John F. Kennedy School of Government, Harvard University, 1991).

4. Charles Krauthammer, "The Unipolar Moment," *Foreign Affairs,* 79, no. 1 (1991), p. 24.

5. This was one conclusion of a large group of specialists who met from May 30 to June 2, 1991, under the auspices of the American Assembly and the Council on Foreign Relations. See the American Assembly report, *Rethinking America's Security* (New York: American Assembly, 1991), pp. 9–10.

6. That is the central argument of my *Securing Europe* (Princeton, N.J.: Princeton University Press, 1991).

7. For an elaboration on these arguments, see ibid., pp. 23–27.

8. See Jorge G. Castañeda, "Latin America and the End of the Cold War: An Essay in Frustration," Chapter 2 in this volume.

9. On this theme, see James Chace, *Endless War* (New York: Vintage, 1984).

10. Jorge Castañeda points out that those who make the trek northward are, by and large, not the unemployed poor but young, enterprising, employed persons who seek the much higher wages they can find in the United States. See Chapter 2 in this volume.

11. See Heraldo Muñoz, "A New OAS for the New Times," Chapter 10 in this volume.

12. See Chapter 2 in this volume.

# 2

# Latin America and the End of the Cold War: An Essay in Frustration

## Jorge G. Castañeda

In early October 1962, Adlai Stevenson triumphantly brandished photographs taken by U.S. U-2s over Cuba. Andrei Gromyko's denials notwithstanding, the U.S. ambassador to the United Nations was conclusively proving to the Security Council and the rest of the world that his government's naval quarantine of the Caribbean island was justified on U.S. national security grounds: There were Soviet missiles in Cuba, and these represented a threat to the United States. It was one of the most effective justifications ever advanced for U.S. intervention in Latin America. The Kennedy administration had the goods on Nikita Khrushchev and Fidel Castro, and it knew how to use them.

Nearly thirty years later, on December 22, 1989, Gen. Maxwell Thurman, head of the Panama-based U.S. Army Southern Command, just as triumphantly brandished what he presented as justification for the U.S. invasion of Panama: fifty kilos of cocaine wrapped in banana leaves found in Gen. Manuel Antonio Noriega's freezer. Even taken at face value, the rationale was arguable: The invasion was an expensive, bloody, and somewhat disproportionate drug bust. But the tragicomic denouement of the Panama affair read like a marvelous parable of the present-day paradox of U.S. involvement in Latin America. The U-2 pictures of the Cienfuegos missile silos convinced the world in 1962 because they were true; in 1989, Noriega's banana-leaf cocaine stash held only Panamanian tamales and did not persuade anybody who was not already convinced.[1]

It is no small irony that the most recent instance of U.S. intervention in Latin America—the Panama invasion—coincided almost to the day with the disappearance of the last vestiges of the Soviet bloc in Eastern Europe. But despite appearances, the Panama intervention contrasted sharply with former examples of U.S. involvement in Latin America. The difference lay precisely in the fact that it was not part of the Cold War, superpower confrontational syndrome. Panama was the first case of overt, direct U.S. intervention in Latin America since World War II that did not possess, in one way or another, a geopolitical, East-West origin or connotation.

The Panama invasion marked the end of the traditional anti-Soviet packaging or ideological justification for U.S. interference in Latin America. It also signaled the resumption, on a different footing, of a long-standing debate on the origins, nature, and consequences of U.S. involvement in Latin American affairs. If the sole motivation for what came to be known over the years as U.S. intervention had always been purely geopolitical—i.e., countering a Soviet threat—then the era of at least a certain type of U.S. intromission was clearly coming to an end. In Fernando Henrique Cardoso's words: "Especially in the case of the Caribbean and Central American nations, the reduction of East-West ideological tension may leave a significant balance: Hereafter 'to fight Communism' will no longer justify the United States interventionist policy."[2] But Cardoso quickly countered this optimistic view with a sobering thought: "This excuse is, as everybody knows, prior to the Cold War, and it may persist. But it won't be a plausible excuse to make war on behalf of democracy. The anti-drug campaign may be perhaps the substitutive asserted reason for U.S. tutelage on the region."

Thus, if the hypothetical level of U.S. interference in the hemisphere's politics was a historical given, straying with only minor variations from a previously established level determined by what Régis Debray has called the logic of domination,[3] then the end of the Cold War and the ensuing elimination of the Soviet "alibi" becomes a much more relative transformation.[4] The disappearance of the other superpower and the experience of the Gulf War lead some Latin American intellectuals, Carlos Fuentes among them, to fear the emergence of a new pax Americana, with U.S. domination enshrined for a considerable time to come. Both views can be found in the literature that has blossomed around the issue, and they are also advanced by the multifaceted and diversely positioned political actors who are either forced or anxious to take a stance on the topic of the day.

With time and reflection, it appears that the ambivalence in most initial assessments was both right and wrong. And the truth lay not in between but elsewhere. Insofar as the United States continued to be a great power—indeed, the only remaining superpower—and that hemispheric intervention could be reasonably defined as the overwhelmingly asymmetrical exercise of power and influence by the United States in myriad fashions throughout the continent to defend and further its national interests (ideological, strategic, economic, political, domestic, etc.), the epoch of interference was far from over. Invasions, covert operations, aid and boycotts, destabilization for those perceived as hostile, and unwavering support for those perceived as constructive—"justice for my friends, the full weight of the law for my enemies," according to Benito Juárez's marvelous recipe—military action when necessary and political measures when sufficient all remained fixtures of hemispheric relations.

But the Cold War had persisted for nearly half a century, determining the type, reasons, and timing of U.S. interventions in Latin America. And when the Cold War ended, the Soviet danger to the United States disappeared. Consequently, nothing could endure unchanged. Those instances of U.S. involvement in Latin American affairs that did stem from geopolitical considerations were relegated to the past, and those that possessed different motivations were now cast in a different light. From 1954 in Guatemala through the Bay of Pigs, the Dominican Republic, destabilization in Chile under Salvador Allende, the contra war in Nicaragua, and the invasion of Grenada in 1983, virtually every instance of direct U.S. intervention in Latin America since World War II had anti-Soviet, anti-Communist, Cold War connotations. Conversely, those examples of intervention occurring after the end of the Cold War—Panama, drug enforcement in Peru—are clearly devoid of those connotations.

More important, perhaps, is the fact that the coincidence in the timing of the Cold War's conclusion and the advent of far more rigid international economic constraints, as a result of both economic globalization and ideological homogeneity, made certain types of U.S. intromission in Latin American simply redundant. In the past, the United States had often threatened or executed direct reprisals against Latin governments for such things as nationalizing natural resources without "prompt, adequate and effective compensation": Guatemala in 1952–1954, Peru in 1968, Chile in 1971. Today, threats and reprisals seem unnecessary. The nationalization would not take place in any case, but if it did, the consequences would be expressed in terms of dried-up credit and investment flows and tense relations with the World Bank and the International Monetary Fund (IMF), rather than in difficulties with the U.S. State Department.

Thus, the effects of the Cold War's conclusion were inevitably mixed for Latin America. The most evidently favorable "Gorbachev effect" for Latin America involved U.S policy toward the region. With the elimination of the reality and perception of a Soviet threat to U.S. security in the hemisphere, the superpower's new relationship with its neighbors to the south redefined the constraints and margins of U.S. policy in Latin America.[5]

The perception of a Soviet security threat either to the United States through Latin America or directly to the nations of the hemisphere was always

a bone of contention in inter-American relations. The importance of the Soviet menace—its nature, relevance, and explanatory value in understanding
Latin American social and political trends—never truly constituted an area of
agreement or understanding between the northern and southern halves of the
continent. Throughout the 1980s, for example, much of the public debate
between the Reagan administration, on the one hand, and those Latin American states involved in Central American peace initiatives, on the other, centered on defining the causes of conflict in the isthmus. At the United Nations
or the Organization of American States or through public statements by U.S.
officials, Washington always sought to present the Central American crisis as
essentially brought on by Soviet involvement. Conversely, the Latin American
mediators would stress the homegrown, so-called autochthonous economic
and social roots of the upheaval in the region.

The anti-Soviet, anti-Communist approach to Latin America was never as
important abroad as it was domestically in the United States. Even at the
height of the Cold War, the United States rarely obtained support from the
rest of the hemisphere, let alone the world, when it intervened in Latin American affairs.[6] Its anti-Soviet vision of the subcontinent's affairs was fully backed
only once: during the Cuban missile crisis, when the Soviet threat to U.S. security appeared undisputable. The suspension of diplomatic and, in many
cases, economic ties with Cuba by most Latin nations was noteworthy above
all because of its exceptionality, responding to powerful, local, anti-Communist impulses. Virtually no Latin American government encouraged analo-
gous U.S. attempts against Peru in the late 1960s or against Chile in the early
1970s. Only the Organization of Eastern Caribbean States supported the invasion of Grenada, and possibly it did so under less than honorable circumstances.[7] The proxy war on Nicaragua after 1981 was backed, at least ostensi-
bly, by several of the Sandinistas' neighbors, but, again, the true motivations
for that support were far from altruistic or entirely homegrown. They were far
more deeply rooted in the desire to accommodate the United States than in
an authentic, local fear of the Nicaraguan "threat." As far as the rest of the
world was concerned, Washington's anti-Soviet rhetoric and strategy in Latin
America was perceived more as a way of defending other interests than as a
true basis for policy. But domestically, to the extent that there was backing for
involvement in the region, it was mainly due to support emanating from those
sectors of U.S. society—the far and center Right—that believed in the reality
of a Soviet threat to the United States "in its own backyard."

As with all ideological foundations for any foreign policy, the U.S. perception of a Soviet presence or menace in Latin America was grounded in a reality. But it also represented a way of rallying a domestic constituency for a policy that often sought other objectives. Anti-Sovietism was neither entirely
cynical and dishonest nor a completely altruistic and always valid basis for intervention in the area. But it was an indispensable ingredient of U.S. policy

toward Latin America. Without it, the Bay of Pigs, the Alliance for Progress, U.S. support for the national security doctrine dictatorships in Brazil, Uruguay, Bolivia, Argentina, and Chile during the 1960s and early 1970s, the successive, multibillion-dollar Mexican debt rescues, and the contra adventure in Nicaragua in the 1980s would be incomprehensible.

Insofar as the knee-jerk, anti-Soviet reaction of the United States was the principal restriction placed on Latin America's autonomy in the international arena, the leeway afforded to the region by the end of the Cold War was obviously enhanced. But in addition to the U.S. security constraint, there has always been U.S. and, indeed, an international economic constraint. Many Latin American elites frequently perceived this restriction as an equally important, if not greater, motive for showing sensitivity to U.S. concerns. The reasoning was and continues to be quite simple: For any Latin American government, there are direct, often immediate, and frequently dire economic consequences of pursuing a policy contrary to Washington's desires or interests. The ferocity of the retaliation depends on the extent and nature of the U.S. opposition to or dislike for the policy in question. The reprisals can range from losing a sugar quota, as happened to Cuba in 1960, to suffering a tuna embargo, as Mexico did in 1980, to an across-the-board economic and financial embargo, as Nicaragua experienced from 1985 onward, or the application of sanctions, like the so-called Super 301 sanctions imposed on Brazil for establishing market reserves on its computer industry. Even this short list indicates clearly that the economic constraint applies equally to countries and governments that are considered enemies of the United States and to those that are generally deemed friendly.

This constraint has possibly been strengthened by the end of the Cold War for even the (false) hope of an economic alternative to participation in the Western financial and economic community has vanished. In an age when everyone follows the same musical score, the penalty for singing out of tune quickly rises. As Latin America's room to maneuver broadens from a geopolitical standpoint, it is narrowing from an ideological, economic policy perspective: The price of any departure from the tenets of free market orthodoxy is exorbitant. Unilaterally suspending debt payments (as Peru, Brazil, and Argentina did at different moments in the 1980s and 1990s) leads to financial ostracism—the cutoff of loans from the international lending institutions, to which debt payments continue to be made, and from official lenders, who also continue to receive interest payments. The effort to protect certain sectors of industry (the Brazilian computer industry, for example) or agriculture leads to retaliation in other spheres of economic endeavor. The desire to continue regulating foreign investment, in the same way that Europe, the United States, and Japan do, implies a sort of international blacklisting, provoking significant disadvantages in the competition for scarce capital.

In the new world order characterized by economic globalization, free market homogeneity, and cutthroat competition for scarce capital and frequently protected markets, the real economic check placed on Latin American autonomy is not the fear or reality of conscious, active, explicit retaliation by the United States. Rather, it is the economic, financial, and, ultimately, political impossibility of straying far beyond the bounds of economic orthodoxy and ideological conformity. The true constraint Latin American elites—and popular movements or oppositions—must cope with today is the perspective of seeing sources of credit, investment, and aid dry up and both sympathy and export markets contract if they follow policies deemed hostile, different, or simply unwise. Nationalizing natural resources, emphasizing social policies, or placing restrictions on foreign trade or investment no longer necessarily invite invasion or destabilization, nor are they even likely to do so. They simply invite financial scarcity and economic ostracism. The political consequences today are much more quickly and automatically unmanageable than they were in, say, Salvador Allende's time, when it took three years, uncounted presidential memoranda, and undercover funding to build a broad constituency for a return to the status quo ante.

Yet U.S. involvement in Latin America persists, despite the fact that the costs of refusing to toe the economic party line have caused most Latin American governments to accede to U.S. wishes. And in the immediate aftermath of the Cold War's conclusion, a substitute for anti-Sovietism in the U.S. policy toward Latin America rapidly emerged: drug enforcement. After the evil (Soviet-Communist) empire to the East, the evil (drug-producing) slum to the South became the new rationale for U.S. involvement.

The emergence of drugs as an important issue in U.S. policy toward the region did not start with the thaw in East-West relations. Drug enforcement had played a significant role in U.S. policy toward Mexico, the Andean countries, Colombia, and Cuba for a number of years. And that role had already been sharply interventionist, providing alibis and motivations for U.S. involvement in the domestic affairs of many Latin American nations. This was already the case with the traditional presence of DEA agents in Mexico. But it became increasingly evident in newer forms of highly intrusive cooperation (including counterinsurgency).

The most disquieting trend in this respect may well have been Washington's affirmation of the unilateral right to prosecute individuals beyond U.S. national jurisdiction. The United States would use whatever means were necessary to bring to justice whomever it considered a criminal, regardless of where the suspect was found and no matter what his or her political or diplomatic status was. It followed that international conventions, principles of common law, and foreign legislations and judicial systems lacked precedence over U.S. rights. Moreover, this interpretation implied that U.S. constitutional rights were only applicable to U.S. citizens and could not be invoked by foreigners if by doing so they limited Washington's ability to protect its national interests.

The February 28, 1990, decision by the U.S. Supreme Court in the *United States* v. *Verdugo Urquidez* case established a legal precedent in this regard, opening the door to multiple forms of U.S. intervention in Latin American affairs. Chief Justice William H. Rehnquist and five other justices ruled that search-and-seizure operations conducted abroad by U.S. law enforcement agents, military personnel, or other government agencies against foreigners should not be restricted by the provisions of the Fourth Amendment of the Constitution. Thus, the Court determined that constitutional rights meant to protect U.S. citizens from the abuses of power by their government were not applicable to foreigners abroad. Simultaneously, the Justice Department issued an internal legal opinion authorizing its agents acting abroad to abduct foreigners in order to bring them to trial in the United States.[8] The document, drafted, according to the *Washington Post,* by Attorney General William Barr, stated that the president and the attorney general of the United States had the "inherent constitutional power" to order the capture of fugitives abroad. It affirmed that "the extraterritorial enforcement of United States laws is becoming increasingly important in order to protect vital national interests."

This policy was first applied in two nearly simultaneous cases: the Panama invasion and subsequent arrest of Noriega in January 1990 and the kidnapping of Humberto Alvarez Machaín in Mexico one month later. Alvarez Machaín was abducted from his home in Guadalajara by bounty hunters contracted by the DEA, who wanted him brought to trial for his presumed involvement in the 1985 torture and murder of DEA agent Enrique Camarena in Mexico. Although the U.S. government's explicit participation in the Alvarez Machaín case was initially less evident than in Noriega's, Attorney General Richard Thornburgh's statements and actions clarified the Justice Department's stand on the issue. When a federal judge in Los Angeles ruled that Alvarez Machaín's kidnapping violated the U.S.-Mexican extradition treaty and ordered him set free, Thornburgh vowed to take the case to the Supreme Court and succeeded in keeping him in prison. The Supreme Court subsequently ruled in the administration's favor, and although Alvarez Machaín was ultimately freed for lack of evidence, this affair provoked a crisis in U.S.-Mexican relations and awakened suspicion and trauma throughout the hemisphere. Behind the Noriega affair and the Alvarez Machaín case lay the same reasoning: Limitations on other nations' sovereignty, as well as the extraterritorial extension of U.S. law enforcement capability and justice, were deemed valid practices in the war on drugs.

Many in Latin America believed that U.S. insistence on drug enforcement was simply a disguise for further domination of the nations of the hemisphere. A *Washington Post*/ABC News poll taken in February 1990 in Colombia showed that 65 percent of those interviewed "suspect[ed] the drug war is a U.S. attempt to control their government."[9] But only with the coming of the drug age in U.S. domestic politics and the elimination of other ideological justifications for U.S. policy in Latin America did drugs acquire their full importance in hemispheric relations. Although the Bush administration paid lip service to the principle of parity between supply and demand as the root cause of the drug crisis, supply-directed policies were easier, cheaper, and more popular to pursue, though undeniably less effective.

It was no accident that the Panama invasion was at least subliminally presented as an action motivated by the desire to halt drug traffic and that its popularity in the United States—in addition to the Panamanian leader's own villainous image—was due largely to the perception of Noriega as a drug dealer. The first U.S. intervention in Latin America without Cold War packaging was also the first attempt by the United States to justify the use of force abroad on the grounds of drug enforcement. And there were sufficient other examples to prove conclusively that drugs had become far more than simply another item on the inter-American agenda. These instances ranged from the deployment of U.S. military detachments to Bolivia in 1987 and the escalation of the DEA presence in the Upper Huallaga Valley through the construction of a second base and the signing of U.S.-Peruvian military agreements with a joint drug-enforcement, counterinsurgency focus[10] and the growing militarization of the Southwest U.S.–Mexican border. They included the failed attempt to send an aircraft-carrier task force to international waters off the coast of Colombia in 1989, the enhanced role of the U.S. armed forces in patrolling the Caribbean drug routes, and the effort to impose an "intrusive" joint statement on the three Andean, drug-producing countries at the Cartagena Drug Summit in February 1990. Drugs were quickly becoming a hemispheric issue with dangerous implications for Latin American sovereignty, as more and more intrusive forms of cooperation were proposed by the United States.

The immigration issue does not yet possess the same urgency or implications, and the absence of a domestic consensus in the United States on this topic leaves open the possibility that it might not ever attain the same status. In addition, its emotional impact is not yet in the same league with that of drugs. But immigration was likely to acquire significant foreign policy implications as the effects of two significant trends of the 1980s began to be felt. The unintended effects of the 1986 Immigration Reform and Control Act only became apparent with time, and the fully foreseeable consequences of ten years of Latin American economic stagnation—widespread unemployment, falling wages, and the ensuing mass exodus to the north—barely began to have an impact in the early 1990s.

Widespread and continuing documentation of formerly undocumented aliens rapidly emerged as one of the most important and immediate effects of the 1986 Simpson-Rodino immigration reform. As a result of the law's amnesty provisions and the special agricultural worker clauses that permitted the legal entry of individuals previously employed in the harvest of perishable agricultural produce, an estimated 2.3 million formerly undocumented Mexicans regularized their migratory status in the United States.[11] The family reunification procedures and other mechanisms that were finally accepted—including a growing number of "green-card marriages"—probably indicate that the total number of documented and undocumented Mexicans approaches 3 million. More importantly, though further away in time, the number of documented immigrants could be multiplied several fold if widespread naturalization takes place in the future and leads to further family reunification.

Similarly, the "new" and fashionable free market policies that included low real wages as a major competitive advantage contributed to maintaining or increasing the magnitude of the flow north, not only from Mexico but also from many other countries. For years, Mexican and U.S. researchers had been compiling data showing that the single most important contributing factor to immigration—illegal or not—was the wage differential.[12] The unemployed do not emigrate: They lack the money to pay the cost of doing so. Those who leave tend to be individuals who already have jobs, either in rural areas or, more frequently today, in large cities, and who choose to leave those jobs in search of higher wages elsewhere. As long as the wage differential between the United States and Mexico, for example, averaged nearly eight to one, enterprising young Mexicans of all social strata were going to continue their trek north. In 1990, the Mexican minimum wage was $.55* an hour, whereas in California, where fully half of all undocumented Mexican immigrants make their home, it was about $4.50 an hour. Similarly, a tenured university professor in Mexico, Brazil, or Argentina, with a Ph.D. and recognized publications, received between $250 and $800 in the early 1990s yet could make $3,000 to $4,000 per month, after taxes, in a major U.S. university.

As the consequences of these trends took hold, reasons became stronger for fearing that immigration would occupy a growing role in U.S. foreign policy toward migration-generating countries, as opposed to remaining a domestic issue with sporadic, secondary foreign implications. If immigration began to be perceived as a significant threat to U.S. welfare, national security (defined in a new sense), and even national identity, the same causes could well produce the same effects. The problem's roots would again be found abroad—in this case, perhaps more justifiably than in the case of drugs—and hypothetical solutions would increasingly be localized in countries of origin. The United States had already pressured Mexico with regard to so-called third-country immigration, that is, the transit of undocumented emigrants from Central

---

*All monetary figures are given in U.S. dollars unless otherwise noted.

America, South America, and Asia through Mexico to the United States. It also demanded that several Central American nations be more forthcoming in deterring migratory flows north. And if Latin American authorities proved unwilling or unable to do what was desired or required by the United States, intrusive U.S. cooperation could follow.

This unfortunate trend could be aggravated if the "Fortress America" thesis or U.S. retrenchment were to be confirmed. Many scholars in Latin America and elsewhere suggested that as regional trading blocs in Europe and Asia emerged and as the United States continued to lose its relative strength in the world economy, it would fall back on its traditional, Latin American sphere of influence in a sort of "hemispheric isolationism." Drugs and immigration would thus not only be used as justifications for intervention and the curtailment of Latin sovereignty but also as ideological coating for a new, purely economic expression of the Monroe Doctrine. George Bush's Enterprise for the Americas Initiative, announced in mid-1990 and proposing the creation of a free trade zone from Alaska to Patagonia, could be viewed (not entirely inaccurately) from this perspective. As the U.S. trade deficit remained stubbornly high and further devaluations of the dollar became increasingly difficult—or, in any case, ineffective in the "dollar-zone"—bringing down trade barriers to U.S. exports in Latin America represented a cheap and quick, albeit partial, contribution to stabilizing U.S. external accounts. Free trade within the hemisphere, coupled with common tariffs applied toward the rest of the world, enhanced U.S. competitiveness without any immediate domestic sacrifice. It was highly revealing that U.S. exports to Mexico, Brazil, and Argentina jumped from $12.6 billion in 1983 to $30.8 billion in 1989, when the trade liberalization policies encouraged by Washington and multilateral financial agencies began to take hold. Similarly, the U.S. trade deficit with Mexico alone, the country that had gone furthest in opening its economy, shrank from $7.9 billion in 1983 to $2.6 billion in 1989 and had become a trade surplus by 1990.[13]

From this perspective, Latin America acquired not more leeway in its relations with the United States as a consequence of the end of the Cold War but less. As the United States retrenched to the Western Hemisphere, it would encroach further on Latin sovereignty, and its relations with Latin America, though no longer shaped by the East-West dispute, would remain strained. They would become a function of a "North-North" economic rivalry but still not be intrinsically important to the United States. Although this view may have been exaggerated—implying that the backward, stagnant Latin economies could substitute for unconquerable U.S. markets in Europe and Japan—it was widely held.

Latin America also suffered an additional effect of the end of the Cold War, perhaps of a more intangible nature but with immediate consequences: the elimination of a counterweight in international affairs that had proved useful in the past to many nations, particularly those governed by center Left regimes. It was much more difficult to be nonaligned in a one-superpower world. Granted, few of the continent's governments had ever truly dared to play one superpower off against another, as regimes in different latitudes had often done. The Indian, Chinese, Egyptian, and even French tactic of flirting with one superpower in order to win the graces of the other was never entirely credible in Latin America, and it was executed only in exceptional or extreme cases. The purchase of Soviet MIGs in the 1970s by the Peruvian military and, more generally, the way in which "during the 1970s the Soviet Union achieved a broader and closer relationship with Peru than with any other Latin American country except Cuba" was one instance of this diplomatic gamesmanship.[14] Another was the long-standing economic relationship between Argentina and the Soviet Union, dating back to 1953 and Juan Domingo Perón's overtures. It led to the sale of Argentine grain to the Soviet Union during the 1980 U.S.-imposed embargo, with "the Soviet Union becoming Argentina's most important commercial partner, absorbing 80 percent of its grain exports and 33 percent of its total exports in 1981."[15] A few other, even less significant examples rapidly fill this short list of precedents.

But the broader idea of a functioning deterrent to U.S. ambitions and free rein was ever present in many Latin American leaders' minds. It seemed self-evident that the existence of "another side," of another superpower militarily and perhaps even politically the equal of the United States, was an adequate, even effective brake on U.S. policy. The United States could not do anything it wanted in Latin America, despite the tacit Soviet acceptance of a U.S. sphere of influence: The 1962 agreement emanating from the Cuban missile crisis regarding the U.S. commitment not to invade Cuba is a good, if somewhat extreme, example of this. The rule of worldwide symmetries, precedents, implicit understandings, and reactions to every action was in play. Whatever the United States did in its sphere of influence could produce similar Soviet behavior in its backyard. Thus, if Washington brazenly intervened in Latin America or disregarded basic rules of international law or behavior, the theory went, the Soviet Union would react to these breaches of conduct, perhaps not in Latin America but certainly elsewhere.

Ronald Reagan's policies in Central America showed this view of superpower rivalry to be naive at best. But U.S. actions in Panama, from the invasion itself to measures implemented against the Nicaraguan and Cuban embassies (not to mention the harassment of the Vatican legation during Noriega's temporary asylum there) demonstrated that things had changed. There was no longer any reason for the United States even to contemplate reprisals elsewhere for blatantly violating diplomatic protocol, immunity, or asylum in Latin America. (There are as many examples of U.S. intervention that occurred regardless of such consequences as there are of interventions that did not take place, partly because of the possible consequences.) The explanation was to be found, above all, in the virtual disappearance of the Soviet sphere of influence and in the end of symmetry in U.S.-Soviet relations, except at the level of thermonuclear confrontation.

The dissolution of any significant counterweight to U.S. conduct in international affairs was inevitably perceived as a contributing factor to the new U.S. flaunting of "might over right." The most moderate sectors of the Latin American political spectrum, chiefly those in government or with government experience and expectations, were evidently more sensitive to the elimination of the counterweight than others. But even the radical Left was affected for it had traditionally argued that submission to the United States was not an unshakable fact of Latin American life precisely because of superpower rivalry. Many, including such fierce critics of the Sandinistas as Mexican poet Octavio Paz, were persuaded that the Nicaraguan revolutionaries' acceptance of elections and their subsequent electoral defeat was directly linked to the termination of Soviet support; that, in turn, was a consequence of the elimination of the Soviet Union as a superpower with worldwide interests, policies, and strategies. The war in the Persian Gulf and the need many Latin American leaders felt to support the United States, either as a result of direct pressure (as was the case with UN Security Council member Colombia) or to ingratiate themselves with George Bush (as Carlos Menem sought to do by sending two Argentine warships to the Gulf), accentuated this sentiment.

The more lucid revolutionary leaders of the Latin American Left also perceived this problem from the outset. Mario Payeras, a former Guatemalan guerrilla leader whose insightful analyses of his country's politics and of regional trends contrast with his inability to rally a constituency around them, sharply formulated the apprehension that many felt. His vision of the post–Cold War world reproduces the ambivalence of his political positions, his people, and his literature. It reflects a fear and hope with regard to a "one-superpower" world that extends throughout Latin America:

> The situation in the world today tends toward a relaxation of tensions. Even if the gringos proceed with their incredible aberrations like in Panama, this does not correspond to the general trend. If the United States interprets events in Eastern Europe as giving it a "free hand" in Latin America, then we will have to defend our sovereignty or reforms with domestic consensus and arms. ... In the postwar, Cold War world, as we knew it, every victory or defeat of one of the two competing systems (socialism and capitalism) has meant a victory or defeat of the other system. But perhaps the experiments in Eastern Europe can escape from this polarity, representing an alternative road, an emerging post-capitalist option? ... (Historically) we will never know what the Soviets would have done if free elections in East Germany in 1954 had given way to a pro-American government.

What we Guatemalans do know is what the Americans did with the Arbenz government, democratically emanated from free elections. For diametrically opposed reasons, the will of both peoples, in that same fateful year, was ignored by the super-powers in the context of the Cold War.[16]

Across the Latin American political spectrum, even the hemispheric Right is affected by this fear of the new world arising from the embers of the Cold War. As pro-U.S. a regime as that of Mexican President Carlos Salinas de Gortari reacted with concern and fright to the fading of the bipolar world. In his own way, Mexican Foreign Secretary Fernando Solana formulated a euphemistic apprehension that, though typically Mexican, is remarkably similar to the one stated by Payeras:

> The world is not going to become a one-sided, uniform world built around a single system of ideas and social and political formulae. The world has been and will continue to be richer and more varied than that. A world of one influence would be uniform and flat, inert, without options, without any possibility of a true exercise of freedom.[17]

Despite the seriousness and potentially negative consequences of these political trends, the greatest concern that the end of the Cold War generated in Latin America was fundamentally economic. As José Aricó of Argentina, one of the continent's most distinguished students of the Left in Latin America, put it: "What role can Latin America play on the global stage as the bipolar world comes to an end and as the Eastern bloc emerges as a fabulous opportunity for investment, as the United States looks East and Europe looks East?"[18] Latin governments and elites (as well as their counterparts in Africa and Asia), particularly those who gambled on external funding for domestic restructuring along so-called free market lines, worried that events in Europe would reduce the possibilities of obtaining the resources they needed. The problem had three separate aspects, but they all boiled down to one: the perception in Latin America that there were more countries competing for the same pie and that there was less pie to go around.

The larger countries feared that private credit and investment flows would be diverted from their region to the new capitalism of Eastern Europe. This was clearly the backdrop for the European and Asian trips in early and mid-1990 by Presidents Salinas de Gortari of Mexico and Fernando Collor de Mello of Brazil, the leaders of the continent's largest economies. As Salinas said, "[We hope that] the splendid signs of change [will] not cloud Europe's global vision nor distract its attention from our continent—and particularly Mexico—nor from other regions of the world."[19] Yet the motivation for their trips and their insistence on the issue stemmed largely from the fear that these events would have exactly those implications. Salinas, for example, justified his changed stance on a free trade agreement with the United States and his efforts to seek such an agreement precisely because funding from Europe was no longer available as a result of the transformation of the Eastern European economies.[20]

In the short run and in aggregate terms, the concern was not well founded. Although some investments and credits originally destined for Mexico and Brazil undoubtedly ended up in Hungary, Poland, or Czechoslovakia, this diverted trickle did not turn into a flood tide overnight. Only in the former East Germany did substantial, real flows of foreign investment immediately materialize and even in this exceptional instance, the money was slower to come and less plentiful than originally expected. The diversion may, indeed, have been most significant for those resource-generating countries that never invested or lent massively to Latin America to begin with—countries of Western Europe and particularly Germany—and least important for the larger, traditional providers of funds—Japan and the United States. Compared to reasonable expectations of both credits to an investment in the major Latin economies (in contrast, perhaps, to what occurred in the cases of Africa and Asia), the net short-term loss to Eastern Europe was negligible. The former Socialist economies were in no condition to quickly absorb large amounts of money from abroad, large corporations and banks did not impetuously plunge into romantic adventures, and there never was much money available for Latin America in the first place.[21]

The Latin American fear of being left out in the cold was more well founded with regard to official and multilateral financial resources. The U.S. Congress, the government of Japan, and the European Economic Community—again, above all, Germany—were far more willing to directly or indirectly channel taxpayers' funds into Eastern Europe than into Latin America. Considerable amounts of U.S. aid were redirected to Europe. Even the $500 million earmarked by the Bush administration for Panama and Nicaragua in the wake of Violeta Chamorro's victory in the latter country's elections in February 1990 was partly redirected by Congress to the "new democracies" of Eastern Europe. Other immediate and conclusive examples of this trend were the U.S. congressional aid packages for Poland and Hungary, the reduction from $10 billion to $4 billion of Japanese support for Latin America through 1995 (the remaining $6 billion were retargeted for Eastern Europe[22]), and the creation of the European Bank for Reconstruction and Development, originally proposed by French President Francois Mitterrand.

This diversion affected mainly aid-receiving Latin nations, excluding the larger economies such as Brazil, Mexico, and Argentina that obtain only marginal official development assistance from the United States and Europe and somewhat more from Japan. The concern was thus greatest for the smaller Latin nations that traditionally counted on U.S. support. In some cases, such as Nicaragua and Panama, they needed it dearly, if only to make up for previous U.S.-wrought destruction. But the other facet of this problem—i.e., World Bank and International Monetary Fund (IMF) resources—did directly affect the entire hemisphere and may have a more devastating, long-term impact on the larger economies than elsewhere.

The World Bank and the IMF had always played an important part in Latin America's funding but never as decisively as in the 1980s and 1990s. The major debt-restructuring packages of the last few years, including the 1990 Mexican and Venezuelan agreements, were all based, in the last analysis, on substituting multilateral loans for the traditional balance-of-payments lending by commercial banks. Moreover, because this process had been under way for some time, principal payments from previous debt deals began to come due as grace periods expired. Given that the World Bank does not roll over capital payments but, in theory, grants new loans to maintain positive flows with its recipients, major new lending to most Latin American countries became a necessity if they were to just stay even, let alone make up for foregone commercial bank credits. The growing importance of multilateral lending was underlined in 1990, when the International Monetary Fund and, to a lesser extent, the World Bank continued lending to countries like Brazil, Costa Rica, and others despite the fact that they were significantly in arrears on interest payments to their commercial bank creditors.

But new entries to these organizations (Czechoslovakia and Bulgaria) or recent ones (Poland, for example), together with more applications and enhanced eligibility for loans by previous members from Eastern Europe (Yugoslavia, Romania, and Hungary), inevitably placed far greater strains on these agencies' lending capabilities. Capital increases for the IMF and World Bank facilitated matters, but even then, the competition for larger funding stimulated by these very increases partly nullified their effect for Latin America.[23] Moreover, events following the collapse of the Socialist world indicated that the policy-based conditionality traditionally applied by the World Bank and the IMF to Latin American nations was being implemented in a much less stringent fashion in regard to Eastern Europe. In the words of one former World Bank official:

> Policy conditionality and, more importantly, evidence of the ability to pursue and implement reforms, appears to be of secondary importance when lenders and donors look to Eastern Europe. A double standard is being applied that falls heavier on the democracies of Latin America than on the would-be democracies of Eastern Europe.[24]

The forgiveness of half of Poland's official debt and the derived reduction in its commercial bank liabilities was perhaps the best illustration of this trend.

Beyond the immediate financial constraint that arose as a result of developments in what was once known as the "Socialist bloc," an additional, intangible, and downside consequence of the Cold War's conclusion for Latin America progressively surfaced. The region suffered from a clear diversion of attention: Latin America was less than ever in the spotlight of world affairs.

And attention was decisive, given the nature of the economic programs put in place by Salinas in Mexico, Color in Brazil, Carlos Menem in Argentina, and Carlos Andrés Pérez in Venezuela. Attention was also crucial given the nature and magnitude of foreign funding that these programs required. The resources that these governments were hoping to attract were private, diverse, and at least partially of small and medium size. Gigantic multinational corporations or megabanks would not make momentous decisions on the basis of headlines or more broadly defined "atmospherics." But small and medium-sized firms or large companies without experience abroad probably do act, to a certain extent, on the basis of general sentiments or awareness and at least a superficially positive business climate. Consequently, disinterest in this context was almost as damaging as scandal, a tarnished reputation, or skepticism. The enormous sensitivity that many of these governments showed with regard to criticism or indifference abroad was highly symptomatic of this.

In fact, the real problem behind the diversion issue was tied to the capital crunch and ensuing rise in competition for and cost of capital in the world during the 1990s. The conversion to a market economy throughout Eastern Europe and the free market reforms promoted and implemented in Latin America placed a severe strain on world capital markets. The forecasted amounts of capital needed to finance the reforms were staggering:

> By 1995 Eastern Europe and Latin America are likely to require about 170 billion dollars per year of external financing; about 110 billion of this is for Eastern Europe, and the rest is for Latin America. ... The conclusions regarding the balance between investment and savings as the potential transfer of resources from the Western countries to the restructuring areas ... are downright alarming. Japanese capital outflows are likely to continue to contract over time. Instead of exporting capital, Germany is likely to import capital. ... In order to satisfy the world's need for extra savings, gross U.S. national savings rates would have to rise from 14% of GDP [gross domestic product] to 18%, without GDP growth falling below 2% per year.[25]

In terms of the cost of capital, as David Roche noted, "the world is short of capital and therefore real interest rates will remain high and there will be piles of new equity issues (particularly privatisations) and less liquidity to buy them with."[26] As Albert Fishlow points out in his essay in this volume, interest rates were bound to rise as a result of this situation. The indirect economic effect of restructuring in Eastern Europe and the Soviet Union was thus much more important than the immediate diversion of funds, even with regard to the multilateral agencies. These agencies were perhaps less pessimistic about the prospects for growth and capital availability in the 1990s. The World Bank, for example, agreed that "the pattern of savings-investment balances across broad country groups is not likely to depart over the medium term from the broad trend established in the past few years."[27] It did emphasize that significant variations would occur country by country and, more importantly, that domestic policy reform would make a dramatic difference between receiving and being denied capital. But again, if every nation in Latin America carries out the same policy reforms, then the competition among them and between the hemisphere and other areas remains equivalent.

Only time will provide answers to three long-term questions regarding the economic impact of the end of the Cold War for Latin America. One involves an upside risk: Will the hypothetical and indirect economic effects of a superpower thaw in the Northern Hemisphere benefit the nations to the south? In theory, a scenario could be easily imagined whereby the conjunction of a substantial peace dividend in the United States and a major reduction in arms spending throughout the world would create a healthier global economic environment. This, in turn, would lead to higher growth in industrialized countries, eventually trickling down to the poorer nations and compensating for any possible, initial diversion of resources. The U.S. recession brought on by higher oil prices, the Gulf War, and the U.S. economy's intrinsic weaknesses has laid this hypothesis to rest.

Secondly and conversely, Eastern Europe's diversion impact could be spectacularly magnified by a true opening of the jewel in the crown: the Russian economy. As both a trade market and a niche for megainvestments in natural resources and infrastructure, the former Soviet Union dwarfs Eastern Europe and Latin America together. Even the greatest imaginable degree of diversion would inevitably be of a reduced magnitude, given the size of the Eastern European economies. This would change were Russia and its associated states to follow a path similar to that pursued by their Eastern European neighbors in economic policy and structural reform and thereby achieve even a relative success in this endeavor. The obstacles in Russia are obviously more daunting, but so, too, is the payoff.

Finally, there is the issue of the Mexican exception. Although many throughout Latin America—and in the United States—agree that the region as a whole would be negatively affected in the long run by the economic implications of the end of the Cold War, they are also convinced that Mexico will be spared.[28] The logic behind this reasoning is geosimplistic: Mexico is no longer really part of Latin America but ever more a portion of an ill-defined but real entity known as North America. To that extent and for reasons deriving directly from U.S. national security considerations applicable only to a border nation, many believe that Mexico will obtain the funding it requires. Private flows, it is thought, will head southward because of Mexico's natural, comparative advantages. Multilateral and official flows depend largely on U.S. votes, vetoes, and jawboning; attention depends on the U.S. media, which always devotes significantly more time and space to whatever happens along the border than elsewhere.

The argument is not absurd. But if the Mexican debt package of 1990 and the relative scarcity of new foreign direct investment—as opposed to portfolio investment—during the Salinas administration were any indication, U.S.-induced funding for Mexico, though undeniable, was evidently finite. Mexico was once again able to borrow money on world markets, albeit at a high price and with substantial U.S. help, but it was experiencing difficulties in meeting direct foreign investment targets. Just as the previous underfunding of Latin America as a whole had been made more acute by events in Eastern Europe, Mexico's underfunding was aggravated but on a lesser scale. Mexico may have been spared utter destitution, but it would certainly not remain indefinitely awash in U.S. funds earmarked "national security."

The underlying, long-term problem lay in the fact that Latin America, Africa, and significant parts of Asia were being increasingly marginalized from the world economy. Most of the factors governing long- and midterm international investment and credit flows had been waning in Latin America for years. With a few very minor exceptions, this region had been excluded, for example, from voluntary commercial bank lending since 1982.[29] In 1990, a reduced group of private or publicly owned companies from selected Latin American nations were able to float small bond offerings in the Eurodollar market but only at exorbitant interest rates that nearly made them the equivalent of newly floated junk bonds. Latin America's exclusion from world capital markets would have occurred regardless of the debt crisis, but that crisis worsened the situation. Similarly, the continent's participation in world trade was also diminishing as trade flows continued to be more and more concentrated within large blocs—i.e., Europe, U.S.-Canada—or in the Pacific Rim. Throughout the 1970s and early 1980s, the region's share of world exports remained stable, at approximately 5.5 percent, but by 1987, it had dropped to 3.8 percent. On the import side, the decline was more precipitous, from over 6 percent between 1975 and 1980 to 3.1 percent in 1987.[30]

From a broader economic viewpoint, Latin America in particular and the nonindustrialized world in general (with the exception of the Asian city-states and China) was ever less relevant to world production. In 1982, Latin America generated 7.1 percent of the world's gross "domestic" product; by 1986, the figure had fallen to 4.3 percent, and it continued to drop as the decade came to a close.[31] Latin America's share of world manufacturing production and of investment and credit was also shrinking. According to the Madrid-based Instituto de Relaciones Europo-Latinoaméricanos, "The most optimistic calculations estimate that Latin America's participation in world-wide direct foreign investment shrank from 13% in 1981–83 to 8% by 1987."[32] The commodities it traditionally exported were less and less crucial to the modern economy. Whatever advantages, beyond cheap labor, that Latin America could offer were either available elsewhere (now in Eastern Europe and China, tomorrow in the Soviet Union) or no longer essential—such as raw materials and cheap energy. The trend was so dramatic that some suggested that, in the same manner that the Great Depression and World War II provided considerable impetus to industrialization led by import substitution by cutting off Latin America from the rest of the world, the contemporary marginalization or "unlinking" could constitute a significant incentive for Latin American economic integration. Turning inward would be foolhardy for each country individually, but the creation of a South American free trade zone or common market was a realistic, distinct possibility, making a virtue out of necessity. The agreement signed in the mid-1980s by Brazil, Argentina, and Uruguay, featuring a commitment to move in the direction of free trade, received a powerful impetus in 1990 from newly elected Brazilian and Argentine presidents Collor de Mello and Menem. Together, they persuaded Uruguay and Paraguay to agree to the creation of the South American Common Market by 1994. While Mexico, Central America, and the Caribbean looked north, hoping to escape the hemisphere's isolation, a Brazilian-led trading bloc in the Southern Cone, including most of the region's economies, paradoxically emerged as one of the more positive results of the broader marginalization process.

But the issue was not purely economic. Politically, Latin America's chief instrument for drawing attention had become obsolete. And attention was indispensable in order to receive the official credits and aid that, in turn, created the conditions that attracted private capital flows. Instability, political extremism, and social chaos remained distinct possibilities in Latin America, but with the end of the Cold War, they were no longer tantamount to a Soviet-inspired geopolitical risk for the United States. Though the importance of Latin America for the United States endured and though there remained easily imaginable, direct negative consequences for the United States of a particular state of affairs in Latin America (essentially through the conduit of drugs or through immigration), the region's post–Cold War relevance was far from established.[33]

Moreover, most of the policy options of the United States and the industrial world have unfortunate trade-offs, or so-called perverse, negative, undesired, and unintended effects. Thus, if economic stagnation is perceived as the chief cause of immigration and drug trafficking, then economic growth provides the solution to those problems. If traditional models of growth are no longer viable, then new, free market, export-led policies fueled by private and foreign investment are recommended. The basic premise for these policies, in the short run at least, is a low wage level that attracts foreign investment, which, in turn, creates jobs and transfers technology. But, of course, the low wage level also stimulates emigration like no other factor. Similarly, as became clear with the (relative) success of the South Florida Task Force against drug traffickers, closing down one drug route (the Caribbean) automatically enhances the attractiveness of others (Mexico). This is also true for coca-leaf cultivation: Eradication of the coca crop in the Upper Huallaga leads to new fields in Peru, and success in reducing Peruvian acreage inspires new coca-leaf production in Brazil.

Furthermore, the type of preoccupation that drugs and immigration stimulate in the U.S. consciousness does not necessarily guarantee a domestic U.S. consensus on providing aid or attention to Latin America or becoming involved in its affairs. Drugs and immigration can generate exactly the opposite reaction: introspection, exclusion, barriers on the borders, and rejection of everything emanating from the South. Instead of stimulating interest and concern, they can lead to indifference or hostility. Finally, whereas the concept of geopolitical risk was applicable to every nation of the hemisphere, albeit in varying degrees, concerns regarding immigration and drugs are not. Indeed, immigration and drug issues may be a basis for U.S. policy only in the case of the country for which such a policy is least necessary, given that nation's power to generate interest and attract attention through other channels: Mexico.

Paradoxically, after so many years of worrying about excessive U.S. involvement in the region, Latin America may soon suffer from U.S. indifference, compounded by the rest of the world's traditional, relative disinterest. Italy still worries about Argentina and Uruguay, as memories of previous emigration linger. The European Left in general expressed outrage or at least concern over human rights violations in the Southern Cone while they existed, but democratization led to boredom. And the Nisei community in São Paulo—the largest in the world outside Japan—can still generate some Japanese interest in Brazil, but it is not enough.

The rise of what several authors called a North-North circuit of investment, credit, and trade that incorporated the former Socialist economies—perhaps including the former Soviet Union and China and excluding the Third World and specifically Latin America, apart from a few "buffer states" like Mexico, Morocco, and possibly Iran—is far from impossible.[34] Trade, investment, and credit could all become concentrated—not entirely but in a higher proportion than ever before—in the Northern Hemisphere. The fear of being "left out," so often expressed by Latin leaders and intellectuals, was a reflection of this possibility. The plummeting interest in Latin America on the part of the developed world's universities, press, business, and politicians was equally derived from this prospect.

And yet, superficial trends and sentiments notwithstanding, the transformation of the modern world (including the Western Hemisphere) into separate, watertight compartments, devoid of any significant influence upon one another, is obviously not a viable scenario for the future.

The direct U.S. economic stake in Latin America today may be less important than ever before, although even this is arguable, given the enduring nature of U.S. energy dependence and the precariousness of Middle East sources. But the noneconomic or "paraeconomic" effect of Latin American affairs on the United States—the emergence of so-called intermestic issues—

seems greater than ever, and it is likely to increase before it diminishes. The North-North syndrome may be valid in strictly economic terms, but from a social, political, and cultural standpoint, it is illusory. The fact that the United States has always proved far less capable of dealing with and being sensitive to economic trends than to other types of transformations will render the process of managing this new American interdependence more complicated. But it will not eliminate it. Nor will the process itself enhance Latin America's leverage: Although its nations, leaders, and thinkers have, in the past, proven more skillful at playing their noneconomic cards, many Latin American leaders today seem to believe that "the business of Latin America is business."

Tragically, this conviction surfaced precisely at a time when Latin elites were more willing than ever before to pay any price to become part of the modern world economy—be it as "the poorest [country] of the rich [group]," as Salinas de Gortari was reputed to have said, or as "a modern First World country leaving Brazil's barbarian capitalism behind," in Collor de Mello's words. As the geopolitical rationale for U.S. policy toward Latin America faded and the European humanitarian motivation dwindled, as rich trading blocs consolidated and Japan looked to China and the former Soviet Union, the economic component of the Latin America policy of the United States and the rest of the world is shrinking. In 1980, 17.9 percent of U.S. worldwide direct foreign investment was located in Latin America; by 1987, the proportion had fallen to 13.7 percent. In 1980, Latin America received 16.3 percent of U.S. exports; by 1987, the percentage had dropped to 12.4 percent.[35] The hemisphere might well face the prospect of "Africanization": condemned to the margins of world financial and trade flows and, inevitably, to neglect and irrelevance.[36]

Latin America thus finds itself today in a sadly paradoxical bind. The end of the Cold War has brought greatly broadened geopolitical leeway, but economic globalization and ideological uniformity have rendered that at least partially meaningless. It has deemed itself obliged to implement economic policies that imply abandoning both traditional development goals and huge volumes of external funding, with only the former assured and the latter largely hypothetical. In consequence, the nations of the hemisphere outdo each other in search of funding, but they quickly run into diminishing returns—it takes greater concessions to obtain shrinking magnitudes of financing—and the harsh reality that in the new world order, Latin America matters ever less in the international equation. For the nations of Latin America, the end of the Cold War has meant high expectations and unexpected frustration.

## Notes

1. William Branigan, "50 Kilos of Cocaine Turn Out to Be Tamales," *Washington Post*, January 2, 1990.

2. Fernando Henrique Cardoso, "United States–Latin America After the Cold War" (paper presented at the workshop on "Latin and U.S. America in the 1990s," Swedish Ministry of Foreign Affairs, Stockholm, Sweden, May 28, 1991).

3. Régis Debray, "Pour en finir avec l'antiaméricanisme" (Lecture at New York University, New York, April 28, 1991).

4. One version of this approach has been critically characterized by Alan Tonelson as "internationalism": "With or without the Soviet threat, internationalists have portrayed America's extensive involvement in Third World countries as a security and economic imperative, resulting from tight, indissoluble links between the Third World's fate and our own. To the extent that these links exist, however, they are largely artificial"; see Alan Tonelson, "What Is the National Interest?" *Atlantic Monthly* (July 1991), p. 49. Debray's deterministic stance stems from his diagnosis: "American originality today derives from its critical size due to the absence of any external counterweight. With the evaporation of its Soviet rival, it becomes necessary to go back all the way to the Roman Empire to find a world as strategically unipolar," ibid. And in the words of another scholar, who wrote an entire book on the basis of the metaphor of Imperial Rome, "American diplomacy has been accustomed to this exercise from the outset: to present with a universal and moral coating operations that are also good business. It proved it from the 19th century, when at the time of the decolonization of Latin America, it invented the Monroe Doctrine to 'protect' the hemisphere. Until now this moralism was for U.S. consumption. From now on, it is addressed to the rest of the world, and must make those that are defended understand that they cannot take advantage of their presumed weakness. U.S. military operations in Central and Latin America in 1990 already bear the mark of this new orientation. Their 'anti-drug' goals gave them a collective tone and showed every country threatened by the drugs that they owed the United States for its drug-enforcement action"; see Jean-Christophe Renin, *L'Empire et les nouveaux barbares* (Paris: Editions Jean-Claude Lattés, 1991), pp. 168–169.

5. In a speech presented at the Mexican Foreign Ministry's Lincoln-Juárez Lectures on March 7, 1990, Henry Kissinger formulated this point in the following manner: "When I began to deal with the hemisphere and to establish contacts in the region, there was an important ideological element on both sides of the divide: in the United States a crusade against Communist penetration in the hemisphere, and in Latin America a fear of U.S. intervention. ... Changes in the continent will have profound consequences, mainly on the United States because as the perception of the Soviet threat in the hemisphere has virtually evaporated, fear as a unifying principle of hemispheric relations has also faded"; see Henry A. Kissinger, "Un mundo en transformación," *Revista Mexicana de Política Exterior,* 27 (Summer 1990).

6. Europe, for example, never really went along with the U.S. anti-Castro policy. "And above all, the United States pushed their allies to adopt a policy consonant with their own. With the Europeans, this did not work at all"; see Jean-Pierre Clerc, *Fidel de Cuba* (Paris: Editions Ramsay, 1988), p. 269.

7. According to Bob Woodward, "CIA records show that at one point 100,000 dollars had been passed to her (Eugenia Charles of Dominica) government for a secret support operation"; see Bob Woodward, *Veil: The Secret Wars of the CIA, 1981–87* (New York: Simon and Schuster, 1987), p. 290.

8. The Mexican Foreign Ministry requested a clarification from the U.S. government regarding the Supreme Court's *Verdugo Urquidez* ruling and the U.S. executive's inter-

pretation of it. No reply was ever made public; there may well never have been a reply at all. For the effects of the *Verdugo Urquidez* ruling on Mexico and Latin America, see Adolfo Aguilar Zinser, *Siempre!* (March 29, 1990).

9. *Newsweek* (Latin American edition), February 19, 1990.

10. The degree of intrusiveness and its effectiveness were well portrayed in a *New York Times Magazine* article on the DEA's presence in Peru. According to the author, "In waging the drug war, the United States has altered the (Huallaga) river's course." As to effectiveness, the same article quoted a U.S. official at the Santa Lucía base as saying that "even if we spend 500 million, we're not going to get the Peruvians to stop growing coca. With that sum I could pave the Upper Huallaga over, but they'd simply move over to the next valley"; see Michael Massing, "In the Cocaine War, the Jungle Is Winning," *New York Times Magazine,* March 4, 1990.

11. Georges Vernez and David Ronfeldt, *The Current Situation in Immigration* (Santa Monica, Calif.: Rand Corporation, 1991), p. 2. The authors indicated that, according to U.S. census figures, there were 4.1 million Mexican-born immigrants in the United States by 1988; in principle, most of them were documented because undocumented Mexicans generally go uncounted by the census.

12. According to an oft-quoted U.S. study of Mexican migration, in 1986, 77 percent of interviewed migrants in Los Altos de Jalisco (a strong emigration-generating area for nearly 100 years) stated that their main reason for leaving Mexico was to improve their income. Only 9 percent gave unemployment as a reason; see Wayne Cornelius, "Mexican Migration to the United States: Causes, Consequences, and U.S. Responses," mimeographed (Cambridge, Mass.: Center for International Studies, Massachusetts Institute of Technology, 1978). According to a Mexican and a U.S. expert, "The determining factor [in migration] is the difference between the wages that Mexican workers receive in the two countries"; see Manuel García y Griego and Mónica Verea, *México y Estados Unidos frente a la migración de los indocumentados* (Mexico, City: UNAM, 1988), p. 56.

13. International Monetary Fund, "Foreign Trade Statistics," *Direction of Trade Statistical Yearbook, 1990* (Washington, D.C.: International Monetary Fund, 1990).

14. Rubén Berríos, "The USSR and the Andean Countries," in Eusebio Mujal-León, ed., *The USSR and Latin America* (London: Unwin Hyman, 1989), p. 352.

15. Aldo C. Vacs, "Pragmatism and Rapprochement: Soviet Relations with Argentina and Brazil," in Eusebio Mujal-León, ed., *The USSR and Latin America* (London: Unwin Hyman, 1989), p. 326.

16. Mario Payeras, interview with the author, Mexico City, February 15, 1990, and "Las revoluciones del Este," mimeographed (January 1990).

17. Fernando Solana, Independence Day speech, September 16, 1990. The fear of and apprehension about a "one-superpower world" was expressed in this way across the entire political spectrum in Latin America. Needless to say, this included Cuba, whose ambassador to the United Nations, Ricardo Alarcón, stated the issue directly: "The US is acting as if they have become the only superpower, the dominant force in the world. ... They are not only doing this unilaterally, but they are using the [United Nations] Security Council for this purpose. This is a very serious development for the entire world"; see *New York Times,* September 22, 1990.

18. José Aricó, interview with the author, Buenos Aires, December 9, 1989.

19. Carlos Salinas de Gortari, "México: Espacio atractivo para la comunidad internacional," address to the World Economic Forum, Davos, February 1, 1990 (distributed by the Mexican Presidency, Office of Information).

20. Carlos Salinas de Gortari, address to the U.S. Business Roundtable, Washington, D.C., June 6, 1990 (distributed by the Mexican Presidency, Office of Information).

21. Disagreement among experts, bankers, investors, and decisionmakers over exactly what the consequences would be for Latin America was evident and widespread from the outset. The first public debate on the issue was perhaps held in the pages of *Latin Finance*, no. 15 (April 1990).

22. "The pool of surplus Japanese capital slated to be recycled to the Less Developed Countries—known once as the Nakasone Fund—is being tapped for bridge loans and export credits for Eastern Europe. When the Japanese assembled the multi-billion dollar facility, about 10 billion was allotted for Latin America. Mexican Finance Minister Pedro Aspo was recently told in Tokyo that Latin America's share has been cut to 4.1 billion, of which Mexico has already received half"; see *Latin Finance*, no. 15 (April 1990), p. 53.

23. In fiscal 1989, the World Bank approved forty-three loans totaling $5.8 billion to all of Latin America. It approved only five loans for $430 million to Eastern Europe in its entirety (three to Hungary, two to Yugoslavia). This ratio is obviously untenable in the new international situation. In relation to total outstanding loans (including approved but disbursed and pending loans), Mexico, Brazil, and Argentina have outstanding loans totaling $36.8 billion (26 percent of all accumulated World Bank credits), whereas the only Eastern European nations owing money to the bank—Hungary, Romania, and Yugoslavia—have $9.2 billion, representing 4.1 percent. See Banco Mundial, *Informe anual 1989* (Washington, D.C.: IBRD, 1989), pp. 173–174, 194–197.

24. Frank Vogl, "Turning Away," *Latin Finance*, no. 15 (April 1990), p. 72.

25. David C. Roche, *The Global Resource Model* (London: Morgan Stanley, Investment Research UK and Europe, December 13, 1990), pp. 81–82.

26. Ibid., p. 6.

27. The World Bank, *World Development Report 1991* (New York: Oxford University Press, 1991), p. 23.

28. This argument is made by both the Left and the Right in the United States. Even a staunch conservative like Mark Falcoff of the American Enterprise Institute stated unequivocally that "with the end of the Cold War, no Latin American country, save one, will be of sufficient value or interest to us to command the kind of attention it did in the past as part of a larger strategic equation. The exception, of course, is Mexico, with whom we share a border"; see Mark Falcoff, "Latin America Alone," *American Enterprise Review* (January/February 1990).

29. The case has been made, convincingly, that this withdrawal of major banks from Latin American lending was part of a deeper trend than the debt crisis alone and that it would have occurred regardless of the debt crisis. "Since the onset of the debt crisis ... officials in both creditor and debtor nations have operated on the assumption that commercial banks would start making new loans to developing country borrowers once the debtors completed their macroeconomic adjustments and restored their creditworthiness. Life may not be this simple. A comparison of the factors that induced banks to begin lending to developing countries in the 1970s with the conditions prevailing during the 1980s and likely in the 1990s suggest that the commercial banks' long-term business

interests may no longer coincide with Latin America's debt service and investment requirements"; see Alfred J. Watkins, "The Impact of Recent Financial Market Developments on Latin America's Access to External Financial Resources," mimeographed (New York: UN Economic Commission for Latin America, 1988).

30. Business International, *The Latin American Market Atlas, 1989* (New York: Business International Corporation, 1989), pp. 5–6.

31. Ibid., pp. 13–14.

32. Instituto de Relaciones Europo-Latinaméricanos, *Europa y América Latina en los 90: ¿Hacia una nueva relación?* (Madrid: Instituto de Relaciones Europa-América Latina, 1989), p. 6.

33. Abraham Lowenthal, for example, eloquently pleaded the case for a new form of U.S. interest in Latin American in mid-1990, given that the "region's supposed importance for the bi-polar struggle virtually evaporated overnight ... and Latin American trends are perceived as no longer having much impact upon the United States. ... U.S. military security is no longer credibly menaced by attack from or through the western hemisphere, but security in a broader sense ... is vulnerable to many Latin American developments ... economic impact, the influence of migration, the region's role in affecting important shared problems [the most dramatic example is narcotics] and from its importance for core values at the heart of U.S. society"; see Abraham F. Lowenthal, "Rediscovering Latin America," *Foreign Affairs* (Fall, 1990), pp. 33–36.

34. See, for example, Peter Smith, "La nueva relación entre México y Estados Unidos," *NEXOS* (February 1990).

35. U.S. Department of Commerce, *Statistical Abstract of the United States, 1989* (Washington, D.C.: U.S. Department of Commerce, 1989), pp. 779 and 788.

36. The term and the tragic analogy—reflecting the African continent's dramatic state of marginalization—emerged simultaneously with the fall of the Eastern European regimes. See Jorge G. Castañeda, "Los efectos del fin de la guerra fría para América Latina," *NEXOS* (December 1989); Alan Stoga, "Poland vs. Argentina," *Latin Finance* (April 1990); or Helio Jaguaribe, "Latin America Is Increasing Its Marginal Condition and Becoming a Sort of Western Replica of Africa" and "The Double Rejection: A Brief Note on the United States and Latin America in the New International Scenario" (Paper presented at the Inter-American Dialogue workshop on "The Changing Global Context for U.S.–Latin American Relations," Airlie House, Warrenton, Va., May 21–22, 1990).

# 3

# A View from the Southern Cone

## Helio Jaguaribe

The international collapse of communism and the implosion of the former Soviet Union have left the United States as the only superpower in the world.

The Soviet Union's internal crisis had its roots in a long-standing disparity between the Communist system's areas of great achievement and the inadequacy of the general condition of the country's infrastructure. The first two five-year plans (1928–1932 and 1933–1937) were able to convert a rural society into an industrial one, although at an intolerable human price. Further development—after the awful sacrifices of World War II—transformed the Soviet Union into a fully industrialized country. In that system, the military was given top priority, making possible such achievements as the explosion of the first Soviet atomic bomb in 1948 and the successful launching of *Sputnik*, the first space satellite, in 1957.

The development of the Soviet experiment, however, was characterized by a large and ever-widening gap between its major achievements and the general conditions of the country. Outside of the military, large sectors remained underdeveloped. The quality of most consumer goods was poor, and there were permanent problems of supply and distribution for many items. The bureaucratic and totalitarian system proved incapable of creating the necessary incentives for most activities, and it was incompatible with innovative efforts and any critical assessment of results. Khrushchev's hope of surpassing the United States in a couple of decades proved illusory, and Leonid Brezhnev's era (1964–1984) was a period of stagnation. When Mikhail Gorbachev came to power in 1985, this great statesman decided that it was time to face realities.

He successfully attempted, in his first years in office, to put an end to the Cold War and to win the Soviet Union international recognition as a peaceful country. He then initiated wide and deep internal changes aimed at transforming a centralized, authoritarian, bureaucratic regime into a democratic federation of autonomous republics, based on a free market economy. These efforts were less successful, however. The disruptive forces unleashed by political liberalization, together with the dramatic drop in production that accompanied the economic changes, brought the nation to a nearly chaotic condition. The final result was the fragmenting of the Soviet Union and its division into fifteen independent republics, bringing to an end Gorbachev's presidential mandate.

Sooner or later, a group of new democratic countries will succeed the former Soviet Union. Russia, as the largest of them, will continue to play an international role. It is hardly conceivable, however, that this nation will attain major international relevance in the next several years. In the meantime, the United States will keep its position as the only operational superpower.

This situation was clearly confirmed by the Gulf War. The violent annexation of Kuwait by Saddam Hussein's troops produced immense international indignation and, except in a few Arab states, a consensus that Iraq's conquest could not be tolerated. But at that historical moment, only the United States, supported by a mandate of the Security Council, had the resolve and the capability to mount a prompt, effective intervention. The broad alliance built by the United States and the participation of several nations, including Egypt and Syria, in the military action underscored the new and undisputed leading role of the United States.

## The New International Scenario

The United States came to this position of world primacy at a historical juncture characterized by many changes in the international scenario. First among them, of course, was the worldwide collapse of communism and the demise of the Soviet Union. With Gorbachev's new policies and reforms, the Communist regimes in Eastern Europe lost both their ideological foundation and the deterrent power that were once encapsulated in the Brezhnev doctrine—Soviet military intervention in support of Communist regimes. In their place, market economies are now being built within an institutional, democratic framework.

Another relevant characteristic of the current scenario is the emergence of postindustrial societies, as the more advanced countries acquire a growing cybernetic capacity. Technology has become the most decisive factor of production, based on extensive use of informatics and robotics. The comparative advantages conferred by cheap, local raw materials are rapidly diminishing. A well-educated work force and an adequate number of highly qualified scientists, technologists, and managers are the new requirements for economic competitiveness.

An important negative consequence of the emerging postindustrial society is a trend toward placing restrictions on the availability and use of knowledge. Since the Renaissance and particularly since the Enlightenment, knowledge has been understood as a universal good, available to all learned men. Scientists have seen themselves as members of an open, international "communauté des savants." Some years ago, a student from an underdeveloped country who was admitted to one of the higher centers of knowledge, such as MIT or Cal Tech, would have access to the ultimate available knowledge in any scientific and technological field. But today, access to applied and applicable knowledge is often restricted by large multinational corporations, protected by patents and legalized secrecy. The mercantilization of knowledge is fast increasing, in step with the growing economic importance of technology.

A third relevant trait of the new international scenario is the formation of megamarkets, such as the European Community, the U.S.-Canada market, and the Japan-Asian system. These are intended to increase the productivity and competitiveness of their members' economies by providing large markets for their products and better conditions for research and development. A liberal discourse is used to argue that the resulting benefits will improve quality and reduce costs and prices for the advantage of both members and nonmembers of the megamarkets alike. There is little doubt, however, that the megamarkets will adopt a rather selective liberalism, insofar as the protection of their own products will be at stake.

A fourth important aspect of the present international situation is the dangerous lack of an appropriate international system for addressing the common interests of humanity. The protection of the biosphere and the whole complex of ecological requirements, the preservation and enforcement of peace in areas of regional conflict (the Middle East, the Indian subcontinent, Africa), health, sanitation, free communications and transport, basic education, human development, international control on drugs and crime, collective resources—all these issues demand an effective and equitable world administration, transcending national frontiers and sovereignties. Although the United Nations is widely acknowledged as the appropriate institution for attending to the collective interests of humankind, it has neither the resources nor the power needed for the job.

A fifth salient trait of the present international system is the deepening of the North-South gap, a problem that is aggravated by the South's immense and unpayable foreign debt. The world cannot remain divided indefinitely between a shrinking group of educated, prosperous countries in the North and an increasingly large, poor, and uneducated South. Nor can the South endure the burden of its debt. Northern cultural values and civilized, prosperous lifestyles cannot subsist surrounded by a world of misery and ignorance. These facts are widely acknowledged, yet no effective international action is taken to halt the deterioration of the South.

# U.S. Problems

In the context of those important changes, the United States must exercise its new status as the only remaining superpower within important domestic constraints.

 The first such limitation is the contrast between the political-military power of the United States and its relative economic decline. For many years, the United States has struggled with large fiscal and trade deficits. According to the 1990 World Bank report, the fiscal deficit for 1988 was in the order of $155 billion, representing 2.9 percent of the gross domestic product (GDP). Although these figures have improved somewhat since then, they reflect a complex set of conditions that have contributed to a long, slow decline in the international competitiveness of the U.S. economy.

A second constraint is a lack of domestic consensus with respect to important collective issues in the fields of politics, social and racial relations, immigration, education, and international affairs. The Vietnam War is responsible for unleashing most of the divisions that have arisen in the United States since World War II. And important changes in the social structure—including the increased distance between the higher and lower strata, new patterns of territorial and urban population distribution, and the concentration of uneducated and poor people in the core of many cities—have significantly contributed to the erosion of the U.S. consensus. The 1992 riots in Los Angeles dramatically illustrated this problem.

Largely because of this breakdown in the national consensus, the U.S. government has been deprived of sufficient domestic support for an active international role. Citizens rejoice to see international demonstrations of U.S. prestige or strength, but they are not prepared to pay an additional price for the performance of related feats. The U.S. government is being called upon to exercise a leading world role—a demand that, as in the recent case of the Gulf War, often requires vast resources—without the possibility of receiving additional contributions from the citizenry.[1]

Another internal limitation on the exercise of U.S. international primacy is the persistent lack of a global and equitable worldview. The United States developed global initiatives, such as the Atlantic Alliance, in response to actual or perceived Soviet threats, but the rapid disappearance of these threats left the nation without a coherent global project. Because U.S. interests in the world are defined primarily by domestic pressure groups, they tend to be understood in piecemeal terms. Lacking an adequate understanding of overall interests or the costs of ignoring them, it is difficult for the United States to adjust its interests to a global framework for a reasonable and equitable world order.

All these constraints are reflected in the current U.S. propensity for maximizing those international advantages that it can gain at very low cost or at the expense of weaker partners—a pattern that has historically characterized declining powers. Episodes such as the invasions of Grenada and Panama and, what is worse, their domestic celebration as national feats are indications of this propensity. The victorious national mood that followed the Gulf War, in which devastating U.S. technology resulted in the death of more than 100,000 Iraqis, is another worrying sign.

## The United States and Latin America

### *The Double Rejection*

One thing that the United States and Latin America have in common in the 1990s is that both are being rejected by Europe, albeit for different reasons and in different ways. Europe used to value the United States as the great protector against Soviet threats, but it endured U.S. strategic and technological superiority with unconcealed resentment. Once the Soviet threat disappeared and the Europessimism caused by the relative stagnation of the Old World gave way to the euphoria of an increasingly prosperous and competitive new Europe, many Europeans started seeing the U.S. presence as an unnecessary, undesirable interference in their national and regional affairs.

In the case of Latin America, the European rejection is related to a growing sense that the Latin countries are a historical failure. These countries were once seen as a promising land of the future that could serve as an arena for expanding European influence, investment, and cultural diplomacy. Increasingly, however, Europe now sees them as badly managed, corrupt, inflation-ridden, debt-wracked, stagnating societies—a sort of slightly better-off Africa of the West.

That double rejection, among many other factors, could induce a closer cooperation between the two Americas. The United States understands that its world predominance, though still significant in political-military terms, is declining in economic and cultural ones. U.S. exports to Europe will fall as the EC expands, and in other world markets, the United States will face superior Japanese competition. In view of these facts, the United States will find it more and more important to consolidate its regional superiority in the Latin American area, and a new good-neighbor policy will be needed to accomplish this goal. From the Latin American side, the European rejection, Japan's inability to surmount its own ethnocentric limitations, the end of the East-West conflict, and the loss of the opportunity to maneuver for Latin America's own advantage mean that the United States is the only major source for investments and technological transfers.

In this context, President Bush's Enterprise for the Americas Initiative seemed attractive for both sides of the Americas. Some Latin American countries are manifesting their effective agreement with the initiative. Mexico had already decided, independently of Bush's initiative, to join the U.S.-Canada common market, and it is now taking the necessary steps. Chile considers its economy already adjusted to the world market and is willing to join a U.S.-led common market. Venezuela, while keeping an eye on its relations with the Southern Cone, is inclined to follow. Uruguay, although deeply committed to Mercosur, is also interested in an open relationship with the U.S. market. The four countries of Mercosur, for their part, made an agreement in June 1991 that adjusted their projected common market to the Bush initiative.

Nevertheless, the initiative is confronted with serious difficulties that stem from the deep differences separating the two Americas and the unpreparedness of the United States to compensate for those differences.

A brief look at the European Community and the way in which it has approached its own internal imbalances is of great interest in understanding the problems between the two Americas. A major difficulty in the integration of the European Community was how to deal with the substantial differences in economic advancement that separated Greece, Portugal, and Spain from the rich members of the community. The EC's answer to that problem has been to adopt two implicit models, which I call the model of factors mobility and the model of systems restructuration.

The model of factors mobility is being applied to Greece and Portugal. Both countries have small populations, and a substantial part of their unemployed labor force customarily emigrates to seek jobs in other countries. Within the European Community, two effects were bound to occur. On the one hand, integration with Europe will increase the unemployment rate in Greece and Portugal even as it upgrades their economic levels as a whole. Goods formerly made in those countries will either be imported from more advanced European nations at better prices and levels of quality or they will be produced in Greece and Portugal by branches of large European firms that operate with higher levels of productivity and lower levels of labor. The result, in either case, will be more unemployment. The unemployed workers, however, will migrate to the richer European countries. There, they will get jobs and eventually replace the guest workers from Turkey and the Magreb, for the good of all concerned European countries.

In the case of Spain, a country with too large a population to permit a massive migration of its citizens to Northern Europe, the implied model of systems restructuration applies. Spain is receiving massive amounts of capital and technology from the more advanced European countries, and key Spanish industries are currently developing at rates that are two to three times higher than the European average. The Spaniards estimate that by the year 2000, they will achieve a level of competitiveness comparable to that of Italy.

In principle, these two models could be transposed to Latin America. If the United States opened its doors to unemployed workers from the smaller Latin American countries and transferred massive amounts of capital and technology to the larger ones, such as Argentina, Brazil, and Mexico, the effects would be similar to those that the European common market is bringing about in Greece, Portugal, and Spain.

As a matter of fact, however, the United States is not likely to apply the European models in Latin America. The reasons have to do with three main differences between Europe and the Americas. First, the relationship between wealth and poverty is different in the two regions. In Europe, a large majority of rich people can afford to help a small minority of poor people, but the poor form a vast majority in the Americas. Second, menial work is no longer performed by the natives of Europe's rich countries. These jobs are done by guest workers from Turkey and the Arab countries, who can be replaced by immigrants from other EC nations. In the United States, on the other hand, there is already a problem of finding work for the unqualified labor force, both native and alien. Finally, the powerful third reason is that the Europeans are united by a common culture. Greece is the cradle of Western civilization, and the Iberian countries are among the major sources of European culture, from Miguel de Cervantes to José Ortega y Gasset, from Luiz Vaz de Camoëns to Fernando Pessoa. There is enough Pan-European solidarity to absorb Greeks and Portuguese in exchange for the disliked Turks and Arabs, and there is enough surplus capital to invest in Spain. There is no solidarity, however, between the United States and Central America and the Caribbean. Moreover, the United States cannot afford to transfer scarce production factors to Argentina, Brazil, and Mexico in large amounts.

## A Pragmatic Approach

President Bush's initiative was not, of course, proposed in a vacuum. Independent of the proposal, important trends were already taking place in the region.

All the small Central American and Caribbean societies except Cuba, pulled by the social and economic weight of the United States, are operating as a sort of informal Puerto Rico. The United States dominates their international trade, their foreign investments, and their tourism, and it is the main destination for their legal and illegal emigrants. It was an exercise of statesmanship by Bush to provide an institutional framework for these undeniable trends.

The terms for Mexico's participation in the U.S.-Canada common market have nearly been agreed upon. In this case, too, the North American Free Trade Agreement (NAFTA) represents the formalization of a preexisting situation. With the Rio Grande as much a frontier as a bridge between two rather complementary societies and economies, the awkward question involves the immense migratory pressure created by Mexicans who want to join the U.S. labor force. It is widely acknowledged that the immigration of a limited number of Mexican workers, particularly for agricultural jobs, is advantageous for

TABLE 3.1   Mercosur Profile

| Country | Population (Million) | GDP | Exports | Imports | Total Trade |
|---------|---------------------|-------|---------|---------|-------------|
| Argentina | 32.7 | 76.5 | 11.0 | 7.0 | 18.0 |
| Brazil | 153.3 | 402.8 | 31.9 | 23.1 | 55.0 |
| Paraguay | 4.4 | 4.8 | 1.2 | 1.6 | 2.8 |
| Uruguay | 3.1 | 7.9 | 1.6 | 1.6 | 3.2 |
| TOTAL | 193.3 | 492.0 | 45.7 | 33.3 | 79.0 |

SOURCE: Helene Arneud et al., *L'Etat du monde, 1993* (Paris: Ed. La Découverte, 1993).

both sides. But the United States would face serious problems—including the displacement of many domestic laborers—if it tried to absorb the many thousands of Mexicans who desire to cross the border. If, as expected, a Mexican-American-Canadian common market accelerates the economic development of Mexico and brings to that country an important flow of capital and technology from the North, then the corresponding job growth in Mexico would substantially reduce the migratory pressure. The willingness of the Mexicans to accept restrictive migratory clauses as a condition of their participation in the common market with the United States and Canada is based on this assumption.

In Chile, which has opened its economy to the world market and diversified its exports from the traditional copper-based products into new lines,[2] such as natural processed foods, there is a wide consensus in favor of the Bush initiative. And Venezuela is trying to follow the Chilean path. While keeping an eye on its relations with the South, particularly in view of the huge Brazilian market, Venezuela is inclined to accept the Bush proposal and join a Pan-American common market.

## Mercosur

The Mercosur is, essentially, an extension of the Brazil-Argentina common market to the other countries of the Southern Cone (see Table 3.1). Uruguay, already a member of that market, is one of the signatories of the Asunción treaty, and Paraguay has joined. Chile is interested in joining the Mercosur, particularly in view of the wide Brazilian market for its food exports, but it does not wish to do so if that would increase its import barriers and thus prevent the formation of a common market with the United States. The four signatories of the Mercosur treaty have agreed to give Chile until 1994 to make its decision.

Although Mercosur is a relatively small market and heavily dominated by Brazil, it provides important advantages for its members.[3] The present level of commercial exchange, even between Argentina and Brazil, is rather small relative to its immediate potential. Indeed, a recently concluded study coordinated by the Instituto de Estudos Politicos e Sociais (IEPES), the "Alvorado

Project," undertaken in Rio by IEPES in 1991, indicated that the present trade figures would be multiplied by 300 percent in a few years if the Mercosur countries adopted a preferential policy toward imports from Mercosur suppliers.

A second benefit of Mercosur is the incentive that it provides for joint ventures among members. Border joint ventures among neighbors, such as the gigantic Itaipu hydroelectric plant between Brazil and Paraguay and the interconnection of the electric networks of Argentina and Brazil, have already become important in the region.

Possibly the most important dimension of Mercosur is its effectiveness in fostering scientific-technological cooperation among its members. Such cooperation is particularly relevant between Brazil and Argentina, both of which have significant and advanced scientific establishments. Each, however, often lacks a critical mass of experts and researchers. In addition, each suffers from inadequate funds and other limitations. A close cooperation between the two countries could frequently solve such problems and lend critical effectiveness to research efforts—for example, in theoretical and applied knowledge in such fields as nuclear energy, informatics, and biotechnology.

The importance of critical effectiveness in scientific and technological research is more than an expression of the new relevance of technology as the key factor of production. It is also necessary to compensate for the legally protected secrecy that increasingly surrounds advances in applied science. The United States is putting pressure on the Latin American countries to sign treaties that would assure long-term protection to U.S. patents and legally protected "intellectual property," i.e., all sorts of innovations in the field of applied science. Without discussing the legal aspects of such policies here, I would add that the obvious effect would be to perpetuate the technological dependency of the South.

From the viewpoint of Mercosur members, the most important prerequisite for technological development is to substantially increase their own research capabilities. Even in the absence of any legal restrictions, countries without a critical effectiveness in scientific and technological research just cannot do anything. And, as the recent Japanese example shows, the development of a strong, autonomous research capability generates positive effects that cannot be stifled even by restrictive international legislation. Limiting such legislation to a reasonable level is, of course, a complementary requirement, but much will always depend on a country's capability for autonomous research.

A fourth relevant aspect of Mercosur is that it enhances, to a degree, the international negotiating capacity of the member countries. In a world of regional megamarkets that are supported by a powerful international trend toward trade liberalization, even as they are territorially protected by essentially mercantilist policies, isolated countries are likely to suffer. Even a relatively small regional market like Mercosur can provide that necessary minimum of mercantilist protection required in today's world. It will also provide a substantive reinforcement to Mercosur members for the renegotiation of their foreign debt.

## Mercosur and the United States

The new liberal fashion prevailing in the world today is reviving the old discussion on the advantages and disadvantages of economic liberalism for developing countries. There is little doubt that, in general terms, economic liberalism optimizes the use of resources on a global scale. It is also widely acknowledged that devoting substantial state aid to less productive economic sectors and attempting to preserve them behind the walls of high tariffs is more of a liability than an asset for the developing countries. The inefficient sectors divert relatively scarce resources to poorer uses, reducing the output ratio of the country and usually contributing to high inflation and the public deficit.

On the other hand, however, the historical and contemporary experiences of developing countries show that a certain margin of protectionism at a certain period of their development is necessary for the creation, expansion, and consolidation of new industries. The Hamilton tariff, the German *Zollverein*, the Japanese practices before and after World War II, and Brazil's experience from the 1950s to the 1970s are some examples of successful protectionism.

In this respect, as on so many other social and economic issues, one is confronted with questions of measure, opportunity, and nuance. Given the wide and growing differences of return between primary and secondary activities— a gap that is being broadened at an extraordinary rate by the technological factor—it is practically impossible for a newcomer to industrial activities to build an industrial system that can compete with that of the well-established industrial countries. The task is even more difficult in the face of patents and legalized secrets of production. Thus, a well-timed and measured protectionist policy is indispensable to creating and consolidating a new industrial society. The crucial goal is to prevent an excess of protection from generating economic inefficiency and technological obsolescence.

Latin American countries, particularly the Mercosur partners, are currently confronted with the task of coordinating two opposed requirements: opening their economies to both the international market and the Bush initiative and selectively protecting their industrial systems and their capacity for technological innovation.

The first requirement addresses the Latin American countries' need to attain a sufficient level of international competitiveness for reasons related to their export sectors, their attractiveness to foreign capital and technology, and the improvement of their domestic efficiency. The second requirement concerns their need to achieve an appropriate level of industrialization and technological development so that they can maintain a satisfactory rate of endogenous growth and approach a state of full employment.

The connection between selective protectionism and full employment is clearly illustrated by agricultural subsidies and import quotas adopted by the members of the European Community and the United States. Such countries are confronted with the reverse of the situation facing developing nations. The Europeans cannot compete with the agricultural productivity of the two Americas; similarly, the United States cannot compete with Latin American countries in certain agricultural areas (for example, Argentinian wheat and Brazilian chickens), and it tries to protect its less competitive industries with import quotas. Conversely, Brazil cannot compete, in general, with U.S. industrial productivity. The main difference between the two situations is the amount of labor involved in each case. Europe spends an immense amount of money, at the expense of its own taxpayers and its foreign agricultural partners, to artificially maintain the employment of less than 10 percent of its total labor force. In developing countries, such as the members of Mercosur, the industrial labor force that needs protecting represents more than double that figure.

The agreement signed in Washington in June 1991 by representatives of the Mercosur countries and the United States was a first cautious step toward combining the two imperatives of openness and protection. The advantage of that agreement is that it establishes a mechanism for consultation, permitting an institutional and rational approach to settling future conflicts of interest between Mercosur and the United States. The disadvantage of the document is that it conceals the nature and extent of the conflicts that will have to be settled.

Institutionalized consultation is a rational way of preserving a space for cooperation without ignoring the inevitability of conflicts of interest. Concealing from the start the nature of the conflicts that are likely to emerge, however, reflects a lack of wisdom on both sides. The United States is playing on its superiority of power, implicitly assuming that it will be able to impose unfavorable conditions on the Mercosur partners. The Latin American countries, meanwhile, are operating on the implied assumption that they will be able to bypass the rules of the game if those rules become intolerable. This is certainly not a sound basis for a long-term understanding between the two Americas.

The members of Mercosur and the United States should engage in a serious general discussion about the conditions under which the opposing imperatives of international openness and selective domestic protection are to be adjusted over time. Only on the basis of a sound and fair treatment of that question can stable and equitable relations be achieved.

## Notes

1. This is a major reason why the United States has collected external contributions for the Gulf War, mostly from Germany, Japan, Saudi Arabia, and Kuwait, amounting to some $40 billion.

2. Chile's exports rose from $6.9 billion in 1970 to $12.9 billion in 1989.

3. The European Community has a population of 323 million and a GDP of about $3.3 trillion, the U.S.-Canadian market has a population of 272 million and a GDP of about $4.3 trillion, and Mercosur has 193 million people and a GDP of $492 billion.

# 4

# Latin America
# and the United States
# in a Changing World Economy

## *Albert Fishlow*

This is a new world, not merely in the vast restructuring of political relationships that has occurred in the five years preceding 1993 but also in the dramatic economic changes that have taken place. Put directly and simply, capitalism has triumphed. What remains are important differences in direction and style—for example between European, Japanese, and American variants—but socialism is dead: Even the adherents of the increasingly successful Chinese model concede that.

For Latin America, the triumph of capitalism has reinforced the need for substantial reductions in the size and functions of the state. Indeed, this requirement was already defined as early as 1982, when the debt crisis first presented itself. The last decade or so has been one of dramatic change in the region. Incomes have declined more than in any comparable period—including the depression of the 1930s—and in the 1980s, for the first time in the postwar era, aggregate per capita income actually fell.

The first portion of this chapter provides a brief reprise of the internal modifications gradually introduced in the region during the last several years. These have focused on increased fiscal discipline, to the point that, in 1993, only one Latin American country—Brazil—faced double-digit monthly inflation. Other important results have included the record Chilean growth of some 10 percent in 1992 and the substantial entry of foreign capital into the region. Both provide substance to the new hopes for launching a sustained advance in income throughout the region in the coming years.

In the chapter's second portion, I take up the dramatic changes in international economic relationships that have occurred in the region. Beyond the successful conclusion of the North American Free Trade Agreement in 1992, virtually all countries have significantly reduced tariffs and eased other protectionist restrictions. For the first time, Latin America as a whole has turned its back on import substitution and is seeking increased participation in world trade. Inevitably, this has meant closer attention to trade with immediate neighbors. A crucial question is the longer-term consistency of Argentine and Brazilian policy with such a strategy of closer hemispheric integration.

The third portion discusses the likely response of the Clinton administration to these new developments. There are four alternatives for the United States. First, it can seek to reinvigorate a global economic policy and reemphasize the importance of GATT. Second, there can be a new focus on regionalism, with formation of an American free trade area extending from the Yukon to the Magellan Straits, as former President Bush proposed. Third, a modified regionalism—a North American Free Trade Area, incorporating Mexico, the Caribbean, and Central America—can deepen and persist. And fourth, NAFTA can be extended to Asia, incorporating Korea, Taiwan, and the rapidly growing economies of Southeast Asia. This last option has received little attention thus far.

At the heart of the matter is the question of whether global economic changes in the 1990s will incorporate and reinvigorate Latin America as a whole or whether new regional divisions will dominate. Will the next decade belong to Chile and Mexico, as the period from 1950 to 1980 belonged to Brazil? The next few years will prove decisive. In a world in which Asian per capita incomes have been increasing at rates of 5 percent each year, there is clear evidence that accelerating growth within the region is, indeed, possible.

## Domestic Restructuring

Latin America emerges from the debt crisis as a much different continent than it was a decade ago. When Mexico defaulted (appropriately enough on Friday, August 13, 1982), the countries of the hemisphere were plunged into searing difficulties that have persisted in certain nations until the present. Growth ceased, and what was proclaimed by some to be a temporary balance-of-payments adjustment turned into the region's longest period of negative development in the twentieth century. By the end of 1992, national income per person, including the negative effects of declining terms of trade, stood at less than 90 percent of its 1980 value.[1]

The process of adjustment passed through four stages.[2] Initially, there was a phase of drastic balance-of-payments correction between 1982 and 1984. This reflected a period of strong reduction in the value of Latin American imports: between 1981 and 1984, these fell by some 45 percent. Indeed, so rapid was the decline that *World Financial Markets* could speak of "lasting resolution of the LDC [less developed country] debt problem."[3] But, instead, that difficulty became worse, ushering in the second phase. This phase, associated with worsening international prices and declining export earnings, exposed a fundamental reality: Banks were not inclined to lend more but rather were committed to reducing their exposure abroad, especially in Latin America. The region therefore was forced to deal with the crisis through a much more fundamental realignment than had been imagined.

The third phase of the readjustment began with the Baker Plan in 1985, which was a tripartite strategy of relying on banks, international institutions, and country adjustment. But in the absence of the much-needed bank support, it eventually gave way to the Brady Plan, which allowed, for the first time, a substantial reduction in country indebtedness to banks. Such a policy became a reality in 1988 when Citibank independently wrote down its balance sheet of loans to various countries, and it was confirmed the following year by the settlement of the outstanding Mexican debt at a price of about sixty-five cents to a dollar. Other countries soon settled at parallel discounts, much greater for small nations like Bolivia and Costa Rica and comparable for those with large debts. The only major outstanding case at the beginning of 1993 was that of Brazil, on which agreement had been reached in 1992, before President Collor's impeachment.

A fourth phase followed, with a sudden, rather unexpected and large flow of external capital into the region in the last half of 1991 and during 1992. The change has been substantial. Estimates for 1992 showed a net movement of capital of well over $50 billion in 1991–1992, equivalent to more than the total for all years from 1983 to 1989.[4] Latin America is again a destination for foreign funds but not entirely for long-term investment prospects. Rather, the dominant motivation has been a combination of high Latin American internal rates of interest and very low U.S. rates, along with the prospect of new Mexican opportunities that will be made available by the conclusion of NAFTA negotiations.

This progression from important surplus to large export balance and back again to new import surplus traces the evolution of the external balance of payments. But what has been left out is of critical importance: the realignment of the domestic economy of the region. This has shown itself in three important changes. First, there has been a structural shift in government fiscal capability and, with it, a decline in the domestic rate of inflation.[5] Brazil is the only country in the region with continuing triple-digit price increases, and its separateness has begun to have repercussions. Second, there has been a shift of ownership from public to private hands. And third, there has been a significant reduction in external tariffs and quotas protecting domestic industry and a much greater reliance on internal productive capability.

The change in fiscal capability and rates of inflation is a major shift in regional patterns. What has happened in most countries is a continuous process, especially over the first three years of the 1990s, years of increasing government control over revenues and expenditures. Another beneficial consequence has come from lower international interest costs: The decline in rates, coupled with favorable results of debt reduction, has brought important benefits. The net impact has been dramatic. The fiscal balance shifted from −7.8 percent of GDP in 1987–1989 to 0.7 percent in 1992 for countries undertaking formal stabilization programs in the region. Even for others, it went from −5.1 to −2.8 percent.[6]

Such improvement was mainly due to increased public-sector revenues. Still, the skeptical position of the UN Economic Commission for Latin America (CEPAL) must be recognized:

> In only a few countries, however, can the fiscal accounts be said to be structurally balanced. For this to be the case, current income must be solidly backed by a stable tax base, which in turn is consistent with a level of current spending that can support the normal functioning of government administration and the provision of basic social services. The tax base must also be able to support the public investment required to revamp and develop infrastructure necessary for economic growth and enhanced social equity.[7]

Clearly, it is still too early to tell. But the major efforts at stabilization in recent years, if continued, promise to respond to a major need of the countries in the hemisphere. It is no accident that price inflation has been dramatically reduced. Indeed, excluding Brazil, overall inflation in Latin America fell to only 22 percent in 1992, less than half its 1991 value and extraordinarily lower than the 900 percent registered in 1990.[8]

Latin America has thus begun to emerge from the 1980s with much greater fiscal and monetary discipline. Contributing to the former is the willingness to entrust the private sector with greater responsibility and control. Sales of formerly nationalized enterprises have accounted for sizable revenues, amounting from 1 percent to 4 percent of total government receipts in recent years. Airlines, telephone and telegraph operations, steel facilities, and countless other enterprises have been turned over to private hands again. In contrast to the pattern of the 1970s, when external debt greatly assisted the state in financing its needs, a radically different model emerged in the late 1980s. It is essential, however, that private investment be sustained and rationalized in new areas of responsibility. Not least of all, there must be regular increases in capital formation. If the shift to private hands is simply a one-time transaction, the projected benefits will not be realized.

Privatization should not be viewed simply as part of the process of fiscal reform for it encompasses a broader conception of the role of the state. Enterprises that should be sold are not merely those that are able to yield an immediate return to public authorities. Rather, the objective must be greater and continuing economic efficiency. The immediate financial gain is small compared to the potential longer-term benefits. To confuse the two goals would be to repeat an error made in the 1970s. At that time, the state expanded its role unnecessarily, using the ability to secure debt finance as its reason. To avoid this mistake, the focus must be on future productivity gains.

The third important policy modification has occurred in the government's strategy for protecting domestic production. Latin America began the post-1950 period committed to import-substitution industrialization. Barriers to free exchange were erected to allow domestic sectors to rise and develop their efficiency. By 1960, it was apparent that protection was not working well; only Brazil and Mexico, with their large sizes and natural limits to trade, had grown. But it was not until the balance-of-payments crisis of the 1980s that all countries in the region converted to freer trade. Tariff reductions in recent years have been spectacular. Virtually everywhere, the value of domestic production subject to restriction has been substantially reduced. So, too, has the average tariff: It now stands at little more than 20 percent, compared to close to 50 percent before tariff reduction began.[9]

This change has contributed to the sharp rise of imports. Between 1990 and 1992, for example, the region's imports grew from $94.4 billion to some $132 billion, an annual rate of increase exceeding 18 percent. (Rising prices cancel out only a little more than 1 percent of each year's expansion.) The only large country whose behavior is at variance with this pattern is Brazil; excluding its slight decline, the region as a whole secured real gains of well over 20 percent in 1991 and 1992.[10]

Latin America is thus a different continent economically than it was a decade ago. Its fiscal situation is much improved, and inflation is now under control for virtually the first time since the 1950s. Its bloated public sector has been compressed, yielding, in the process, revenues to public authorities much in need of them. Its external barriers to trade have been substantially removed in recent years, and a commitment to greater competitiveness has emerged. These changes are due to the brute force of the readjustment imposed upon the region. Faith in the planning ability of domestic managers has evaporated. Instead, as elsewhere around the globe, a new reliance on markets is becoming the rule.

The question for leaders in the region is what strategy of international integration is likely to be the most effective in stimulating growth in future years. Substantially, but not unanimously, the answer has been to seek greater association with the United States. For the first time since World War II, closer economic links in the Americas are a distinct possibility.

## A New Strategy of Regional Integration

On June 27, 1990, President Bush announced his Enterprise for the Americas Initiative, formally opening the prospect of a free trade agreement ranging from the Yukon to the straits of Patagonia.[11] This measure, like its much earlier (1982) predecessor, the Caribbean Basin Initiative, rested on three bases: investment promotion, aid accompanied by debt reduction, and the elimination of trade barriers. The centerpiece of the new initiative and its greatest departure from past policy was its trade provisions.

First, Bush offered closer cooperation with the Latin American countries in the Uruguay Round, including the promise to seek deeper tariff cuts for products of special relevance. Second, Bush announced that "the United States stands ready to enter into free trade agreements with other markets in Latin America and the Caribbean, particularly with groups of countries that have associated for purposes of trade liberalization."[12] Finally, given that such a step was likely to be too drastic for some countries to consider, Bush also offered to negotiate bilateral "framework" agreements that would permit more incremental discussions covering particular issues of relevance.

By the end of 1990, seven countries had negotiated such bilateral framework agreements with the United States—Bolivia, Chile, Colombia, Costa Rica, Ecuador, Honduras, and Mexico. Subsequently, an agreement was concluded in 1991 that added a first regional grouping, the Mercosur, involving four countries as a unit—Argentina, Brazil, Paraguay, and Uruguay. By 1993, there were a total of fifteen framework agreements covering thirty countries, including one with the thirteen members of Caricom (the Caribbean Common Market). But real attention was focused in the first instance on free trade with Mexico. Agreement to move ahead was signaled in September 1990 when Bush notified Congress of his intention to negotiate a free trade agreement with Mexico.

Two years of negotiation were required, involving not only the United States and Mexico but also Canada, with whom the United States had concluded an earlier pact that went into effect at the beginning of 1989. A final agreement was reached in August 1992, subject to approval by a new Congress in 1993. The prospects for approval were enhanced by President Clinton's decision, announced during his campaign, to accept such a pact, provided that the issues of the environment and labor standards were simultaneously addressed. What is needed is a joint commitment for new expenditures along the border, as well as a program to assist U.S. workers who may face unemployment as a result of the pact.

Mexico's decision to press for closer association with the United States was motivated by three factors. Despite the fact that trade between the two countries was relatively free—especially after Mexico began to liberalize trade in 1985—an accumulation of adverse U.S. decisions affecting bilateral exchange began in the 1980s. Moreover, an agreement would lock in a variety of wide-ranging economic reforms that Salinas wanted to continue and consolidate. Integration meant permanence for a more liberal Mexican economic model. But there was also a third motive: to influence positively the perceptions and expectations of the private sector, both foreign and domestic.

Though foreign investment increased after 1987, it did not respond as affirmatively to the Mexican debt agreement and other policy changes as the government had hoped. Salinas was also discouraged after visiting Europe at the beginning of 1990 and noting that region's preoccupation with the new challenge of Central Europe and a corresponding lack of interest in Mexico. But some believed that the prospect of free trade, by encouraging new flows of capital (primarily but not exclusively from the United States), could stimulate a needed increase in domestic investment. How accurate such an assessment would be, at least in terms of foreign flows, is demonstrated by a simple comparison of subsequent capital intake: In 1991 and 1992, foreign flows of capital grew to more than $20 billion, permitting an increase of some 50 percent in imports.

The rest of Latin America now has to decide on its response to the prospects of new trade linkages; whether other Latin countries will join is not clear. Chile has already indicated its desire for free trade with the United States and has been accepted as a second potential partner; talks will await a decision on NAFTA. But despite the apparent interest of other countries, adherence to NAFTA is still very much a debatable issue for there are costs as well as potential benefits.

The gains are associated with the possibility of assured access to the U.S. market and the prospect for increased investment, to exploit this new boost in comparative advantage. I emphasize this dynamic effect for, given the already substantial reduction in tariffs and trade limitations throughout the hemisphere, the static advantages represent a trivial percentage of national income. They derive from one-time increased trade created by lower barriers. But it is to the future and to a continuing expansion that one must look. Exactly because Latin America offers the prospect of lower costs and because of its substantially lower income, it stands to be the largest beneficiary of continually growing trade.

On the other side, three principal costs confront the countries of the region. First, any close alliance automatically limits national macroeconomic policy. Renunciation of the use of trade and exchange-rate instruments inhibits the ability to operate independently. It is no accident that Mexico and Chile are moving rapidly to lower inflation rates, making them more comparable to U.S. values, or that Argentina has adopted a gold standard to fix exchange rates. These adaptations become a necessary component of policy. And such limitations are seen by adherents as advantages rather than costs.

Second, benefits from a closer association may not be distributed evenly: It is the likely attraction to future investments that will be decisive for individual members. Indeed, it is this reality that serves as a disciplinary device, limiting national economic autonomy. There is no assurance that all countries will derive significant benefits. Indeed, unlike the previous emphasis upon domestic markets, the possibility of effective export is what counts at this point.

Third, protection levels in Latin America will have to change more radically in order to conform to lower U.S. values. But the much larger share of U.S. trade in Latin American imports, rather than the reverse, simply emphasizes the much greater adjustment that will be necessary in these countries. And it raises the issue of whether there will be additional sources of finance to help meet the burden. In the absence of new investment, agreement will simply mean the mass entry of exports from the United States.

Preliminary calculations support this emphasis on dynamics and adaptability as the crucial factors determining future success. One recent study shows that the one-time increase of Latin American imports to the United States would be less than 10 percent if all trade restrictions were removed.[13] The implicit maximum gain in Latin American income would then be less than 2 percent. Further, the only two large beneficiaries would be Mexico and Brazil. Note, as well, that the positive effect gained by the United States is smaller by one order of magnitude: in the range of .1 percent.

Indeed, one reaction to such calculations is the conclusion that "in view of the limited potential of the free trade area (FTA) approach, Latin American countries might do better by assigning relatively greater importance to multilateral liberalization efforts within the GATT."[14] This assessment correctly places a much larger part of the decision on the ability of Latin American countries to derive gains over time by attracting investment and increasing their trade. The choice depends on whether a new association with the U.S. market can set in motion a more rigorous commitment to effective policy than a GATT reduction can. Recall that Latin American participation in world exports has declined by two-thirds since 1950. The appeal of a regional trade option lies in its potential to define and discipline a new economic strategy that can reverse that unfortunate history.

In framing the Latin American response, the countries of the Mercosur, particularly Brazil, will play the central role. These countries stand apart from the others in the region, differentiated by the limited extent to which they are integrated into the U.S. market and, in the case of Brazil and Argentina, by the high inflation rates they have been subject to in recent years. It is not entirely accidental that these two countries have been the last to agree to a debt renegotiation, in contrast to Mexico's initial acceptance in 1988 and Chile's willingness to assume its obligations in full. Moreover, in the GATT round, Brazil has been quite active in opposing U.S. positions and attempting to pursue a more independent course.

Calculations of the static gains from export expansion, as already mentioned, show that Brazil can increase its exports by a greater percentage than any other country, precisely because it is trading manufactured products subject to higher duties. But the absolute value of such benefits is still a full 50 percent greater for Mexico. Note, as well, that these two countries alone capture some 90 percent of the aggregate advantages to the region. But these refer to immediate gain; the dynamic effects deriving from continuing investment and greater growth are far more significant.

On this issue, both Winston Fritsch and Roberto Bouzas agree, but both opt for a more independent stance. The former favors emphasis upon GATT negotiations and effective continuation of the subregional arrangement; the latter goes beyond but only to the extent of "promoting a transparent accession mechanism as part of NAFTA."[15] It remains to be seen, however, whether the effects of Mexican accession and a speedy Chilean entry thereafter mushroom well beyond the immediate gains from more efficient trade. Should that begin to occur, there is little doubt that both Argentina and Brazil would reevaluate their initial positions and seek early inclusion. In turn, that would require macroeconomic stability, which would become a new and significant pressure on the internal policies of both nations. Argentina would have to confront its exchange-rate overvaluation, and Brazil would have to deal with its high rate of inflation.

What we see within the region, then, is uncertainty but a strengthening commitment to the possibility of freer trade. What we see in the United States is less clear, particularly since the election of President Clinton. No broad strategy is evident, beyond the commitment to support NAFTA.

## U.S. Options

The turn to regionalism in U.S. trade policy was somewhat accidental, the result of two independent circumstances. It was, to begin with, part of a U.S. effort to push the Uruguay Round of GATT negotiations to a satisfactory conclusion. There is little reason to believe that a major new advance focusing exclusively on the hemisphere was an expected result of Bush's initiative. Furthermore, Mexico's early willingness to move ahead was more the product of a fear that new freedom in Eastern Europe would deter needed U.S. investment, rather than a belief in the virtues of integration. Thereafter, other potential hemispheric partners soon joined. But this new direction of policy, in conjunction with Europe 1992 and efforts by Japan to stimulate closer alignment with the Asian nations, opens up the question of its future.

Is there still hope for the Uruguay Round? And even if concluded, can it continue to serve as the principal focus for new U.S. trade initiatives? Increasingly, these two questions lead to negative conclusions. There is mounting pressure within the United States for greater protectionism and a more vigorous pursuit of specifically national objectives. That the U.S. balance-of-trade deficit with Japan is again rising does not help. And trade tensions with Europe are proliferating. All this seems to signal the end of a model of global free trade.

But that analysis misses two realities. First, a third Asian bloc is unlikely. ASEAN countries and others in the region well appreciate that their economic future is better served by maintaining both the United States and Japan as active sources and active market possibilities. On its side, the patterns of recent trade confirm strong U.S. interest and commitment in this part of the world. Second, the increasing role of foreign investment is crucial. Capital mobility promises to assure consistency between regional integration and the goals of global liberalization. What is sometimes forgotten is that fully half of all U.S. investment abroad is in Western Europe, and during the 1980s, East Asia matched Latin America in terms of the volume of capital received.[16] Regionalism is not equivalent to a rejection of important outside interests.

A U.S. global concern remains, but it may now be advanced through a greater regional focus, rather than through the traditional GATT route. Whether or not there is a successful conclusion to the current global negotiations, trade interests are now likely to have a more self-conscious regional dimension. NAFTA opens a new path. But another question immediately emerges: What kind of regional approach will be undertaken? Will it feature Mexico alone, Mexico in conjunction with Central America and the Caribbean, or the Western Hemisphere as a whole?

Here, the answer seems to be clear. The United States has agreed to negotiate with Chile next, not with the range of smaller countries in Central America and the Caribbean. These nations remain on the list of applicants but without substantial appeal for early action. They already have the advantages of the Caribbean Basin Initiative, concluded back in 1982—a measure that was initially motivated primarily by security, rather than economic, concerns. It was consequently handicapped by the exclusion of key merchandise from free trade and the elimination of investment incentives. But the absence of the continuing strong political pressures that were its initial motivation and the lack of powerful economic interests requiring accommodation suggest that this modified route is unlikely to evolve. If it did, it would suggest diminished U.S. interest in pursuing a hemispheric route, rather than a means to that end. For the United States—but not, to be sure, for the countries of the region—trade and investment are much too small to be significant. Now that Central America is no longer seen as the next breeding ground for Communist expansion, economics is likely to dominate in defining policy.

This, then, makes a hemispheric free trade area the likely central policy focus, assuming congressional approval of NAFTA. Here, a core issue is the form that such a widened structure might embody. Will it be "hub-and-spoke" structure, centered around the United States and extending out to later acquisitions individually? Or will it take the shape of Richard Lipsey's ideal "plurilateral regionalism"?[17] Economists are virtually unanimous in their preferences for the latter or, more exactly, in their opposition to the former.[18] A hub-and-spoke model, in which the United States would negotiate separate treaties with each successive member, would grant it tariff-free access to all the others; each of the partners, however, would face continuing limitations in their relations with other members, hence creating possibilities for trade diversion. In addition, investment in the United States is given a relative advantage via free access to all other countries, although access among members remains limited. Finally, "in the hub-and-spoke model the United States is placed in a superior bargaining position. It negotiates separate agreements with each of its smaller partners so that they have no chance to make common cause against it in areas of mutual, small-country interest."[19]

This analysis of the limitations, however accurate it may be, incorrectly exaggerates potential economic losses and neglects important political gains. Countries joining a hemispheric group would typically have a much larger bloc of trade with the United States than with other countries. The only exceptions to such a rule are Bolivia, Paraguay, Uruguay, and Argentina; the last has a much larger trade and is much closer to conforming to the general rule. Furthermore, all the countries (again excepting Bolivia, Paraguay, Uruguay, and Argentina) already have preferential arrangements with a neighboring group, so that virtually all privileges would automatically extend. In this regard, it is noteworthy that Chile, about to negotiate with the United States, has already concluded a free trade treaty with Mexico. Others would do the same. Consequently, even without an identical free trade treaty, the degree of discrimination is likely to be miniscule.

Partners may prefer a multilateral free trade agreement to a hub-and-spoke system, but how might it come about? It seems plausible that after a series of countries have negotiated access to the U.S. market, generalization to a common free trade arrangement could follow. Is there a real possibility of negotiating such a common agreement at the outset? Actually, it is likely to be much easier to obtain a generalized free trade arrangement at the end, rather than at the beginning, of the relationship. Once the principal countries have agreements with the United States, subsequent entrants could be asked to sign on to the plan. Such a sequencing arrangement is merely intelligent politics, which seem to dominate the maximizing economics in this matter. Indeed, imagine the mechanism for negotiating the accession of new members subsequent to Chile under other circumstances: It would involve either such simplicity or such complexity that a new multilateral agreement would be necessary each time.

Thus far, the focus of this chapter has been limited to a Western Hemisphere group. But that is not an inevitable scenario. One could well imagine that, after Mexico and Chile join a free trade group, the next petitioner might be Taiwan or Korea. Lipsey is clear on this point: "To preserve the outward-looking image and reality of the WHFTA [Western Hemisphere Free Trade Association], countries outside the Western Hemisphere that met the preconditions should be welcomed."[20] For he sees such a trade thrust as inherently consistent with general trade liberalization. But extension of the agreement in this direction would imply something very different for the future of the hemisphere. Instead of setting forth preferential market access as a potential and rational reward for making hard domestic decisions, it would alter the picture. Being part of the hemisphere would be no advantage and yield no special privilege.

Once again, the politics and the economics diverge. If the Clinton administration intends to proceed with a Western Hemisphere model, it must clearly give precedence to regional members. Otherwise, the model becomes one of selective negotiation—like that with Israel—and it loses any regional significance. The real question is the extent to which a WHFTA can become a mechanism for assuring better domestic policy throughout the region by demonstrating the close relationship between the initial step and greater trade access. Mexico and Chile are two obvious cases. Brazil is another, where the gains from better fiscal policy can bring international—and not merely domestic—rewards.

For the United States, the free trade model might offer a genuine chance for Latin American nations to renew their growth and productivity. In the initial years, the U.S. economy would continue to expand, driven by the repressed demand for its exports in the region. Ironically, calculations indicating advantages for poorer neighbors ignore their desperate and long-postponed need for new investment. Eventually, a return flow of imports would mount but hardly so soon as to cause great concern. Such a policy, aggressively pursued, holds the promise of broad hemispheric allegiance. Certainly, the large number of countries interested in adhering to such a model provides a basis for greater regional solidarity that at any time since the proposal of the Alliance for Progress. It would be tragic were it not actively promoted. The United States has no international reason not to assume aggressive leadership. The real issue is consistency with domestic politics.

## Conclusion

Latin America has passed through a difficult decade, but the light at the end of the tunnel finally seems visible. In the changing world economy now taking form, the region must soon choose its options. Clearly, future success requires a much greater outward orientation than was characteristic earlier: On this, there is virtual unanimity. And in turn, there is an equal recognition that much greater macroeconomic stability is required. The real question is whether to pursue much closer association with the United States or, as in the past, to seek to further diversify the economic ties of the region.

For the United States, there is an equally significant moment of decision. The Reagan-Bush policy of relying upon government deficits as the basis for economic expansion has now fully run its course: Combined, the votes for President Clinton and Ross Perot represented a large majority in the last election. And administration proposals for approaching closer budget balance are central items for policy discussion. What remains to be decided is trade policy, at both the global and the regional levels. There is agreement on the need for competitiveness and productivity advance. But will competition and productivity be enhanced through higher protection and more attention to exclusively domestic interests?

A Western Hemisphere Free Trade Association offers a common direction to both parts of the region in search of new approaches. It is a way to integrate Latin America more effectively and to revive necessary capital formation in both the North and the South. It is equally a way to check protectionist tendencies in the United States, while boosting current exports of capital goods. It does not imply that the rest of the world is a loser. A tripartite division of world markets, so much feared in some quarters, is unlikely to occur. And it may well be that a new regional emphasis is required to assure the continuing expansion of global trade.

The 1990s will probably see an ongoing effort to reconcile globalism and regionalism, rather than an exclusive commitment to the latter. This is all to the good. Insistence upon a regional route as a single alternative is a potentially dangerous course, without a firm economic basis. It would be desirable neither for the United States nor for Latin America, depriving both of important and positive roles in the world economy in the next decade. Regionalism must become a route, rather than an alternative, to globalism.

## Notes

1. United Nations, *Estudio economico de América Latina y el Caribe, 1991*, 1 (Santiago: CEPAL, 1992), p. 18; CEPAL, "Preliminary Overview of the Latin American and Caribbean Economy, 1992," *Notas sobre la economía y el desarrollo*, no. 537/538 (December 1992), p. 39.

2. For a summary of literature prior to the new commitment to debt reduction, see my essay, "From Crisis to Problem: Latin American Debt 1982–87," in R. Wesson, ed., *Coping with the Latin American Debt* (New York: Praeger, 1988), pp. 7–18. For the subsequent evolution of the Brady accords, see International Monetary Fund, *International Capital Markets: Developments and Prospects* (Washington, D.C.: IMF, 1991 and 1992). Argentina and Brazil are the latest adherents.

3. *World Financial Markets* (October–November 1984), p. 1.

4. CEPAL, "Preliminary Overview, 1992."

5. See, for example, "Fiscal Adjustment in Developing Countries," *World Economic Outlook* (Washington, D.C.: IMF, May 1992), Annex V and subsequent reports.

6. Ibid.

7. CEPAL, "Preliminary Overview, 1992," p. 2.

8. Ibid., p. 8.

9. CEPAL, *Estudio Económico, 1991,* Table 13.

10. Ibid., Table 15.

11. This discussion is based upon Albert Fishlow and Stephan Haggard's *The United States and the Regionalisation of the World Economy* (OECD Publications Centre, 1992), pp. 25ff.

12. George Bush, "Remarks Announcing the Enterprise for the Americas Initiative," White House press release, p. 1011.

13. Refik Erzan and Alexander Yeats, "U.S.–Latin America Free Trade Areas: Some Empirical Evidence," in Sylvia Saborio et al., *The Premise and the Promise: Free Trade in the Americas* (Washington, D.C.: ODC, 1992).

14. Ibid., p. 129.

15. Winston Fritsch, "Integración económica: Conviene la discriminación comercial?" in Roberto Bouzas and Nora Lustig, eds., *Liberalización comercial e integración regional* (Buenos Aires: FLASCO, 1992), pp. 37–53. Roberto Bouzas, "U.S.-Mercosur Trade," in Saborio et al., *The Premise and Promise,* p. 267.

16. See Fishlow and Haggard, "The United States and Regionalisation," pp. 18–19.

17. Richard G. Lipsey, "Getting There," in Saborio et al., *The Premise and Promise,* p. 108.

18. See, for example, Carsten Kowalczyk and Ronald J. Wonnacott, "Hubs and Spokes, and Free Trade in the Americas," National Bureau of Economic Research (NBER) Working Paper No. 4198, October 1992.

19. Lipsey, "Getting There," p. 108.

20. Ibid., p. 114.

# PART TWO

*The Prospect for
New Partners*

# 5

# Europe and Latin America in the 1990s

## *Alberto van Klaveren*

Contrary to the assertions of its Latin admirers and some well-intentioned but overly rhetorical Europeans, Europe did not play the leading role in Latin America during the 1970s and 1980s. Nonetheless, it continues to be one of Latin America's most important foreign partners, second only to the United States. Europe's share in Latin American trade, for example, has stabilized at around 20 percent, more than three times that of Japan.

Despite the appalling economic crisis in Latin America and the existence of other geographical priorities for most European countries, the European continent became the main source of sorely needed foreign investments in the region during the second half of the 1980s. British, Dutch, and Spanish banks took advantage of generous debt conversion schemes, Spain's telephone company took over some of the major local companies in its sector, and the main European airlines—not U.S. airlines—acquired a number of the Latin American flag carriers that were up for privatization. French, German, Spanish, and other European enterprises are now successfully competing with their U.S. counterparts for major public works contracts in the region. Europe holds nearly one-third of Latin America's foreign debt, a share not far below that of the United States. During the latter half of the 1980s, Europe also became a main supplier of foreign assistance to Latin America. In 1989, development cooperation received from Germany, Italy, and the Netherlands surpassed that received from the United States. In a less encouraging trend, European arms suppliers replaced their powerful U.S. competitors by the 1970s, taking advantage of Washington's policy to control and limit sophisticated arms transfers to the region.

In the political realm, the presence of European governments, political parties, and nongovernmental organizations (NGOs) in Latin America has increased considerably during the last decade. These political actors—relatively new in the region—clearly do not form the "third option" or the alternative to the United States so ardently proclaimed by some European politicians (who usually did not hold significant governmental responsibilities) and intellectuals. However, they do represent a permanent influence in the region, rivaling or collaborating with other external actors. Madrid, Rome, Bonn, and Paris compete with Washington as required, and sometimes they are the preferred destinations for Latin American presidential and ministerial visits. And of course, Europe is still a source of inspiration for many political groups in Latin America, which feel closer to European political traditions and models of economic and social organization than to other external referents.

To be sure, the importance to Europe of Latin America is more a reflection of its global prominence and of historical links than of any extraordinary commitment to the future of the region. It is true that Latin America is the most Westernized and even Europeanized area of the Third World, and certainly it is the only one in which Europe can recognize—to a certain extent—its own political and cultural values. Nevertheless, awareness of this affinity tends to be limited to countries such as Spain and Italy and to some particularly sensitive political sectors in other nations. Beyond that, Latin America receives little political attention in European governments and public opinion and tends to be seen as just another trouble-ridden area of the Third World—one for which, moreover, the United States is primarily responsible.

In economic terms, Latin America is a low priority for Europe. The region's share in European trade, investment, and finance has steadily decreased during the last years. And European enthusiasm over the Latin democratization process during the 1980s has faded lately due to the continuous governability problems that affect countries such as Brazil, Argentina, Peru, Colombia, and most of those in Central America. Political attention to the region has also been reduced by the newer and surely no less demanding democratization processes taking place in the neighboring countries of Eastern and Central Europe.

Nor does Europe have major strategic interests in Latin America. Indeed, even Spain, a nation with so many ties to the region, has greater security and economic stakes in North Africa and the Middle East. Unlike the United States, no country in Europe has vital national security concerns in the region, although it would be a mistake to altogether deny European territorial and security interests in the area.[1]

Taken together, these contradictory trends of a continuing European presence in Latin America and the region's low priority in European foreign concerns reflect the asymmetrical nature of interregional relations. Hopes for redressing this asymmetry were high in the 1970s and the beginning of the

1980s, but Latin American expectations—often unrealistic—concerning their European partners were not met. Commercial trends and problems were not altered; Europe did not adopt a more flexible position with regard to the debt crisis; development cooperation flowing from Europe, although substantial, was not and could not be a remedy for the region's severe economic problems; and, in general, Europe was unwilling and probably unable to confront its Atlantic ally over any major and significant conflict affecting a Latin American country.

As the 1990s began, Europe once again became the central stage of the most important changes in the international system since World War II. On the one hand, it witnessed the dismantling of the former Soviet bloc and the fall of seemingly unmovable Communist regimes. On the other hand, the member countries of the European Community are involved in the design of a new European "architecture" represented by the implementation of the European Single Market and the adoption of the Maastricht Treaty on European Union, unfulfilled projects that had been pending since the Treaty of Rome was signed in 1957.

In this changing situation, new questions arise. How are these global and regional trends affecting European–Latin American relations? Will new developments in Europe further slow the already weak momentum in interregional relations? To what extent will these new factors lead Europeans to rely even more heavily upon U.S. initiatives in their policies toward the region? And how, if at all, can Latin America attract more European attention, given this situation?

## The 1980s: From Illusion to Realism

The early 1980s seemed to herald a new period in interregional relations. Governments, political parties, and most sectors of European public opinion supported the democratization processes developing in Latin America, putting an end to a long tradition of indifference with regard to the political fate of the region. If Europe had generally been aloof in the past regarding the issues of democracy and the protection of human rights in the region and if economic interests tended to prevail over political commitment, Europeans in the 1970s started to show more concern for democratic progress in the region. They began denouncing gross human rights violations, distancing themselves from authoritarian regimes in countries like Chile and Argentina, supporting democratic political parties, sending aid to local NGOs, and strengthening relations with the new democratic governments that were emerging in the region.[2]

To be sure, this policy was carried out with pragmatism and due consideration for other, more traditional European interests in the region, and political goodwill was not transformed automatically into economic support for new Latin American democracies. Nonetheless, it marked a significant change in European attitudes toward political development in the region, and more importantly, Europe was playing a valuable role in Latin America's struggle for democracy.

European commitment to democracy and human rights in Chile contrasted with the initial collaboration of the Reagan administration with Augusto Pinochet's regime. In Argentina, European rejection of the military regime differed not only from the U.S. and Argentine military cooperation in Central America but also from the Soviet reluctance to condemn the dreadful human rights record of the Argentine dictatorship. European-dominated political internationals also adopted active policies toward the region, supporting their Latin American members, recruiting new affiliates, and getting involved in the major external and internal issues affecting the region.

As a consequence of this new European involvement, several Latin American countries paid greater attention to Europe. Raúl Alfonsín's government in Argentina, a country that has traditionally been more oriented toward Europe than to other areas of the world, placed great hopes on the development of a special relationship with European countries such as France, Spain, Italy, or Germany. Although Brazilian views were tempered by earlier disappointments, Europe continued to play an important role in Brasilia's foreign policy, in the context of the diversification of its external links and due to increasing problems with Washington. Social Democratic and Christian Democratic governments in Venezuela also strengthened their links with Europe, collaborating in some joint ventures in Central America. Costa Rica, whose foreign relations had traditionally been focused on its neighbors and the United States, began to cultivate new relationships with several European countries. Under the Sandinista leadership, Nicaragua also looked—with considerable success—for political support and economic aid from Western Europe. Even before coming to power, the main political parties in Chile had high expectations for European political and economic support in the event a democratic reconstruction occurred in their country.

Although the European political presence increased significantly in the region, many of the initial expectations could not be met. Often as rhetorical as their Latin American friends, Europeans did not make it clear that their concern for the region had to compete with many other international responsibilities and that they could not alter the low priority given to Latin America in most of their foreign policies. On the other hand, Latin Americans, always too prone to seek special relationships with major powers and to make unrealistic appeals for international solidarity in a world system governed by other rules, did not make a sober and sound assessment of the real possibilities of their relations with Europe. This situation led to frustration and mutual recriminations, leading some external observers, especially in Washington, to rejoice and many from the two regions to overlook significant progress in European–

Latin American political relations.[3] Thus, although Latin America did not rise significantly in European foreign policy priorities, it is no less true that it is the only area of the developing world with which Europe has a solid and dense network of political links, often of a transitional rather than intergovernmental nature.

The European role in the Central American conflict was a clear demonstration of the potential for and the limitations of interregional relations during the 1980s. In October 1984, the historic conference of the foreign ministers of all the member countries of the European Community (accompanied by representatives of various EC bodies) and their colleagues from Central America and the Contadora Group inaugurated a process of interregional cooperation that reflected the European will to contribute to the solution of difficult and conflictive problems.

Indeed, this political will was less natural than may be thought. After all, European countries did not have an important interest or historical presence in the area; they tended to view it, correctly, as the backyard of its great Atlantic ally. In fact, European interest in the Central American conflict stemmed from the fact that it presented one of the few cases in which Europe was able to adopt a truly common stance, enabling it to play a proper and more autonomous role in a major international conflict. This role also seemed necessary to the extent that Europeans felt their U.S. ally was following an erroneous and dangerous policy that could increase international tensions and lead to a very costly conflict.[4]

During the 1980s, most European countries did not hide their discrepancies with respect to U.S. policy in Central America. In the case of Nicaragua, Europeans generally disagreed with the U.S. blockade of the Sandinista regime and U.S. support for the contras; they sought a peaceful solution to the conflict. Although differences concerning the political situation in El Salvador tended to diminish, it is worth recalling both the French-Mexican resolution of 1981, which recognized the rebel movement as a "politically representative force" that had to be included in any political solution in the country, and the considerable European Christian Democratic involvement in the country.

In more general terms, Europe participated through the peace process in the region—first through the Contadora Group and afterward with the Esquipulas agreements—and its role was specifically mentioned in the 1987 Esquipulas agreement. European forces have also had a prominent role in the verification of the subsequent peace processes, and they collaborate actively in the area with other Latin American countries such as Mexico and Venezuela. But the European role in Central America was not crucial and could even be qualified as discrete.[5] This area was certainly not a primary interest for Europe, and political and economic resources invested by nations on the Continent were limited. The assertion that Western Europe would never endanger its alliance with the United States due to this or any other regional confrontation was also confirmed.[6]

However, Europe now has a presence in a region in which it had been conspicuously absent earlier, and both the EC and several of its member states are providing development cooperation that, although limited, is directed toward rural development, aid for refugees, and the strengthening of regional integration.[7] Europe's supportive role in the regional peace process during the 1980s also had an important legitimizing function, in the sense that Washington's main allies in the world offered a different option for resolving the regional crisis. This option coincided with that favored by the rest of Latin America through the Contadora Group and, later, its Support Group.

Indeed, it was precisely these external coincidences that established the bases for a new political dialogue between the member states of the EC—acting through European Political Cooperation—and the Rio Group, which was finally institutionalized in December 1990 by means of the Rome Declaration. It is clear that these regular contacts between the foreign ministers of both groupings still stem from rather rhetorical appeals to "the joint role that the EC and Latin America are called to play in the international society of the future,"[8] yet this framework provides a useful forum for discussing the main international issues that both regions face.

Even though European security interests in Latin America have never been very high and are not comparable to those of the United States, the extension of security concerns to areas such as environmental protection and drug trafficking has added new dimensions to the relationship. Environmental issues have become high priorities in European politics and, obviously, are permeating Europe's foreign policies, particularly toward Latin America. Similarly, although drug trafficking seemed a typically U.S. obsession to most Europeans during the early 1980s, there now seems to be a new awareness in Europe about the seriousness and complexities of this problem. Thus, in a major departure from its traditional policy toward Latin America, the EC decided in 1990 to grant preferential treatment to exports from the main drug-producing nations—Bolivia, Colombia, Ecuador, and Peru—during a four-year period, suspending the application of tariffs and other trade barriers in order to encourage them to diversify away from the narcotics traffic.[9] The EC also supplies development aid for the prevention and treatment of drug abuse. Meanwhile, several European countries are assisting Latin American nations in their struggle against drug trafficking, establishing regular mechanisms for information exchange and international cooperation and providing equipment and training. Moreover, European countries have been active in promoting alternative cultivation in the Andean countries. Gradual but growing diversion of cocaine exports from the United States to European markets will most likely lead to increased collaboration in this field.[10]

The evolution of European–Latin American economic relations during the 1980s was less positive but far from gloomy. After a long period of decline in the relative importance of interregional trade, such commerce stabilized during the 1980s; in 1989, Latin America was supplying around 6 percent of EC imports and receiving around 3.8 percent of EC exports.[11] These figures were far below those of the United States (11 percent of total imports and 12.5 percent of total exports) but higher than those of Japan (4.2 percent and 3 percent, respectively). The EC's share in Latin American exports was 21 percent (the corresponding figures for the United States and Japan were 41 percent and 5.9 percent), whereas it provided 17.4 percent of the region's imports (the figures for the United States and Japan were 17 percent and 6.4 percent). However, trade between both regions has grown considerably in recent years, showing significant surpluses for Latin America. The EC is still the largest trading partner for several important Latin American countries, including Brazil, Argentina, Chile, and Colombia. The last two countries and Mexico have also been fairly successful in developing new "niches" in the European markets, thus contradicting negative predictions about the closure of European markets for Latin American products. Nonetheless, it is also true that the only general preferential instrument available to Latin exports to the EC—the General System of Preferences (GSP)—has been losing importance and now only covers a minor part of Latin American products, excluding agricultural raw materials and exports specified as sensitive for the EC, precisely because of their high level of competitiveness with European production. The Common Agricultural Policy (CAP) of the EC has not only represented a formidable trade barrier to the major export products of several Latin American countries but has also led to the loss of third markets because of highly subsidized competition from Europe.

Although Europe was directly involved in the Latin American debt crisis, it showed a rather distant and more passive attitude in general than other large creditors, like the United States and Japan. Although many European leaders declared their preoccupation and even solidarity with Latin America on this issue, these expressions of sympathy did not translate into policy—despite the fact that the combined voting power of the European countries in the IMF (traditionally led by a European director general) and the World Bank is greater than that of the United States. In some specific cases, European creditors condoned the public debt, but their approach to the large debtor countries has been very orthodox, even though stricter banking regulations have led to less exposure and vulnerability to debt defaults.[12]

During the 1980s, European direct investments in Latin America evolved more favorably than did trade, particularly from a Latin American perspective. Although Europe's investments concentrate massively in the countries of the Organization for Economic Cooperation and Development (OECD), their relative weight in Latin America has increased, mainly as a consequence of the decline of U.S. investments in the region. The European country that has been most active in this field and that is directing a larger portion of its investments in the developing world to Latin America has been the United Kingdom, which is somewhat ironic given the little interest it has in the region in terms of other fields.[13] Other important sources of investment are Germany and, predictably, Spain and Italy.

Latin America does not occupy a privileged position in the development assistance programs of the European countries and regional organizations. In fact, these nations and groups dedicate, on average, a lesser share of their aid programs to the region than does the United States or even Japan. However, Europe's size alone made it a main source of development cooperation for the region during the last decade. Although the impact of this assistance should not be overestimated, it has provided valuable support for social projects in Central America and the Caribbean and in countries such as Bolivia, Peru, and Ecuador.

Over the years, European development cooperation in Latin America has changed considerably. During the 1960s, it was mainly oriented toward the support of the developmentalist models in force at the time; during the 1970s, it was inclined toward alternative models favoring grass-roots development and nongovernmental organizations. In the 1980s, it began to include the private sector, as well. Accordingly, the previous emphasis on traditional assistance programs, aimed mainly at areas like rural and community development, food aid, technology transfer, and training, has been supplemented by industrial and economic cooperation, directed toward the establishment of joint ventures and the mobilization of financial resources and seed capital for the private sector.[14] These new forms of cooperation do not replace the previous ones, but they do tend to add a new dimension, especially vis-à-vis the more advanced countries of the region. They are reflected in the new EC guidelines for cooperation with the developing countries of Asia and Latin America and in the cooperation agreements signed by the European Community with Argentina, Chile, Mexico, and Brazil.[15]

Similarly, new forms of economic cooperation are combined with investment promotion in the ambitious framework agreements that have been signed during the last several years by Italy and Spain with the economically more advanced countries of Latin America. These agreements have been aimed at mobilizing substantial flows of European funding for the promotion of investments, joint ventures, and other forms of industrial cooperation.

Although most of these trends and facts do not constitute a special or preferential set of economic relations and although Latin America's relevance for Europe has continued to decline, the Continent retained an important presence in the region during the last few years. In fact, it even improved its position in such fields as investments and development cooperation. Thus, in many Latin American countries, Europe's weight can be compared to that of the United States, and it has usually exceeded that of Japan.

## European Interests and Actors

Among all the countries of Europe, Spain places the highest priority on Latin America in its foreign policy and in its international economic relations, though there has been a decline in trade similar to that observed for Europe in general.[16] During the last decade, Spain has increasingly directed itself to its own European environment. But this new and very dynamic European projection has actually allowed Spain to enhance its profile in Latin America, where, despite some recurrent emotional recriminations, it is perceived as a defender of the region's interests in Europe, particularly before the usually more distant European Community. In addition, Spain's special relationship with Latin America is perceived and consciously used by Madrid as a foreign policy resource to improve the country's status in the world, a perception that seems to be confirmed in the occasional (but not very decisive) consultations on Latin American issues that Washington, Moscow, and other European countries have held with Madrid.

At the EC, Spain has actively played its role as advocate of Latin America's interest—lobbying to obtain a new political framework for relations with Latin America, contributing decisively to the inclusion of the Dominican Republic and Haiti in the new Lomé Convention, and obtaining a modest increase in Latin America's share in the EC's development programs. However, Madrid has been considerably less helpful in aiding Latin America to fight European protectionism.

Bilaterally, Spain unfolded a diplomatic offensive over the last few years that culminated during the almost mythical year of 1992.[17] This offensive included frequent visits to the region by King Juan Carlos I, Prime Minister Felipe González, and other authorities, as well as intensive political contacts and the special cooperation agreements. Spain has also given special treatment to some of its Latin American debtors, not only forgiving part of Bolivia's debt but also granting some concessions in the renegotiation of the Mexican debt. Although trade has not followed the flag, investments have. Major banks and the few Spanish enterprises with multinational pretensions are taking strategic positions in the most advanced Latin American countries. In 1990, the Spanish government established the Quincentennial Fund at the Inter-American Development Bank (IDB), allotting $500 million for development projects in Latin America.

Spain has also played an active diplomatic role as political mediator in Central America, contributing to the peace process in the region and facilitating political dialogue aimed at resolving internal conflicts in El Salvador, Nicaragua, Guatemala, and Colombia.[18] Although its development cooperation programs tend to be rather modest and do not equal those of a country like Holland (for which Latin America is not a high priority), the programs do have a high profile, benefiting from cultural and political advantages and good public relations campaigns.

Germany has never given the region as high a profile as Spain has, but it is the top European economic power. For that reason and because of the political links that Germany established early on with diverse Latin American sectors, it has had a primary importance in the region for several years.[19] Germany is, by far, Latin America's most important trading partner and source for development cooperation in Europe, and although its role in the financial and investment sectors is less salient, it has kept its position as the main European economic power in Latin America. The intense activity of German political foundations in the region is well known, as is the presence of numerous NGOs. During the first half of the 1980s, Germany was the main force behind European–Central American economic and political cooperation, which was promoted personally by Foreign Minister Hans Dietrich Genscher. This interest has tended to decline over the last few years as a consequence of the more urgent priorities in Central and East Europe, but Bonn is still a relevant actor. Traditionally, Germany has also had strong relations with Brazil, Latin America's economic giant and one of the main destinations of German emigration, and its presence in Southern Cone countries such as Chile, Paraguay, and Argentina (which also include important colonies of German descent) has been considerable.

Italy's emergence as one of Europe's economic powers has been visible in Latin America, an area that received large flows of Italian emigrants well into the 1950s. Italy now ranks as one of the region's most important trading partners in Europe; Italian multinationals are extending their operations in Latin America; a fairly substantial part of Italy's arms exports to the developing world are directed to the region; and Italian aid has become one of the main sources of development cooperation.[20] Although less active, rich, and organized than their German counterparts, Italian political parties have also strengthened their links with fellow Latin American Christian Democrats and Socialists. As mentioned earlier, Italy initiated a series of ambitious bilateral cooperation agreements, designed to establish special associative relationships, which in practice exhibit rather modest results.

British interests in Latin America have declined considerably over the last decades, but some are still relevant despite reduced political attention from Downing Street and Westminster.[21] London-based banks hold the largest part of Latin America's debt with European creditors, and trade with the region is still significant, especially for Latin America. Despite little political interest and almost constant opposition in the EC to initiatives in favor of Latin America, the level of British expertise and academic activity concerning the region is still far above the European average.[22] The Foreign Office's long experience in Latin America is also evident in British diplomatic activity in the region, although it was not able to foresee the escalation of the Malvinas conflict at the beginning of the 1980s. Britain even has some secondary strategic interests in Latin America, centered in the defense of the Malvinas and protection of Belize in Central America.

Like other European countries, France does not place a high priority on Latin America in its foreign policy. Most economic and political resources directed toward the developing areas tend to favor French ex-colonies in Africa, a preference that has also been evident at the EC, where France has occasionally shown a negative attitude toward strengthening EC relations with Latin America. However, during the 1980s, France continued to be an important trade partner for the region, French multinationals maintained their presence, and arms sales experienced considerable growth. Moreover, French groups have held an important stake in large public works in the region, ranging from subway systems to electrical stations. Development cooperation has tended to decrease but is still significant. France even has strategic interests in the area, centered on the protection of its territories in the Caribbean and French Guyana, with its space center in Korou. Always inclined to grand political gestures and ambitious foreign policy designs, France played an active role in initial European involvement in Central America, strongly criticizing U.S. intervention in Nicaragua and actively supporting the peace process. However, political changes in France in the mid-1980s led to a lower profile in the region. President Mitterrand has also shown a special preoccupation with the debt crisis in the region and, in more global terms, with the need to resume the North-South dialogue, but these expressions of solidarity have not led to concrete policies.[23]

Smaller European countries have also maintained a certain presence in Latin America. As one of the main ports of entry to the richest part of Europe, Holland is one of the major trading partners for Brazil and Argentina, and Dutch multinationals keep an important presence in Latin America. The decision of the government in The Hague to increase development assistance to Latin America has made the Netherlands one of the major sources of development cooperation. And former colonial links are still relevant in troubled Suriname.

During the 1980s, Scandinavian countries, especially Sweden, were prominent in the field of development assistance and in providing political support to revolutionary regimes such as Sandinista Nicaragua and, to a lesser extent, Cuba. But political changes in those countries and in Scandinavia itself have made these less important recently.

The countries of Eastern and Central Europe have had lesser roles in Latin America, with the exception of the now-defunct German Democratic Republic, whose rather substantial cooperation programs with Cuba have not been taken over by the Bonn government due to the nature of the Castro regime.

Across the Atlantic, Latin Americans have shown an interest in strengthening relations with the new democracies emerging in that part of Europe. Mexico became one of the founding members of the European Bank for Reconstruction and Development (EBRD), and the foreign ministers of the Rio Group met with their colleagues of Eastern and Central Europe in Budapest in 1990, agreeing on a joint work program to intensify mutual relations.[24] More urgent priorities on both sides and weak prior relations have not prevented them from making significant progress.

European–Latin American relations have also had nontraditional protagonists. First, of course, is the European Community, which is gradually increasing its direct presence in the region. EC direct cooperation programs are particularly relevant in Central America, as a consequence of the San José process, but they have also been visible in the EC's support of integration processes in South America.[25] Obviously, the EC is already Latin America's obligatory bargaining partner in trade and fisheries issues. Beyond that, it is seeking a more prominent role in political issues, as well, trying to articulate some form of European consensus with respect to the region. These new functions will require a major revamping of the rather modest and not very efficient Latin American services of the executive body of the EC, the Commission. Taking into account European interest in the democratization processes in Latin America and strong party links between the two regions, it is no accident that the European parliament has been the most sensitive institution of the EC with respect to Latin America. However, its area of responsibility within the community is still rather modest.

The second category of nontraditional actors is composed of political parties and the myriad NGOs that are involved in many aspects of interregional relations, including religious institutions, charities, political foundations, labor unions, pressure groups, special lobbies, and academics.

In the past, European policies in Latin America have focused on two different groups of Latin countries. The first group consists of those in particularly conflictive areas, such as Central America and, to a lesser extent, some countries of the Andean subregion. Cuba could also fit into this category, although it represents a special case and has received less European attention than Central America. (This difference is not so much a consequence of lack of European interest in the political situation on the island as the result of Europe's relative lack of leverage there, as well as Cuba's reluctance to discuss its political future with any European partner.) The second group consists of the larger countries of Latin America, such as Brazil, Mexico, and Argentina. Despite its more limited dimensions, Chile could also be added to this category because of its relatively high profile in European–Latin American political relations.

European perceptions, objectives, policies, and instruments tend to vary from group to group. Thus, with regard to the first set of countries, European policies assume a greater political content and, to a certain extent, are directed toward crisis situations. With the second set, more traditional and permanent interests prevail, often centering on economic issues.

During the 1980s, the Central American conflict represented one of Europe's top priorities in Latin America. However, the peace process in the isthmus has shifted interests and needs from the political to the economic field, a change that requires Europeans to translate their initial political interest into comparable economic commitment. The Andean area has been a European priority in terms of development cooperation, and it is also gradually receiving more political attention. However, the size of the Andean states, the intractability of their crises, and a certain lack of previous historical involvement have discouraged a larger European role. To be sure, cooperation with Colombia is increasing significantly, Bolivia has been especially successful in attracting European development aid, Peru's worrisome economic and social situation is a matter of European public concern, and the EC Commission is supporting the Andean Pact. But commitments are limited, and there is a degree of pessimism about the possibilities for recovery for countries like Peru.

Although Europeans are not overly optimistic about the prospects for the larger countries, their policies and interests tend to be more stable and substantial in these cases. Relations with Brazil continue to represent a sizable part of Europe's relationships with Latin America, despite the perpetual economic crisis and political mismanagement in that country. To a lesser extent, the same is true in Argentina, which is attracting a considerable flow of new European investments and which is linked to Europe even by family ties. As for Mexico, it is probably the Latin American country that has attracted the most economic interest in Europe lately, given its improving economy and its imminent integration into a North American Free Trade Area. Relations with Venezuela are guided by conventional economic interests, which could increase in the future, but there are also some political elements, attributable mainly to party links. In the case of Chile, strong previous political links with Europe and the combined effect of its democratization process and successful economic situation make it a privileged object for special European consideration.

Policy instruments utilized by Europe vary according to these two very broad categories of countries. In the first case, there is a certain tendency to use emergency programs and measures and to contribute directly to crisis management. Thus, the European presence in Central America has been especially visible in terms of supervision and verification of the peace process, whereas development cooperation has been directed toward mitigating the effects of political crisis (e.g., refugee aid), economic reconstruction, and regional confidence-building, including the revitalization of Central American integration. Linkages between European and Central American political parties and NGOs have also been an important instrument for establishing and strengthening relations between the two areas.[26]

In contrast, trade and investment have played a minor role, due to the limited potential in these areas and the lack of significant previous links. In the Andean area, Europeans have resorted especially to development aid, which has been concentrated on Peru and Bolivia and probably has had more impact in the latter case. Party links have played a lesser role, except in Ecuador, and some NGOs are active in such areas as human rights protection. As mentioned earlier, special cooperation programs and actions are developing with respect to selective issues like the prevention and control of drug trafficking. However, policy instruments tend to be more restricted, and the European presence is less visible. Regarding Cuba, Europeans have few policy instruments, and, after some involvement in the 1980s, they now seem less capable and, most likely, less inclined to engage themselves in the uncertain future of the island. However, considerable investments in the tourism sector could give Spain and other European countries a new leverage in Cuba.

As to the second group of countries, policy instruments are less crisis oriented, development cooperation is less relevant, and the European presence tends to engage a broader spectrum of actors, especially in the private sector. Particularly in the larger countries of South America, trade plays a very important, although controversial (because of strong Latin complaints about European protectionism), role. Investments are significant, at least from a Latin American perspective. The debt crisis is still an obstacle to normal financial relations with Brazil, but it does not pose problems with respect to other major countries. As already mentioned, in the case of the major South American countries and Mexico, there is also a certain tendency to establish special framework agreements to promote investments; these are favored especially by the Southern European countries but resisted by Germany, Britain, and Holland, which prefer to rely on the interplay of market forces. NGOs are particularly active with respect to ecological issues in Brazil, whereas party links are relevant in Chile due to the symbolic nature of its political process.[27]

## Latin American Interests and Actors

Latin American interests in Europe are generally similar to European ones in Latin America. The difference lies not so much in the nature of the interests but in their relative weight and relevance for each region. From the Latin American perspective, Western Europe is important as a trade partner, as a source for foreign investments, as a financial counterpart, and as a provider of development cooperation. From the perspective of domestic politics, Western European political actors have been perceived as supporters (and occasionally as valuable allies) in the struggle for democratization. European political institutions and practices in fields such as decentralization, labor relations, civil-military relations, or even parliamentarianism are sometimes considered as models to be followed. From a foreign policy perspective, Europe has played an important role in Latin America's search for the diversification of its international relations. Although Europe has been unable and unwilling to become an alternative to the United States in the region, it has been and continues to be a crucial component in any Latin American design for a more balanced set of external economic and political relations.

Naturally, the relative weight of each of these factors varies from case to case. For Brazil, Europe is especially important in terms of its economic and foreign policy interests but less so in its domestic politics. For Central America, Europe is still a fairly secondary economic partner, but its political and even strategic relevance in the peace process should not be underestimated. In Argentina, Europe's importance as a trade partner surpasses that of the United States, and strategic interests are also present in the South Atlantic area. Chilean relations with Europe not only include important economic interests but also have a domestic politics dimension due to the historical affinities between Chilean and European political parties. In contrast, despite having acquired an associate status with respect to the EC, the Dominican Republic's relations with Europe are still weak.

Several Latin American countries have, at times, attempted to develop active European policies. Brazil, for example, pursued a European option in the 1970s, seeking a special relationship with Germany.[28] In addition to strong trade and investment links, it was to include a strategic dimension, consisting of an ambitious nuclear cooperation program that provoked strong reservations in Washington. The European option did not work out as planned, and, particularly in the nuclear area, it became a source of permanent frustration; nevertheless, during the 1980s, Europe continued to be an important factor in Brazil's already diversified external relations.[29] Despite protectionist tendencies in Europe, Brazilian-European trade relations have remained very substantial, accounting for approximately 30 percent of total trade between the two regions. European investors have also increased their activities, often forming joint ventures with Brazilian businesses. However, recent Brazilian perceptions about future relations with Europe tend to be pessimistic, and its policy is more defensive than offensive, focusing on the possible negative impact of the Single European Market and discrepancies concerning Brazilian environmental policies.[30] Bad press in Europe about Brazil's present economic and political situation also nurtures this defensive stance, which contrasts with its traditionally dynamic and optimistic outlook toward Europe.

Argentina's historical orientation toward Europe has been less obvious during the last decades, but it is still visible. Although the outcome of the Malvinas War led to a profound revision of Argentina's foreign priorities, this reorientation did not necessarily imply a distancing from Europe. On the contrary, Buenos Aires was able, to a certain extent, to isolate the conflict with Britain from its other European relations. The conviction of most other European partners that London's position on the Malvinas was characteristically rigid and obstinate contributed to this result. Thus, during Argentina's transition to democracy, Western Europe occupied a significant place in the country's foreign policy design. According to Roberto Russell, Europe was seen as a crucial actor in the search for more diversified international relations and as a counterweight to U.S. influence in the region.[31]

In fact, under the leadership of President Alfonsín and his foreign minister, Dante Caputo, Argentina insistently looked for a special relationship with European countries such as Spain, Italy, Germany, and France. Not coincidentally, both Spain and Italy initiated their respective series of framework cooperation agreements in Latin America with Argentina, and, in both cases, there are explicit references to special relationships. Buenos Aires also attempted to convince Germany of the need for a major cooperation agreement with Argentina, but German authorities explicitly discarded this possibility, explaining that Bonn preferred to rely on other mechanisms to develop mutual relations.[32] Alfonsín and Caputo's romantic visions about the European role in Argentina and Latin America have been tempered by reality, but the country has continued to develop its links with Europe, especially in the areas of trade, investment, and finance. In contrast with his predecessor, President Carlos Menem has placed more emphasis on economics than on politics with respect to Europe and has focused his quest for political alliance on Washington.

In the past, Mexico's links with Europe were not as strong as those of the Southern Cone countries. Trade, investments, and finance are overwhelmingly focused on the United States, and traditional political nationalism and extreme sensitivity to foreign opinions about the country's politics have prevented a closer political relationship with Europe. However, from the 1970s on, Mexico (like other Latin nations) has viewed Europe (and Japan) as a partial economic and political counterweight to the United States. Under the Salinas administration, Mexico has, in fact, become one of Europe's most active and dynamic Latin American partners, attracting new investment and allowing for a certain diversification of Europe's oil supplies. The conclusion of a free trade agreement between Mexico, the United States, and Canada may paradoxically spur Mexican relations with Europe, which sees Mexico as a platform through which it can gain access to the North American market. Accordingly, Mexican perceptions about the future of its relations with Europe tend to be more positive, although fears of increasing protectionism and the image of "Fortress Europe" still remain.[33]

With its relative concentration of exports on the European markets, its close political relations with the Continent, and its often difficult relations with the United States, Chile has, at times, searched for special relationships with Europe. However, though Eduardo Frei's administration made special efforts to establish such relationships and only Western Europe supplied the

Unidad Popular government with sorely needed economic aid, relations with Europe were marred by moments of frustration.[34] Expectations with respect to development aid were not met, in part because they were excessive and did not take into consideration the country's relatively higher social and economic indicators within the Third World and the Latin American context. On the other hand, as Chile developed its export capacity, complaints about European protectionism also rose to the fore, even though part of Chile's positive foreign trade balance is attributable precisely to its trade with the EC. Be that as it may, Patricio Aylwin's administration is pursuing a European policy focused on promoting trade, fighting European protectionism, attracting European investments, and procuring development cooperation in especially sensitive social areas. Political links were reinforced during President Aylwin's European tours in 1991, 1992, and 1993.

Although the other Andean countries have fewer advantages than Chile, all of them are interested in strengthening their European connections. The EC is Colombia's second-largest trading partner, and in the long term, this country has had one of the most successful Latin American experiences in exporting to European markets. Sound economic and financial management of successive governments in Bogotá has also contributed to this fairly good performance. But the Colombian government has also insistently tried to increase Europe's involvement in its struggle against drug trafficking. It was Colombia that induced the EC to approve a special regime for its imports from the Andean area. And cooperation with Spain, Italy, and Great Britain in efforts to control drug trafficking has also increased. Colombia's interest in engaging Europe more actively in this task is shared by Peru and Bolivia. Indeed, these two countries have procured most of their sorely needed development aid from European sources in recent years.

Central America has also been very receptive to a gradually increasing European presence in the isthmus. Early hopes in the Social Democratic parties and other circles of the Left that Europe would be an alternative to the U.S. presence have been abandoned. However, Central American governments have attached considerable importance to their dialogue with the EC and its member countries in the context of the San José process, and they are coordinating their positions more effectively than in the past. Several governments have also initiated bilateral cooperation programs with specific European countries, covering a broad range of activities from grass-roots development to institution-building and police training.

In a very different context, Cuba has also looked toward Europe as a useful partner in its almost desperate quest to diversify its international economic relations. Cuba was, for many years, able to maintain pragmatic and normal relationships with most European countries, despite the U.S. blockade. However, changes in the international context and growing disillusionment on the part of many sectors of the European Left that had traditionally been somewhat sympathetic toward the Cuban Revolution have marred relations. Inexplicably, despite this unfavorable context, Cuba not only allowed but also contributed to the escalation of a bilateral diplomatic crisis in 1990 with Spain, the Western European country with which it had previously enjoyed its friendliest relations. As a consequence, the EC, responding to Spain's request, suspended its mostly symbolic cooperation programs on the island until bilateral relations cooled off.[35] The reasons for the Cuban attitude have never been explained satisfactorily, but the fact remains that Havana lost ground in Western Europe just when its traditional allies were faltering.

Latin American countries are also attempting to strengthen collective action with respect to Western Europe, especially the EC. Although it is clear that there is a profound asymmetry between the weak and rather ineffective Latin American regional institutions and their European counterparts, some progress has been made. Thus, especially in the political realm, the Rio Group has proven to be an important forum for political contacts between both regions. Its institutionalization in December 1990 represented a success for Latin America, which has no comparable framework for regular consultation and political cooperation with any other region or group of countries in the world.

Although political dialogue between both regions is consolidating, no similar progress can be observed in economic negotiations. However, it is debatable whether comprehensive interregional economic dialogue is as important for Latin America as many of its regional institutions proclaim. The region's main economic problems with Europe are commercial, and it is obvious that these can only be solved in the context of global negotiations. In such negotiations, the region has to establish tactical alliances with more powerful economic blocs and groupings, such as the Cairns Group or the United States in the field of agricultural trade liberalization. On the other hand, Latin America's economic interests in many areas are not uniform, due to growing diversity and heterogeneity in the region. Colombia and Brazil have different perceptions concerning the liberalization of services, and Bolivia's interests in development cooperation contrast with Chile's insistence on trade liberalization. And the EC's special treatment of the Andean countries not only has met with criticism among the associated countries of the Lomé Convention but was also qualified as discriminatory by the Central American countries, Chile, and Argentina.

## Looking into the Future

Europe is going through a period of profound changes, but these changes may not have a very decisive impact on its relations with Latin America. To begin with, no "grand design" for the region will be altered for the simple reason that this design never really existed. Several changes in emphasis are evident in both the economic and the political sphere, yet they do not seem to lead to a qualitative change in interregional relations—neither for better, as some Europeans want us to believe and many Latin Americans expected during the 1980s, nor for worse, as some particularly negative and defeatist critics in both regions have warned. European–Latin American relations will most likely experience only incremental change.

It is true that Europe's political attention is now focused much more sharply on Central and Eastern Europe than on Latin America; further, the permanent state of crisis in the Middle East and the increasing instability in the strategically sensitive countries of Northern Africa's Maghreb are also putting pressure on European foreign policies. But it is by no means evident that this attention has been diverted from Latin America, a region that never has been particularly high in European priorities. But from a Latin American perspective, it is not really so important to know how high the region ranks in European priorities (although that question obsessed many politicians and scholars in the region); rather, the question involves how relevant Europe is for the region and particularly how useful the Continent has been for the diversification of Latin American international relations. Viewed from this second perspective, the balance is more positive than negative.

In economic terms, the completion of the Single European Market can be expected to bring additional diversion of exports from Latin America, if only because each deepening of European integration has historically had that effect for Latin America. However, this negative dimension could be offset by the likely expansion of demand caused by economic unification. Obviously, the effects will vary from sector to sector. Some preliminary studies are already differentiating between possible growth areas, which could include half of the total trade, marginal areas representing some 22 percent of all trade, and problem areas that would include some 28 percent.[36] Obviously, all estimations in the field are extremely tentative, but the general picture does not confirm the threat of a Fortress Europe, at least for Latin America. Yet the outcome of the Uruguay Round could affect interregional trade to a much larger extent than the Single European Market. And of course, it is difficult to foresee Latin America's capacity to adapt to changes in Europe. But if we consider the experiences of Colombia, Mexico, or Chile (but only during the last years), the outcome could be fairly positive.

The completion of the Single Market will likely accentuate the tendency of European investment to concentrate in its own internal market, but it is unlikely that this will affect investments in Latin America due to their marginal character for Europe. Similarly, the gloomy predictions about investment diversion from Latin America to Eastern and Central Europe have not been confirmed. Rather, the economic and political conditions prevailing in the latter area do not seem more favorable than those in Latin America, and most of the former Communist countries are just beginning to adjust their economies to introduce market mechanisms.

The debt issue is likely to decline in importance in Latin America's relations with Europe, as with other powers or regions. In the view of the European financial community, internal adjustment, not external support, is already allowing some important debtor countries to emerge from the crisis. On the other hand, European money markets are playing an important role in supplying fresh money to the region.

European development cooperation in Latin America appears stable. No major increases seem to be in store, but present levels should be maintained. What may be expected is a greater shift from traditional aid programs to new forms of cooperation in the industrial, technological, and educational sectors. Institution-building could represent another growth area, provided that democratization processes in the region continue to consolidate.

In the long term, an economically and politically stronger Europe will inevitably seek a more salient role in the developing region with which it has more historical and political affinities. Individually, the weight of some European actors in Latin America could gradually change in the coming years. Thus, it seems fairly obvious that Germany is concentrating more on its internal challenges and looking more to its eastern neighbors. Some changes in regional priorities are already evident in German political foundations and NGOs, but it would be an exaggeration to say they are abandoning the region. On the other hand, Spanish involvement in Latin America is likely to remain and even to grow, if not in trade then in equally important investment flows. The Italian presence in Latin America depends not only on the country's foreign priorities, where Latin America ranks in an intermediate place, but also on the capabilities of its state, which may need a major restructuring during the 1990s. For France, Great Britain, Holland, Belgium, and Scandinavia, no major changes seem likely in the coming years with respect to Latin America. And as for Portugal, apart from its special relationship with Brazil, its limited resources probably will not permit a significant change in its low profile in the rest of Latin America.

European priorities in the region are also undergoing some shifts. Changes in the political situation in Central America have diminished attention on that area, though economic aid has increased slightly and though Europeans continue to be involved in supervising the peace process and mediation efforts in countries like El Salvador and Guatemala. Among the larger countries of Latin America, Mexico will most likely continue to attract European attention, whereas the strengthening of relations with traditional partners such as Brazil and Argentina will largely depend on internal conditions prevailing in those countries. Relations with Chile will likely stay at their present positive level, but there are no hopes of constituting any kind of special relationship.

It is also likely that Western Europe will increase its collaboration with other OECD partners with regard to Latin America. Old discrepancies between the United States and its European allies over Latin issues have decreased considerably. During the 1980s, Washington viewed European engagement in Central America with distrust and skepticism, but in the 1990s, European powers are being invited to participate in some aspects of the Enterprise for the Americas Initiative and in international programs for the reconstruction of Central America. Political contacts between European nations and the United States that cover sensitive internal situations in the countries of the region are also increasing. Thus, the Atlantic triangle continues to be one dimension of European–Latin American relations, in a scheme that also includes Japan when economic enterprises are involved.[37]

Changes in Europe are not likely to make a major difference in interregional relations, but internal conditions in Latin America could well do so. In effect, most of the countries of the region will continue to maintain their interest in Europe, as part of their quest for greater diversification of their external links. Hopes for special relationships and appeals to European solidarity will gradually be replaced by more realistic and concrete appraisals of the potential for interregional relations. However, substantial progress in specific areas will depend more on economic and political conditions prevailing in Latin America than on mere political will. Europe's interests in the region could increase significantly if Latin America recovers the dynamism it showed during past decades and if it is able to preserve and deepen its democratization processes. It is obvious that Europe can assist Latin America in confronting those tremendous challenges, either by itself or jointly with the United States and other important foreign partners of the region. But success will depend on the Latin Americans themselves, not on their foreign friends. It is not that Latin America has been "abandoned" or "left alone."[38] Rather, what must be abandoned are delusions and mirages about nonexistent external benefactors and special relationships that never developed with Europe or even with the United States.

## Notes

1. José Miguel Insulza, "Los temas estratégicos in las relaciones entre Europa y América Latina" (Paper presented to the workshop on European studies at the Tenth Annual Meeting of the Member Centers of the RIAL Program, Montevideo, October 1988), p. 2. See also Atilio A. Borón, "Los intereses político-estratégicos de Europa Occidental y la cooperación eurolatino-americana," Documento de trabajo EURAL no. 31 (Buenos Aires, 1988).

2. Alberto van Klaveren, "Europa y la democratización de América Latina," *Nueva sociedad,* 85 (September–October 1986), pp. 134–140.

3. See, for instance, Howard Wiarda, "Europe's Ambiguous Relations with Latin America: Blowing Hot and Cold in the Western Hemisphere," *Washington Quarterly*

(Spring 1990), p. 154, where he asserted, "Whether Latin American intellectuals like it or not, the region has been thrown back into the arms of the United States."

4. On this subject, see Wolf Grabendorff, "Central America: A Dilemma for US-European Relations," *Harvard International Review,* no. 1 (November/December 1986), pp. 37–39.

5. See, for instance, Abelardo Morales, "El discreto encanto por Centroamérica en el Viejo Mundo," in Atilio Borón and Alberto van Klaveren, eds., *America Latina y Europa Occidental en el umbral del siglo XXI* (Santiago: PNUD/CEPAL Proyecto de Cooperación con los Servicios Exteriores de América Latina, 1989).

6. José Miguel Insulza, "Europa, Centroamérica y la Alianza Atlántica," *Síntesis,* 4 (1988), pp. 264–279.

7. For a solid analysis on EC development cooperation in Latin America that places special emphasis on Central America, see Guido Ashoff, "La Cooperación para el desarrollo entre la Comunidad Europea y América Latina: Experiencias y perspectivas," Documento de Trabajo IRELA no. 20 (Madrid, 1989).

8. The phrase is from the "Conclusions of the Council and the Representatives of the Governments of the Member States on the Development of Relations Between the European Community and Latin America," June 22, 1987. Spanish version reproduced in *Síntesis,* 4 (1988), pp. 350–353.

9. *Europe* (Brussels), October 25, 1990, and *El País* (Madrid), October 31, 1990.

10. William Drozdiak, "Cocaine's New Focus: Europe," *International Herald Tribune,* April 12, 1991.

11. These figures were obtained from the Institute for European–Latin American Relations (IRELA) in Madrid.

12. For a general analysis of Europe's involvement in the debt issue, see Gunnar Wiegand, "Western Europe and the Latin American Debt Crisis," IRELA Working Paper no. 12 (Madrid, 1988).

13. On British investments in Latin America, see the article by Soviet economist Olga V. Gridchina, "El capital británico en América Latina: En busca de expansión," *Revista de estudios Europeos,* no. 11 (July–September 1989), pp. 158–169.

14. For an early but still valid analysis, see Hubert Julienne, "Cooperación económica entre la Comunidad Europea y América Latina," Documento de trabajo IRELA no. 4 (Madrid, 1987).

15. On this subject, see IRELA, "Relaciones entre la Comunidad Europea y América Latina: Balance y perspectivas, Febrero 1989–Marzo 1991" (Base document prepared for the Tenth Interparliamentary European Community–Latin America Conference, Seville, April 2–6, 1991, Chapter 7), and Guadalupe Ruiz-Giménez, "La construcción de la nueva Europa y sus relaciones con América Latina (Paper presented at the workshop on "European Policies Towards Latin America in the New International Context," organized by AIETI, IRELA, RIAL, and CIDOB, Barcelona, October 4–6, 1990).

16. José Antonio Alonso and Vicente Donoso, "Perspectives de las relaciones económicas España-Iberoamérica–Comunidad Europea," *Pensamiento Iberoamericano,* no. 13 (January–June 1988), pp. 161–177.

17. *El País,* January 8, 1990.

18. On Spanish policy in Central America, see Francesco Bayo and Aníbal Iturrieta, eds., *Las relaciones entre España y América Central (1976–1989)* (Madrid: CIDOB and AIETI, 1989).

19. On the German role in Latin America, see Esperanza Durán, *European Interests in Latin America* (London: Royal Institute of International Affairs, 1985), pp. 24–26, 43–46, 71, and 88–91.

20. On Italian policy in Latin America, see Massimo Micarelli, "Las relaciones entre Italia y América Latina," Documento de trabajo IRELA no. 20 (Madrid, 1989).

21. Thatcher is not the only one responsible for this lack of interest in Latin America, an area that she visited only once during her long reign, on a trip that was placed in the global context of the North-South Dialogue in Cancún. Indeed, on August 23, 1988, *Financial Times* reported about the previous day's celebration of the first general debate on Latin American affairs in the House of Commons in thirty-eight years, adding that no significant conclusions had been reached. However, in 1992 Prime Minister Major visited Colombia and Brazil, becoming the first serving British prime minister to visit South America.

22. Thus, the best recent volume on bilateral relations between a European country and Latin America is Victor Bulmer-Thomas, ed., *Britain and Latin America: A Changing Relationship* (Cambridge: Cambridge University Press/Royal Institute of International Affairs, 1989). No equivalent studies exist for countries such as Spain, Germany, or France.

23. See, for instance, Mitterrand's declarations during his visit to Venezuela, Ecuador, and Colombia in 1989, as reported by *Le Monde*, October 14, 1989.

24. *El País,* April 13, 1990.

25. For a general assessment of European–Central American relations, see Roberto López, "Las relaciones económicas entre la Comunidad Europea y América Central durante los años Ochenta: Balance y perspectivas," Working Paper no. 5/90 (Madrid: IRELA, 1990), and Klaus Bodemer, *Europea Occidental—América Latina: Experiencias y desafíos* (Barcelona: Editorial Alfa, 1987), especially Chapter 2.

26. For an interesting and balanced analysis of the role of European Socialist parties in Central America, see Eusebio Mujal-León *European Socialism and the Conflict in Central America* (New York: Praeger, with the Center for Strategic and International Studies, 1989).

27. I have dealt with this aspect in more detail in "Chile y Europa Occidental: Entre el apoyo a la democracia y el realismo económico, in Heraldo Muñoz, ed., *Chile: Política exterior para la democracia* (Santiago: Editorial Pehuén, 1989), pp. 189–206.

28. Wolf Grabendorff, "Brazil and West Germany: A Model for First World–Third World Relations?" in Wayne Selcher, ed., *Brazil in the International System: The Rise of a Middle Power* (Boulder, Colo.: Westview Press, 1981), pp. 181–200.

29. On the frustration of the "European option" during the Geisel administration, see Miriam Gomes Saraiva, "A Opcáo Européia e o projeto de Brasil potencia emergente," in *Contexto internacional,* 11 (January–June 1990), pp. 95–117.

30. See Geraldo Holanda Cavalcanti, "O Brasil e a Comunidade Economica Européia," *Síntesis,* no. 12 (September–December 1990), pp. 185–208, and Sergio Sobrinho et al., *Al Europa de 92: Possíveis consequencias do proceso de unificão* (Brasilia: Cuadernos de IPRI, 1990).

31. Roberto Russell, "Argentina y Europa" (Paper presented at the workshop on "European Policies Towards Latin America in the New International Context," organized by AIETI, IRELA, RIAL, AND CIDOB, Barcelona, October 4–6, 1990).

32. *Ambito financiero,* July 22, 1988.

33. See Esperanza Durán, "Memorandum sobre la política de México hacia Europa" (Paper presented at the workshop on "European Policies Towards Latin America in the New International Context," organized by AIETI, IRELA, RIAL, and CIDOB, Barcelona, October 4–6, 1990), and IRELA, *Las relaciones entre México y la Comunidad Europa,* Informe de conferencia no. 5/90 (Madrid: IRELA, 1990).

34. Manfred Wilhelmy, "Chilean Foreign Policy: The Frei Government, 1964–1970" (Ph.D. diss., Princeton University, 1973), especially pp. 247–251.

35. *El País* and *El Independiente* (Madrid), June 20, 1990.

36. "A Test of Partnership: The Impact of the Single European Market on Latin America in the 1990s," Institute for European–Latin American Relations, Preliminary Study, Madrid, July 1990. For a more detailed and authoritative analysis, see *El mercado unico Europeo y su impacto en América Latina* (Madrid: Institute for European–Latin American Relations, 1992).

37. Wolf Grabendorff and Riordan Roett, eds., *Latin America, Western Europe, and the U.S.: Reevaluating the Atlantic Triangle* (New York: Praeger/Hoover Institution, 1985).

38. See for instance the rather melodramatic and inadequate title of the volume edited by Alvaro Tirado Mejía, *América Latina se ha quedado sola* (Bogotá: Fundación Santillana para Iberoamérica, 1989). The title has been taken from Gabriel García Márquez' speech accepting the Nobel Prize of Literature in Stockholm, 1982.

# 6

# Russia and Latin America in the 1990s

## Sergo A. Mikoyan

What importance, if any, will Russia have for Latin America during the rest of the 1990s? After a period that extended from Fidel Castro's triumph in Havana to the end of the 1980s, when it was often argued that the Soviet Union was an important factor and influence in Latin America, do the events in Moscow in 1991 bring that influence entirely to an end? Are Latin America and Russia still relevant for each other in any significant ways? Or are both now completely free of an apparent association that was the product of Washington's paranoia and pressures, as well as their own initiatives? These are the issues I will illuminate in this chapter, with the hope that my impressions and opinions may provide insights and perspectives lacking in many contemporary accounts of Russian–Latin American relations.

As a Russian specialist on Latin America whose interest in the region began with a visit to Havana more than thirty years ago, I work now from a vantage point in Washington. That fact itself reflects our changing world, and I believe it has helped me comprehend U.S. misconceptions and myths about Russian–Latin American relations, as well as some of the half-truths that had so much power in Moscow. My goal is to avoid such myths and to put Russian–Latin American relations into a realistic perspective. First, I present a brief review of the historical background, and then I turn to current and prospective relations as they are emerging after a period of kaleidoscopic international change, especially the ground-breaking transformations in my country. The full international implications of what happened in Moscow in August 1991 cannot yet be determined for the changes in Russia are, as yet, unfinished. Enough has clarified, however, to permit some ordered, if tentative, assessments.

# Myths and Realities of the Past

Soviet Russia was originally conceived as an international entity with a historic mission to determine the future not only of Russia itself but also of Europe and, indeed, of the whole world. And it certainly did, though hardly in the ways that Vladimir Lenin and his Communist cohort intended. The failure of communism in Russia in the 1990s should not lead us to underestimate the impact on the world of the seventy-four years that were started by the October Revolution in 1917.

Latin America was one of the areas of the globe least influenced by "the Red October," but it began to feel something new and significant in its social and political consciousness after 1917. On the surface, little changed. But the deeper we look, the more we see that the seeds of stormy future events had been sown. Some subtle, mysterious ideological impact (mysterious because we are speaking about geographically remote countries, populated by masses of backward and often illiterate people) began much earlier and was more profound than any influence that stemmed from subsequent Soviet diplomatic maneuvers or actions in foreign policy.

That is why it is difficult to agree that "in fact, nobody but Soviet Communist party members and their self-seeking followers elsewhere ever saw the events of October 1917 as a momentous event except in determining the rulers of the Russian empire."[1] If this were true, the breakup of the Soviet system would not be a momentous event either, apart from determining the rulers of Russia and other successor states. But few would defend this sort of interpretation of perestroika and the subsequent events in the USSR, Eastern and Central Europe, and many other areas of the world. Of course, what we have seen is not the end of history but the end of one era and the beginning of another. And we cannot afford to wave aside the importance of the USSR experience.

Many who were never Communists or Communist followers would agree with Abbot Gleason, who pointed out that he was educated with the conviction that "the Russian revolution was the most important event of the twentieth century"; he still believes that "in a way all progressive transformations of the twentieth century were closely connected to what happened in 1917."[2] But this is not to say that the Soviet regime achieved any great successes regarding democracy or the well-being of the people, especially when compared with capitalism.

Certainly, the very existence of the self-declared Socialist state for more than seven decades had a huge effect on the rest of the world, both because of its nature and because of its relations with other countries. The radiation of ideas and ideals from Moscow could be compared with the light of a star from another galaxy, whose rays were still illuminating distant objects while back at the source itself, warmth and light had been cooling and fading. It is in this context that we should acknowledge how correct Fidel Castro was when he said that without the October Revolution in Russia, there would not have been a Cuban Revolution. The Cuban Revolution came to illustrate more vividly than anything else how the Soviet Union's ideological influence outlasted the revolutionary fervor in the USSR itself.

The Cuban Revolution; the progressive military regimes in Peru, Panama, Ecuador, and Bolivia (with abortive elements of such regimes in Honduras and El Salvador); the Socialist government led by Allende in Chile; the urban and *selva* ("jungle") guerrillas in Brazil, Peru, Argentina, Bolivia, and Colombia; the revolutionary movements in Central America and the Caribbean— there was not a single area in the Americas where Washington felt free of the threat of troublesome developments somehow linked to Moscow.

Moreover, Cuba actually became a close Soviet ally that Moscow supported and tolerated. A very stubborn myth was that Havana became a mere pawn in the Soviet strategic chess game. In reality, Cuba knew that Moscow could not afford a quarrel with Havana even when it challenged Moscow's presumed supremacy quite openly. Still, it was an alliance, in spite of all the difficulties and headaches on both sides.

In short, the ghost of communism was more than a goblin—it was real enough to serve as a reminder of how expensive neglecting the poor and needy in Latin America might prove to be. And Fidel Castro did what he could to sustain this belief.

At the same time, the continent did not receive tremendously close attention from Moscow before 1991. It was not a proving ground or even a *place d'armes* for aggressive and expansionist communism. This is an example of the lasting and presumably convincing myths that served as a basis for policymaking in many countries, especially the United States. Surely, Moscow had some wish to expand as far as the Western Hemisphere, but the rulers in Moscow were realistic enough not to dream of turning the Caribbean Sea into a Communist lake—having the Socialist island of Cuba there was enough.

Grenada and Nicaragua were surprising gifts, which caused mixed emotions in the Kremlin. On the one hand, the gifts were welcomed because they gave some advantages to Moscow within the framework of the worldwide confrontation.

First, with the situation in Nicaragua, the Moscow rulers felt they had made some gains vis-à-vis the rulers in Beijing. The Chinese efforts to undermine the Soviets' image and influence in the Third World and especially among leftist movements sometimes seemed to the Kremlin no less important than the confrontation with the United States. This factor is often underestimated by Western analysts.

Second, Nicaragua proved useful in another context. The "dirty" war in Afghanistan had given the United States an obvious and very effective instrument to undermine the international stature of the USSR. But instead of recognizing its own stupidity and retreating from Afghanistan, the Kremlin used the situation in Nicaragua to turn the headache back on the U.S. government by equating the contras with the *mujaheddin*; and again, the Soviets tried to improve (this time, rather successfully) Moscow's image in the Third World. But Soviet aid to Nicaragua did not reflect an attempt at any real expansion in Central America. Moscow regarded such an outcome as improbable, despite Castro's hopes.

To be sure, had the domino theory begun to materialize in Central America by itself, the situation would have been happily greeted in the Kremlin. But pragmatic self-interest dictated a moderate approach to the events in the Western Hemisphere (Chile in 1970–1973 is a convincing example). Pursuing an aggressive line, instead of a conservative one, would have been too dangerous. The chances for failure would have been great, and failure could have eliminated any prospect for bilateral talks with the United States concerning the arms race and other issues. It could only add financial burdens without any significant gains. Paradoxically, Moscow became about as committed as Washington was to the idea of "no more Cubas."

In sum, the Soviet involvement in the Americas was never as great as portrayed in U.S. policy circles. To the extent that Moscow exported revolution, it sent little more than ideology.

Still, the existence of the Soviet Union raised any liberation movement to a potentially global scale. The ghost of communism could, at any given moment, be revitalized into a mighty warrior. That myths could easily become realities for the Soviet Union was undeniably a factor in Latin America by virtue of its involvement in and commitment to Cuba, its ties with the Sandinista government in Nicaragua, its links with Communist parties and progressive movements, and its usefulness for Latin American leaders as a point of leverage with the United States.

## Perestroika and Soviet–Latin American Relations

The one-sixth of the globe covered by the Soviet state was not the only place deeply transformed by the events that Gorbachev's perestroika process touched off after the spring of 1985. These events forced a reassessment of national interests and values by the Soviet regime, the end of the Cold War, and, finally, the burial of the ideology itself at its home in Moscow. Eastern and Central Europe and peripheral parts of Asia were shaken by the explosion that shook the world between 1989 and 1991. Latin America, distant as it is from Moscow, was also affected by the blasts of that explosion.

These blasts had varying effects in different parts of the Latin American continent and in different strata of its population. The failure of the ideology was perhaps the most significant blow for the leftist forces and the most welcome surprise for conservatives.

The breakdown of the USSR and the strange zigzags of Russian foreign policy, however, were something of a blow to centrist governments, as well. Clearly, those governments and the forces that back them see the end of the Cold War as a generally positive development: There is no more danger of a global nuclear war, nor is there a danger of subversive activity directed or encouraged by Moscow.

But at the same time, many countries have lost the opportunity to play on the confrontation between the two superpowers. Insofar as some countries could show that they belonged to "the gray zone" for which each side—but especially the United States—felt it necessary to struggle, "special treatment" was usually secured: Economic aid, loans, concessions in foreign debt and trade tariffs, preferential prices, military aid, political support, and other benefits were all potentially available. All this did not, of course, come automatically. Still, it was much easier to expect favorable "understanding" on the part of Washington when a mighty, dangerous, unpredictable, and mysterious adversary existed on the other side of the ocean.

Today, there seem to be few such opportunities on the horizon, and the impact of Russia on Latin America has diminished and become more complex. Under such circumstances, does anybody care about South and even Central America nowadays?

Moreover, one possible future scenario could cause the interests of Russia and Latin America to be conflictive instead of more or less compatible. The two may become competitors for U.S. financial aid, loans, and other assistance. In such a situation, at least three considerations promise to give the advantage to Russia: Washington's belief that democracy is stable and irreversible in Latin America, Washington's confidence that it can substantially influence domestic developments in Russia, and the fact that Russia is still a nuclear superpower and must be reckoned with and assisted. A countervailing consideration may be that Latin America is closer than Russia, and of course, Mexico will always be something of a "special case." As Michael G. Wilson put it, "After Russia, Mexico is possibly the most important country to the U.S. foreign policy."[3]

In any case, nobody can expect a general lull on the Latin American sociopolitical horizon as a result of the events in Russia. Zbigniew Brzezinski once acknowledged that Latin America, especially Central America, was the region for which Marxist theory and practices were most appropriate.[4] This remains true today. Of course, under the guise of leftism or because of a misunderstanding of the essence of the term *leftism*, different kinds of fanatics, cynics, and even corrupted elements can be very active. The Sendero Luminoso is an example. There should be no illusions: There is no guarantee whatsoever that the leftist trends will evaporate because of the hot blasts of the Moscow explosion in August 1991. On the contrary, new activists on the Left cannot but appear here and there—and not because they "failed to read in the papers about the sad end of Communist totalitarianism," as the president of Colombia, Cesar Gaviria, put it.[5] The other side of the story is that Russia will hardly be of any importance for the new Left on the Latin continent. Jorge Castañeda gave an excellent analysis of the prospects of the leftist movements in Latin America, which are no longer connected with "the Red Giant."[6]

It is obvious that Reagan was wrong from the beginning to suppose that crises or sociopolitical unrest in the world were connected with subversive activities masterminded in Communist capitals. But the most curious thing is that this simplistic explanation, born in the mind of a former movie actor who was counseled by the authors of the "Santa Fe manifesto," has found sanctuary in the former USSR. Nowadays, it is almost impossible to write or speak persuasively in Russia (except to a narrow community of Latin American specialists) in defense of the Sandinistas, of the Cuban Revolution, of Allende's government (many believe that he usurped power in a Castroist way!), or of anybody or anything that was portrayed in a positive light in Russia before August 19, 1991. "The arm of Moscow" has become an obsession for many people in Moscow itself, as critics try to discover in the Communist party's archives proof that every liberation movement in the Third World had been provoked, organized, and directed by the KGB.

An immediate result of the putsch in Moscow was a kind of revolution in the consciousness of many people, especially those in official circles and the mass media. To be against everything that was praised earlier became a must for almost any politician or journalist, with the exception of extremely stubborn ones. Even before the putsch, in 1989–1990, this trend was visible.[7] August 1991 made the trend almost irresistible.

However, this atmosphere in Moscow will not last. It should be considered as a natural backlash against the tiresome, untruthful, openly biased, or contradictory official propaganda of the past. A more thoughtful and impartial approach, based on common sense and generally recognized liberal democratic interpretations of world processes and events, will come in time. And this development will surely affect foreign policy issues, including those connected with Latin America.

Gorbachev's domestic reforms and his global "new political thinking" had their most direct and visible impact on the Soviet Union's relations with Cuba. However, even this inevitable development was initially minimized and delayed by bureaucratic and political inertia and internal compromises, as reflected in the early 1990 Gorbachev-Castro summit and the USSR-Cuba treaty. Indeed, the treaty of May 1990 looked like something from the beginning of the 1960s or the late 1970s. It seemed strange, however, after 1989. But this was not because the Cold War had ended for Cuba—regrettably, it had not.

However, an ideological rift between the Soviet-Russian leadership and certain leftist forces in Latin America could be traced in *comandante* Fidel

Castro's initially cautious, then openly negative attitude toward perestroika at its very beginning. Given the worldwide background, the summit in Havana in May 1990 was doomed to be a disaster. Surprisingly, the summit brought a multifaceted treaty that appeared to forge a stronger and closer relationship than the two countries had known under Brezhnev. But this was a misleading illusion, involuntarily created by the two leaders.

The treaty was a realization of plans conceived at least two years earlier in the apparatus of the Central Committee of the Communist Party of the Soviet Union (CPSU) and of the Foreign Ministry. Bureaucrats "preparing" the visit were eager to make their contribution "a new stage" in relations between the two countries; they were far more interested in accomplishing their own goals than in assessing the rapid changes going on in the USSR and considering how those changes might affect Soviet-Cuban relations. The feeling that the almighty apparatus could go its own way was still strong. That is why the summit brought one of the most seemingly productive treaties between the USSR and Cuba even as it ushered in the most serious cooling of actual relations. In fact, the treaty became outdated at the moment of its signing. Thus, another myth was substituted for reality.

Personal incompatibility between Mikhail Gorbachev and Fidel Castro was only the first sign of strain in the Soviet-Cuban romance on the governmental level. Indeed, a cooling in the relationship was unavoidable due to the general direction of Gorbachev's reforms. The "general lines" of the two leaderships became irreconcilable. Nevertheless, Gorbachev would not have broken Soviet-Cuban relations altogether and would have upheld at least some parts of earlier obligations and treaties if domestic developments had been proceeding in a more orderly way. He believed that the relationship with Cuba, though changed substantially, was important in the context of world politics.

However, the putsch of August 1991 altered everything. Coming back from his Foros detention, President Gorbachev was so demoralized by his vengeful rival Boris Yeltsin that he failed to follow basic diplomatic and ethical rules of behavior. Unilaterally, without even bothering to inform Castro beforehand, he declared on September 12, 1991, in the presence of U.S. Secretary of State James Baker, that he intended to withdraw the Soviet military brigade from Cuba.

The statement was evidently forced and premature. First, it was unclear how large the Soviet military brigade actually was. Second, even as of January 1993, almost 1,500 soldiers were still in Cuba. Obviously, the military was not willing to cooperate in such a hasty retreat. Finally, the full withdrawal was scheduled by President Yeltsin for the second half of 1993.[8]

For thirty years the presence of these troops on the island has been little more than a symbol of the friendship that the two countries established in 1962, in the immediate aftermath of the missile crisis. Actually, they were no longer necessary to protect Cuba from a U.S. invasion. Moscow, at least, did not think such an invasion plausible, though the incursions into Grenada and Panama led Cuban leaders to believe that their country might be next.

In 1991, Cuba still had the highest per capita defense budget in the hemisphere. Its defense forces in 1992, after all African expeditions were curtailed, remained among the strongest in the Americas, at 175,000 people.[9] Of course, Cuba had no illusions that it could defeat U.S. forces, but its leaders wanted to make sure that any potential invasion would be long and bloody enough to make it unaffordable. Fidel Castro never regarded direct Soviet military help as a serious possibility—even when Nikita Khrushchev promised "to send the Baltic Fleet."

### 1991 and After: Russia's Changed Role in Latin America

What can be expected now, after the end of the Cold War, the breakup of the Communist ideology in Moscow, and the demise of the USSR as a superpower?

Gorbachev and Eduard Shevardnadze had a vision for the strategic direction of Soviet foreign policy. The end of the Cold War was their primary goal, and this dictated many of their decisions. I cannot say that Latin America occupied an important place in their minds, though the Cuban connection could not be simply dismissed. But immediately after August 1991, an obvious vacuum of strategic thinking emerged. This was quite understandable: Even traditional, stable states cannot always boast of strategic vision in their foreign policy, and for a country based on dogmatic ideology to lose that ideology so abruptly made a certain period of disarray and confusion inevitable. Moreover, the first Russian government after August 1991 was a government of amateurs, including Foreign Minister Andrei Kozyrev. Here was a textbook example of the "Peter principle."[10] As a result, the new government found it difficult to think clearly about preserving its own interests.

As far as Cuba was concerned, the Russian foreign minister made clear his intention to annihilate any specifics of the prior Russian-Cuban relations. He even tried to introduce an adversarial attitude toward Cuba, which was considered necessary for a final resolution of differences with the White House's world vision. The most scandalous example was Russia's vote on the UN resolution for lifting the U.S. embargo toward Cuba in November 1992: Russia abstained, while the majority of countries, including many U.S. allies, voted in favor of the measure.[11] After the first shock passed, policies like this prompted objections on the grounds that they contradicted Russia's basic interests as a great power and ignored the obvious diplomatic advantages of the relationship with Cuba as a way to balance Washington's pressure on Russia's weakened international position.

What scenarios may be predicted for the 1990s? If Kozyrev remains at his job for long (which is extremely unlikely), his policy of "infantile pro-Americanism" may continue for some time.[12] But Kozyrev may feel pressured to make corrections in this area, and political considerations may be interpreted differently. Much will depend on the correlation of forces in the decisionmaking bodies.

However, economic realities are stronger than the fluctuations of any opportunistic official. On one hand, Russia's economic situation has brought an end to the preferential trade conditions that were extended to Cuba in the 1960s. Not only will Russia be unable or unwilling to extend economic aid or preferential prices to Cuba, but the steady decrease in oil production that has been under way for several years will deny Cuba any hope for extra oil imports from Russia. At best, Russia will fulfill its trade obligations, but any interruptions that take place may mean much more for Cuba than Russian oil industry czars can imagine.

On the other hand, economic needs will dictate continuity in normal trade relations. Russia does not have enough sugar for its population, and the disruption of economic relations with Ukraine, which has always produced more sugar beets than Russia, means that shortages of sugar will be felt even more profoundly. The sugar shortage has also been acute in a number of other republics. That is why it was easy for Cuban foreign trade delegations to sign trade agreements with Russia and other republics.

This was the essence of what President Yeltsin told George Bush when the latter asked why Russia would not halt its imports from Cuba altogether. It was not the whole answer, but the Russian president evidently wanted to give a neutral, purely economic reply that left aside political aspects of the problem. In reality, however, Russia and Cuba may remain rather close politically, though their relationship will not be what it once was.

Neither country wanted the Russian military to cut short its relations with Cuba. In January 1992, a whole group of U.S. representatives—Robert McNamara, Raymond Garthoff, Raymond Cline, Arthur Schlesinger—accompanied by Sergei Khrushchev and myself, were invited by Cuba's Defense Minister Raul Castro to his headquarters in Havana. Among other curious things, Raul showed us a red telephone, connecting him with the Defense Ministry in Moscow. He even picked up the receiver and was immediately talking with somebody speaking Spanish in the Russian General Staff.

Evidently, nobody in Moscow wanted to be deprived of an opportunity to use Cuban ports for the Russian navy and trade and fishing fleets in the Atlantic. And actually, the United States wanted from Russia more than it could have hoped for from its closest allies. The first repercussions of the Torricelli Act—the "Cuban Democracy Act" intended to tighten U.S. pressures on Cuba, signed by George Bush on October 27, 1992—showed that though the American-Cuban Foundation had proved its growing influence on the U.S. Congress, no close allies of Washington wanted to take the act into consideration.[13]

Very important developments in Russian-Cuban relations will occur in connection with the nuclear power plant near Cienfuegos. Just several months prior to the November 1992 agreement with Russia (which will be discussed later in this chapter), Castro declared that construction of the plant would be stopped for financial reasons. Everybody understood the significance of the decision: Problems connected with security and the general context of relations were not mentioned, but they clearly played a role. By the end of 1992, Russia held talks with Cuba, proposing to continue the construction. The arguments were the following: (1) Almost 90 percent of the work had been done; (2) if the construction were stopped, much of the completed work would perish, and any future attempt to continue would cost a great deal more; (3) Cuba needs new sources of energy anyway because it cannot afford to import all the oil it needs (the power station would save one million tons of oil); and (4) other participants could be invited in order to minimize security and financial problems (French companies had been asked to contribute and allegedly gave their preliminary agreement). Ultimately, Cuba reacted favorably. It is clear that such a change could not have taken place without Castro's approval, and by the same token, the proposal could have come only from the highest authorities in Moscow.

The November 1992 agreement solved a number of problems, providing a stable market for Cuban sugar and assuring a steady supply of spare parts for the Soviet military and other machinery. Last but not least, it changed the psychological environment for the Cuban-Russian relationship in the 1990s. The agreement signaled changes in Moscow's Cuban policy, imposed by quarters beyond the Ministry of Foreign Affairs.

The agreement, signed on Russia's part by Deputy Prime Minister Aleksandr Shokhin, a representative of the old military-industrial complex, established the Inter-Governmental Commission on Commercial, Economic, and Scientific-technological Cooperation. The commission is supposed "to give an impetus" to Cuban-Russian economic relations. The two sides agreed to set up a special working group for dealing with "mutual obligations"— which certainly means, among other things, the problem of the Cuban debt to Russia.

What is especially important for the future is the decision by Russia and Cuba to strengthen the legal basis on which their bilateral relations were established. The accord also gives a legal and permanent status to the Russian radioelectronic center in Lourdas. Washington has been assured that the center's intelligence functions will be strictly limited; it will be used for other purposes, including radio transmissions for Latin America, weather monitoring, and information.

Perhaps it was no accident that the agreement was concluded just days after Bush signed the Torricelli Act regarding Cuba and days before the presidential elections in the United States, when Clinton's victory seemed assured.

Such variations in Russian policy are quite explicable. President Yeltsin, very inexperienced in foreign affairs, listens to anybody around him who claims to understand these matters. And claimants came in battalions. Oddly enough, an obscure professor of "scientific communism" from Sverdlovsk (the city in the Urals now called by its old name, Yekaterinburg) became responsible for supervising all foreign relations on behalf of the president himself. Then the star of Guennady Burbulis began to fade. As for Kozyrev, he was appointed the Russian minister when that job was absolutely unimportant because Eduard Shevardnadze was still the Union minister, and his survival at the helm of the new Russia's international affairs has surprised even some of the people who recommended him for the job.

Clearly, the situation could continue to change in any number of ways. The groups that the Western press regards as simply conservatives (irrespective of their diverse opinions on many domestic issues) but that claim to be more patriotic than the present leadership may expand their influence from economic development to problems of foreign policy. Some signs of such expansion can already be seen. Many of their international visions are shared by "proven democrats." Furthermore, some of these groups recognize the importance of the Third World, and this will undoubtedly lead to a reevaluation of the Kremlin's Cuban policy in favor of a more tempered approach. The November 1992 agreement may prove to be just the first signal of such a change.

Russia's cultural contacts with Cuba and other Latin American countries are evidence that a scenario of this type may well develop. The role of the "creative intelligentsia" in politics has always been very strong in Russia, though foreigners sometimes have trouble appreciating its true significance. Even the temporary trend of ignoring cultural and academic fields, prevalent among nouveaux riches in the new Russia, cannot make the old cultural traditions disappear. Consequently, intellectuals in different fields will contribute greatly to what is usually called a "civilized" approach to various issues. As far as Cuban-Russian relations are concerned, it will mean that thirty-year-old cultural ties will continue to work in favor of a lasting friendly attitude toward Cuba. The same trend will, to a great extent, define relations with the whole Latin American continent.

Not too much will depend, I believe, upon domestic developments in Cuba. The personality of Fidel Castro may be a difficulty if he persists in his hard line on dissidents and demands for a multiparty system. Yet Cuba is not experiencing serious disturbances like the civil wars in the former Soviet Union and Yugoslavia or the Tiananmen Square massacre in China. And the Russians will understand better than the Westerners how difficult the transition from dictatorship to democracy can be.

Even if Yeltsin manages to strengthen his own authoritarian hand, he will feel pressure to develop a sounder, more thoughtful foreign policy with certain strategic directions and goals in world affairs. Such a policy has certainly been missing since August 1991 and especially since the disappearance of Mikhail Gorbachev and Eduard Shevardnadze from the key positions in that field.

Of course, Russia will need Western aid for a long time. In theory, this need should make it obedient to U.S. demands concerning Cuba. But such obedience is contrary to Russian traditions, and real U.S. aid is not felt very directly in Russia. The public is coming to realize that this aid is more talk than action, and the Clinton administration, which may well dominate the political scene in the United States until the end of the century, is not expected to do more than George Bush and James Baker did. Instead, the White House and Congress will have to pay more attention to domestic needs. The World Bank's activities in Moscow are rather limited, and the Western European countries, which are quite active in Russia, will never make Cuba a problem. The consolidation of Europe will make these countries even less willing to follow the U.S. anti-Cuban obsession. Russian leaders know that the West European aid and investments have been and probably will remain more important than U.S. assistance.

That is why there are grounds to expect at least a partial return to relatively friendly (but not longer "brotherly"!) relations with Cuba. The relationship will not have the old anti-U.S. flavor, however; instead, it may resemble the Spanish-Cuban relationship.

### *Russia and the Continent at Large Through the End of the Century*

Russian relations with every Latin American country will be affected by changes in the former USSR. A good example is Mexico. The traditional friendship between the two countries, which dates almost to 1917, was based partly upon romantic ideas about the two revolutions that gave birth in that same year to new images of each state. Both images were seen through rosy glasses, but the concept worked: Public opinion disregarded the actual results of the "unfinished revolutions" as far as relations between the two countries were concerned. Furthermore, many well-known and respected Russian cultural figures have visited Mexico since the 1920s, and many Mexican muralists, writers, singers, dancers, and other cultural leaders have visited Russia. This factor depends little upon political changes inside Russia, however dramatic they are.

Nonetheless, the special relationship also had a political basis in terms of both countries' confrontations with the United States. Although the confrontation was open and dangerous on the part of the USSR, it was covert and undeclared on the part of Mexico. The latter case was more of a "defensive" animosity that stemmed from both historical and contemporary grievances. In any case, maintaining a friendship with the Kremlin served Mexican national interests.

Interestingly, President Salinas de Gortari looked troubled when, in his address to the General Assembly of the United Nations on January 11, 1992, he said that the end of the Cold War has resulted in the military domination of *one* power, while in Latin America, old sources of instability still exist.[14]

When Mexico invited the delegation of the Supreme Soviet of the Russian Federation to visit in October 1992, it looked like an attempt to maintain relations with the main successor state of the Soviet Union. Mexico was clearly not using a "Communist card," but its government sees Russia as a power like Japan, France or Germany—still significant politically, though almost useless economically. The delegation was received very warmly and had meetings with industrial and agricultural departments. The head of the delegation, Vice-Chairman of the Supreme Soviet Sergei Filatov, made an optimistic statement about the developing Russian-Mexican relations.[15] He even declared that President Yeltsin was going to visit Mexico in the first half of 1993.

"Distant neighbors," as the United States and Mexico were rightly termed by Alan Riding, are becoming less distant nowadays.[16] And of course, there is no longer a confrontation between Moscow and Washington. The North American common market and the Russian-U.S. political cooperation seem destined to undermine political interests based upon common animosity. This should be regarded as a positive development in the post–Cold War era.

But the real Achilles heel in Mexican-Soviet relations is the absence of serious mutual economic interests. Russia, at present, has nothing to offer the Mexican economy, which is closely tied to North American capital and technology. Mexico's export goods are mostly oriented toward the United States, and its capital can hardly be active in Russia at a time when Mexico must prepare to cope with the NAFTA common market and competition from the North. Indeed, Filatov's optimism does appear very realistic. But Mexican capital may eventually find in Russia a new market in which there is no North American competition.

Strange is it may seem, the countries of Central America have slightly brighter prospects, both economic and political. Their traditional exports— bananas and coffee—are being imported in Russia in growing quantities, thanks to the new economic conditions there. Under the old "commanding-administrative system," which kept most prices in the country fixed, the price of bananas was extremely low: 1 ruble, 10 kopecks per kilo (cheaper than apples, which were produced in the USSR itself or imported from neighboring Hungary or Poland). This made the import of bananas unprofitable for the bureaucrats from the Ministry of Foreign Trade. Given their basic approach— "the coefficient" between dollar and ruble prices—that kind of import did not deserve to be seriously developed. The situation with coffee was "corrected" when the fixed price in the USSR was doubled in the 1960s from 4 to 8 rubles and then more than doubled in 1972 to 18 to 20 rubles per kilo. Now that small private trade exists and prices for tropical products are no longer controlled centrally, it is profitable to import bananas and coffee at all times of the year.

These changes help Central American countries, Colombia (exporting 84 percent of its coffee crop), and Brazil (exporting 60 percent of its coffee) both directly and indirectly. Although German, Austrian, Swiss, and other firms sell more coffee to Russia's small traders than do Colombian or Brazilian firms and although Central American firms simply cannot be found in Russia, those European countries can be expected to increase their own coffee imports as a result. The same is true for bananas. The establishment of direct trade contacts with Costa Rica, Nicaragua, Honduras, Colombia, and Brazil is very desirable because it will decrease exceptionally high prices by eliminating a whole chain of intermediaries.

The process is gaining momentum gradually, but it will not become really important until big corporations within the former USSR accumulate capital and acquire the ability to transport and preserve tropical goods. Russia needs several years to work out the logistics of private trade in tropical food products.

What are the political factors currently in play in countries south of Mexico? Oddly enough, the end of Soviet military aid to Nicaragua and the repudiation of the Communist party's rule in Moscow did not cut short the Russian role in Central America. For example, the Russian mission to the United Nations continued to take an active part in the whole process of peace talks in El Salvador. And the Farabundo Martí Front of the Salvadoran insurgent Left is inclined to trust the Russian delegation in New York far more than any other mediator in the talks with the U.S. government. The front has also approached Moscow through the Cuban Embassy there.

For the foreseeable future, Russia can expect the following:

1. Stable relations with Nicaragua in spite of all the domestic changes in both countries (the Russian write-off of $2.4 billion out of the total Nicaraguan debt of $3 billion is a good example);
2. Comparatively trustful and easy relations with the leftist forces in the area, including armed movements like the Farabundo Martí Front. Even after all the difficulties in El Salvador—such as the inability of President Alfredo Cristiani to meet the UN demands concerning the Salvadoran army—are solved, these movements will still be important for the Sandinistas to remain in Nicaragua; and
3. A good chance to continue the participation in the peace process in Guatemala because, again, the Guatemalan guerrillas are likely to trust Russia.

The parallel processes of democratization in Russia and in a number of Latin American countries have lifted serious earlier obstacles to their political cooperation. The end of the Cold War was a little belated in Latin America; the psychological climate for relations with the Soviet Union and Russia could not but change radically after the events of 1989 and 1991. Anticommunism, as a basis for policy toward Moscow, had to die when communism collapsed as dominant ideology in the Russian capital. Moreover, some Latin American governments that are still fighting the leftist ideology—including Colombia, Chile, and Guatemala—are eager to use their relations with Russia to undermine revolutionary or radical trends at home.

Relations between Russia and Brazil undoubtedly have an important future in a number of fields. The belated computing explosion in Russia shows that the computer industry might be a very broad field of cooperation, in which a good deal of capital may be accumulated. Brazil has been seeking Russian scientific and technological assistance for big computers, and at the same time, it can help Russia feed its own enormous appetite for cheap personal computers.

True, by the beginning of 1993, only a few dozen Brazilian companies were active in Russia, mostly in trade or joint ventures. (The hotel industry dominated Brazilian investments.) But there are numerous fields of business activity that could be mutually beneficial. One example may be the joint venture between the MIG design bureau in Moscow, which has traditionally produced fighting planes, and a Brazilian company to produce a small business jet. Some cooperation in the military industry could also emerge between Russian enterprises and Brazilian companies. This would not be a tremendously happy development, but economic considerations may push it forward.

In November 1992, air communications between Russia and Brazil were, at last, established (after many years were spent gaining Brasilia's permission for Aeroflot to land in Rio de Janeiro on the way to Buenos Aires). Now, Aeroflot and Transbrazil will connect Moscow and Saint Petersburg with Rio, São Paulo, Salvador, and Porto Allegre, for both passenger and cargo flights.[17] The latter flights will undoubtedly facilitate direct relations.

Politically, no obstacles to closer ties remain. The interest in such ties was obvious even in earlier times, when both countries had authoritarian systems. Now, when both are striving to build democratic societies, the countries have added grounds for cooperation. As the foreign minister of Brazil said in November 1992: "Brazil is interested in the best relations with the states of the Commonwealth of Independent States. With some of them we may have rather active trade."[18]

Ironically, more and more scholars, journalists, and even officials in Russia have come to the conclusion that big Third World countries like India and Brazil are better models for Russian development than the United States is. The Brazilian practice of inviting transnational corporations to invest, which was once criticized in the Soviet Union, now seems a good model for adapting. Brazil's ability to achieve some features of a developed country and to compete on world markets in both raw materials and industrial goods is impressive to Russians, whose industrial goods are too poor in quality to be competitive (except in the military and a few other fields).

Sometimes, of course, trade, free of state control, brings difficulties that are quite normal for countries with free markets. Thus, the uncontrolled export of natural resources from the former Soviet Union caused trouble not only to the governments of the commonwealth but also to Brazilian producers. During 1992, for example, about 3,000 tons of ferrochrome were imported to Brazil from Russia, Ukraine, and Kazakhstan at prices 33 percent lower than those of local producers. As a result, the Brazilian producers applied to their government for protection against such dumping.[19] In sum, then, there are viable prospects for enhancing the existing trade relationship with significant economic exchange, including the flow of capital from Brazil to Russia and of high technology from Russia to Brazil.

Closer economic relations may also be possible with other, more developed Latin American countries whose economies are compatible with that of Russia, among them Argentina, Colombia, and Peru. Peru already cooperates with the Soviet Union in military equipment, and there is little doubt that the cooperation will continue. First of all, ties of this kind inevitably continue for the sake of obtaining spare parts and making renovations. Second, the Russian armaments will remain competitively priced and sufficiently sophisticated for Peruvian needs.

Venezuela never had promising trade relations with the USSR. As an oil exporter, however, Russia cannot be indifferent to this Latin country. As Venezuelan Foreign Minister Armando Durán declared:

> Venezuela has a clear interest in the future of these new nations [of the commonwealth], particularly so since they constitute the basis of the principal oil producing and exporting country in the world. Any development in this critical area of the international economy concerns us directly and we feel compelled to insure that future developments preserve the stability and transparency of the world energy market.[20]

The minister had good grounds to feel troubled, but he certainly did not have the means to influence the situation. For a whole year, the export of oil from Russia was out of control, and as a result, world prices dropped significantly (from $24 to $18 per barrel by the beginning of 1993).

Relations with Argentina were always normal despite the country's cruel military dictatorship. This was one more proof of Moscow's opportunistic policy, which considered imports of grain and meat more important than political solidarity with democratic or even leftist forces. Until the land reform in Russia succeeds in increasing the grain crop (which is unlikely to happen in the near future), Russia may import grain from Argentina, as well as from the United States and Canada. One field of cooperation that has been opened by political changes in Russia is military contacts. In October 1992, Argentine Defense Minister Antonio Herman González paid a visit to Moscow, where he met with Vice President Aleksandr Rutskoi, Chairman of the Supreme Soviet Ruslan Khasbulatov, Defense Minister Pavel Grachev, and Chairman of the Constitutional Court Valery Zorkin. González visited the General Staff Academy and the powerful Union of Industrialists and Entrepreneurs, and he invited Minister Grachev to visit Argentina as soon as April 1993. González's utterances at his lunch with the press in the Moscow hotel Metropol were rather contradictory but still significant. In spite of the expressed wish of his government to join NATO, he said that "Argentina is not going to follow somebody who is striving to the world hegemony." He declared that the goal of his visit was not to purchase armaments, but he did not rule out trade cooperation in the military-technical field: "The exchange or purchase of military technology will be studied," said the minister.[21] Evidently, political changes in both countries paved the way for exchanges that could not have seemed possible before, even in the immediate aftermath of the Falklands War. As in the case of Mexico, we can suppose that Argentina now sees relations with Russia as an important diversification of its international entourage.

Chile's prospects as Russia's economic partner are, unfortunately, not very bright. The fast-developing economy of this country is based on its U.S.-oriented exports, and a free trade agreement between Chile and the United States is being discussed. Accordingly, Chile will not be interested in selling to or buying from Russia; even the few commodities that could be a basis for such trade will fit perfectly into the country's economic relations with her northern neighbor.

Elsewhere in Latin America, however, the Russian tradition of importing grain, meat, and leather from Uruguay, Argentina, and Brazil has a good chance of developing. Ecuador and Colombia have been main suppliers of bananas to Russia, and Bolivia always sold some metals to the Soviet Union. Colombia imported Soviet cars and trolley buses, and a Panamanian company used to buy Soviet cars such as Ladas and Nivas, selling them throughout the continent at very low prices. All these trade patterns could either continue or resume before long.

Contrary to most Western expectations, however, there would be no stabilization of the ruble. Any normal and stable economic interaction has been very difficult. Changes in the Russian government and in the approach to reforms on the eve of 1993 gave the country a real chance to develop a more sound basis for its internal economic policy and, hence, for its foreign economic exchanges. Though the catastrophic situation created by inflation will probably not be overcome in the near future, a Russian economic recovery can optimistically be expected by the mid- to late 1990s. That kind of a "Russian economic wonder" is possible because of the country's rich natural resources and high educational and technological levels.

# Some Conclusions on U.S.-Russian Relations

Leftist forces in Latin America may soon be able to put aside the shock of the Communist regime's defeat in the USSR. The Communist ideology has gone, but Moscow's ruling circles are regaining their sympathy toward liberation movements and the Third World's struggles for elementary national rights. Here, I should make it clear that there are different factions among these ruling circles. That is why such an assumption should be understood only within the context of the internal struggle in the decisionmaking bodies of Russia itself. This power struggle, as usual, is more visible in concrete issues of domestic or foreign policy.

In no case will the struggle lead to a resumption of the Cold War or a new confrontation with the United States. More likely, Russia will model its international posture along the lines of the French example—in the "worst" case, from the U.S. point of view, that of Charles de Gaulle's time.

How might these trends in the Russian approach to Latin America influence U.S.-Russian relations? This is an important question because U.S.-Soviet confrontation on the Latin continent used to be a substantial element of the Cold War. Even though this was mostly due to mutual misperceptions, the matter poisoned every attempt at détente. Even after the end of the Cold War in 1989, conflict over the Russian role in Latin America was affected by the détente policies boldly pursued by Gorbachev and Reagan, Gorbachev and Bush, and Yeltsin and Bush.

If the "infantile pro-Americanism" does not continue to dominate Russian foreign policy but is overcome by sober and independent minds in Moscow, the U.S. government will have to face different facts, not all of which will be pleasant or easy to sell to conservatives. Trade and economic relations with Cuba, especially the existence of the Russian radioelectronic center there, will certainly be difficult issues for the U.S. government because of the pressures of the Cuban-American lobby.[22]

A continuing Russian political role in Central America should be easier to accept. With the end of the Cold War, any peaceful Russian contribution should not only be tolerated but also welcomed. Whatever jealousy remains in this area is nothing more than a relic of the Cold War attitude. And the Russian relationship with South American countries should cause no significant discomfort at all: It should eventually be as acceptable to the United States as the involvement of any other European country.

# Appendix: Communiqué (Unofficial Translation)— Joint Announcement on the Results of the Russian-Cuban Intergovernmental Negotiations, November 3, 1993*

Russian-Cuban intergovernmental negotiations were held on November 2–3 in Moscow. The Russian delegation was headed by Deputy Chairman of the Government of the Russian Federation A. Shokhin, and the Cuban delegation was headed by Deputy Chairman of the Council of Ministers of the Republic of Cuba L. Soto. A broad range of issues was reviewed in the course of the talks. The two sides reaffirmed their intention to develop their ties on a renewed basis, on the principles of sovereignty, equality, self-determination, non-interference in internal affairs, mutual benefit, and the balance of Russian and Cuban interests. Principal attention was given Russian-Cuban trade and economic relations. The sides agreed that these relations would rest on the universally recognized principles of international trade. They agreed with the need for giving these relations a significant impetus in the interests of economic development of both states, in particular, by diversifying the recently existing structure of trade, and developing new forms of trade and economic cooperation, including compensatory operations, industrial cooperation, and establishment of joint ventures. To coordinate these efforts, the sides decided to set up an intergovernmental commission on trade, economic and scientific-technological cooperation.

The two sides also discussed the problem of settling their mutual obligations. In order to develop a concrete program and ways for dealing with the problem, they agreed to set up a special working group within the framework of the aforementioned Commission.

The sides deemed it advisable to update the Treaty as the legal basis of their bilateral relations and to intensify their mutual efforts at adapting it to new realities.

They also discussed other bilateral issues and some vital international problems.

In the course of the talks the two sides reaffirmed their mutual interest in continuing the presence of the Russian radioelectronic center on the territory of the Republic of Cuba. They signed an agreement to that effect.

As a result of the negotiations, the sides signed Intergovernmental Agreements on trade and economic cooperation, and on commercial shipping, plus a Protocol on trade volumes and payments for 1993.

---

* *Source: Izvestia*, Moscow, November 5, 1992.

Both sides stressed that the talks they held and the resulting agreements meet the interests of both countries, reinforce the new character of Russian-Cuban relations, and have contributed to lending them a sustained and predictable nature.

The talks were held in a constructive and businesslike atmosphere, in the spirit of searching for mutually acceptable solutions that meet both sides' interests.

## Notes

1. Jack Perry, "The Russians Aren't Coming," in Wayne S. Smith, ed., *The Russians Aren't Coming* (Lynne Rienner, Boulder, Colo., and London, 1992), p. VIII.

2. *The Atlantic*, November 1992, p. 30.

3. "Agenda for Latin America and the Caribbean, Memo to President-elect Clinton" (Washington, D.C.: Heritage Foundation, January 13, 1993).

4. Zbigniew Brzezinski, *The Grand Failure: The Birth and Death of Communism in the Twentieth Century* (New York: Scribner, 1989).

5. *Washington Post*, November 9, 1992.

6. *Latin America*, no. 12 (1990), pp. 52–61.

7. An illustration of this "other-way-around" approach is the visit of a Soviet delegation, including a member of the Supreme Soviet, to Chile in 1990. The delegation called on General Pinochet and praised him for the economic successes of his country. Those democrats did not even understand that this was like congratulating Stalin on the successes of industrialization in the USSR or praising Hitler for eliminating unemployment in Germany.

8. See the appendix preceding the notes.

9. *Latin American Weekly Report* (London), no. 43 (November 5, 1992), p. 8.

10. For years, he had been an excellent apparatchik under the auspices and guidance of Vladimir Petrovsky (deputy-minister under Shevardnadze and now deputy secretary general of the UN). Then he made his name known by publishing a "revolutionary" article, reevaluating different aspects of Soviet foreign policy according to the new political thinking, in *The Mezhdunarodnaya Zhizn*, a pale Moscow shadow of New York's *Foreign Affairs*.

11. *Washington Post*, November 9, 1992.

12. The quote belongs to the Russian ambassador to the United States, Vladimir Lukin. He did not address the remark to Kosyrev directly; responsibility is, of course, wholly mine. See a very thoughtful article by Stephen S. Rosenfeld, *Washington Post*, November 13, 1992.

13. *Latin American Weekly Report* (London) (October 8, 1992), p. 9.

14. *New York Times*, January 12, 1992.

15. Tass, October 22, 1992.

16. Alan Riding, *Distant Neighbors: Portrait of the Mexicans* (New York: Knopf, 1985).

17. *O Estado de São Paulo*, November 2, 1992.

18. Tass, November 18, 1992.

19. Tass, January 5, 1993.

20. *Venezuelan News & Views,* February 1992, Washington, D.C., p. 8.

21. Tass, October 15, 1992.

22. During Senate hearings for the confirmation of Warren Christopher as secretary of state, Senator Jesse Helms tried to press the future secretary with extreme demands concerning Cuba, which could jeopardize relations with Russia. His questions alluded to the presence of Russian advisers in Cuba and even the nuclear plant in Cienfuegos, which was, as Senator Helms implied, of a dubious character and allegedly capable of having a military importance. However, Christopher resisted Helms's pressure. He agreed with Senator Paul Sarbanes that the presence of Russian advisers could be regarded as a "refraining factor"; see Hearing of the Senate Foreign Relations Committee, January 14, 1993.

# 7

# Japan and Latin America: New Patterns in the 1990s

## Barbara Stallings and Kotaro Horisaka

By the early 1990s, most Latin American countries had embraced a new economic and political openness. As a result, international relationships have become even more significant than in the past, but the characteristics of those relationships are far from clear. Latin Americans are more willing to acknowledge the key U.S. role in the hemisphere, but their desire for a counterbalance to U.S. hegemony has not disappeared. With the collapse of the Soviet bloc and Europe's new concern with its own problems, the most obvious source of diversification is Asia, particularly Japan.

Indeed, Japan has already become an important actor in Latin America. During the last two decades, it has risen to second place behind the United States as a trade partner for many countries. Its banks are the largest holders of Latin American debt, and its corporations have invested heavily in natural resources and some industrial sectors. The Japanese government has become the largest lender to Latin America, both bilaterally and through its contributions to the international financial institutions.

Many Latin American leaders have sought to expand these activities, and Tokyo has become a prominent destination for presidential journeys. These leaders want to increase Japanese government loans for infrastructure projects, as well as to interest private Japanese firms in investing in Latin America. They are also trying to open Japanese markets to more Latin American exports. Carlos Salinas has been particularly active on this front because the Mexican government views expanded ties with Japan as a crucial complement to the North American Free Trade Area. Chile's aggressive approach toward Japan acquired a presidential imprimatur in late 1992 when Patricio Aylwin took a large delegation to Tokyo.

126

The Japanese, by contrast, have become extremely cautious about involvement in Latin America. The enthusiasm Japan had for the region in the 1970s and early 1980s has diminished, even as the overall Japanese role in the world economy has expanded enormously. As a consequence, Latin America's share of Japanese overseas activities has fallen off, replaced by booming Asian countries, the increasingly integrated European market, and the United States. In part, the change was due to the debt-driven recession in Latin America after 1982, but the problem is deeper. Japanese business feels betrayed by Latin America: Promises have not been kept, contracts have not been honored, and payments have not been made. The distance and lack of experience that always separated Japan and Latin America somehow seem greater than before. Increased frictions with the United States—in whose "backyard" Latin America is seen to reside—weigh heavily in Tokyo's decisions concerning the region. And uncertainties persist about Latin America's ability to achieve long-term economic and political stability.

Nonetheless, Japan has not given up on Latin America altogether, although it has become much more particular about its activities as seen in the evolving geographical and sectoral foci. At the same time, there has been an increasing tendency to acquire an "insurance policy" through stepped-up coordination with both the United States and the international financial institutions. These trends suggest that there are limits on the role Japan can be expected to play in Latin America in the 1990s, but they also imply that countries meeting certain conditions can gain access to the capital and even the markets of Japan.

## Japan's New Role in the World

Japan, like Germany, plays a peculiarly asymmetrical role in the contemporary world. By many indicators, its economic strength is second to none, but its international political presence is slight, and its military role is smaller still.[1] Only in Asia has Japan been willing to assume the responsibilities of a major political power. In general, it continues to defer to the United States, although less so than in the past.

Japan is the world's second largest economy, with a gross national product (GNP) of $3.4 trillion in 1991; this represents 14 percent of world output (compared to 25 percent for the United States). This figure is especially impressive because only twenty-five years ago, Japan accounted for a mere 5 percent of world output.[2] There were also major shifts in the structure of the Japanese economy over that period. The role of agriculture declined substantially, and services increased their weight. Within the industrial sector, light and basic industries were outpaced by technology-intensive sectors. Thus, goods such as textiles, clothing, paper, wood, steel, and nonelectrical machinery were displaced as leading products by electronics, transportation equipment, and precision instruments.[3]

The rapid growth rates were stimulated by high investment ratios, which, in turn, led to new technological advances and increases in productivity. Robotics, for example, were invented in the United States, but they were much more quickly put to work in Japan. At the same time, Japanese research and development has become more heavily focused on basic research, rather than concentrating on adapting inventions for industrial use as occurred in the past. Recent studies show that in basic sciences, Japan is catching up with the United States in many fields; even in dual-use military technology, it has become a serious competitor.[4]

Within the rising trend of economic growth, two external shocks caused temporary setbacks: the oil price rises of the 1970s and the dramatic appreciation of the yen after the Plaza Accords in 1985. In both cases, however, productivity increased to surmount the problems. Following the oil shocks, a major program of energy conservation was undertaken that eventually resulted in absolute, as well as relative, declines in the energy/output ratio. The same was true for other raw material inputs. Likewise, after the yen appreciation, cost-cutting measures of various kinds led to more efficient industries.[5]

These production shifts helped fuel changes in Japan's external accounts. The traditionally positive trade balance grew to enormous size in the mid-1980s and, after shrinking at the end of the decade, burgeoned again. Because the Japanese trade surplus mirrors the U.S. deficit, most international attention has focused on it. More important in the long run, however, is the corresponding increase in Japanese capital outflows. During the 1984–1990 period, Japan's long-term capital exports outpaced even the trade surplus, reaching a peak of $192 billion in 1989; *net* long-term flows had peaked at $137 billion in 1987. By the latter year, Japan had become the largest assetholder in the world, as well as the major capital exporter.[6]

The largest share of Japanese capital exports has gone toward the purchase of foreign securities, especially U.S. Treasury bills, which have financed an important part of the U.S. budget deficit. Second, direct foreign investment (DFI) has been of growing importance. DFI picked up with the yen appreciation in the mid-1980s, which made domestic production relatively more expensive than production abroad and led to the relocation of important facilities to Asian countries. In addition, U.S. pressures with respect to the trade imbalance led to the decision to open plants in the United States rather than continue to rely on exports. A third type of capital export was loans. Although Japanese private banks continued to send money abroad, an increasing share of foreign loans originated with the government, through both an expanded commitment to official development assistance (ODA) and the $65-billion "recycling" program.[7]

Japan's global economic importance thus skyrocketed during the 1980s, but its political presence has failed to increase commensurately. At the most general level, the Japanese have yet to develop a "vision" about how they would like to see the world organized. In more specific terms, they have not put forward any major initiatives but instead support those of the United States. The overall impression is still one of a country trying to avoid alienating anyone, rather than a nation providing leadership.

A number of factors help explain the discrepancy between Japan's economic and political positions. First is the speed with which the economic—and especially the financial—changes came about. The general expectation was that the yen appreciation would take many years to overcome. In reality, the production impact was short-lived, and Japan was turned into the major capital exporter almost overnight. Second, the long-ruling Liberal Democratic Party (LDP) has been unable to overcome its internal problems, a prerequisite to taking a strong international stance. Scandals have wracked the leadership, increasing factional struggles, and the party lost control of the upper house of the Diet. Third, the long-standing policy of subordinating politics to economics, especially in the international sphere, meant that little political knowledge and expertise were accumulated.

Japan's fundamental policy since World War II has been to ally itself firmly with the United States and thus avoid the need for independent action. This policy worked as long as Japan remained a minor player, but its increased economic importance led to new demands and expectations that have yet to be fulfilled. In the international financial institutions, for example, Japan has increased its contributions substantially, but expectations that it would use its augmented voting power to propose new policy directions have been frustrated. Likewise, Japan agreed to "untie" most of its loans from the required purchase of Japanese exports, but it has been slow to use its aid to promote a broader political-economic agenda. Moreover, despite Japan's obvious self-interest in maintaining an open trading system, its delegation has not played any major role in moving the GATT negotiations forward.[8]

At the beginning of the 1990s, the Japanese were beginning to articulate and advance some key principles. At the G-7 summit in July 1990, Tokyo announced its intention to renew economic assistance to China and avoid warmer relations with the Soviet Union, despite contrary views among their allies.[9] The Gulf War, however, reversed this process. Not only was Japan unable to reach agreement on sending troops or even noncombatants to the Gulf, it was almost unable to agree on its usual fallback position of sending money. The eventual decision to participate in future peacekeeping operations was a divisive one.

These political setbacks have been reinforced by recent economic problems. The dramatic fall in the stock market and land prices, the resulting weakness of the banks, and the most serious recession of the postwar period have diminished Japan's interest in events beyond its borders. This is especially true for regions—such as Latin America—that the Japanese government and companies do not perceive to be of central importance.

## Japan and Latin America: A Historical Sketch

Insofar as Latin America wants to try to obtain a significant share of Japan's markets and capital in the 1990s, it is essential for Latin leaders to understand the history of Japanese interactions with the region. The twentieth century reveals a shift in the type of activities over time; it also reveals a change from optimism about relations to pessimism.

Japan's first interest in Latin America came at the end of the nineteenth century, when the region was seen as a place to send emigrants to help combat poverty, overpopulation, and unemployment problems at home. Needing labor, Latin America responded with some enthusiasm and became the main recipient region. By the onset of World War II, over 200,000 Japanese citizens had left for Latin America, mainly for Brazil but also Peru and Mexico. Conditions were difficult, especially during the war, but most of the immigrants remained. When Tokyo renewed its interest in finding homes abroad for people after the war, Latin America offered the only positive response. By the early 1960s, most emigration ceased as economic conditions improved in Japan itself, but the presence of Japanese descendants (now numbering over one million in Latin America) continues to be important to the government and the general public. The fact that Latin America accepted more Japanese migrants than any other region has given it a positive image in Japan.[10]

Latin America was also attractive to Japan as a trade partner in the early postwar period, initially as a supplier of raw materials and then gradually as a market for exports. Indeed, during the mid-1950s, Latin America's role as a trade partner was at its peak, with the region purchasing 9.2 percent of Japanese exports and providing 9.8 percent of its imports (or 9.5 percent of total trade). The total trade figure gradually declined to 7.0 percent in the 1960s, 6.2 percent in the 1970s, and 4.5 percent in the 1980s (Table 7.1). Much of this trade was handled by the giant Japanese trading houses (*sogo shosha*). These firms established subsidiaries in the largest Latin American countries in the 1950s and gradually moved into the medium and smaller countries later on.[11]

The type of goods traded has remained similar throughout the postwar period: Japan exports industrial goods in exchange for raw materials. The main changes have been an increase in the sophistication of the Japanese industrial exports and occasional moves to semiprocess Latin America's raw materials before shipping them to Japan. Principal items that Latin America exports to Japan include petroleum, iron ore and steel, ferroalloys, copper, aluminum, coffee, salt, and forestry and fish products.[12] There has also been little change in Japan's trading partners. If the registry of Japanese ships in Panama is excluded, Brazil has continued to be the largest trade partner. Mexico became more important after its oil exports began in the 1970s, and Chile has recently increased in significance.[13]

TABLE 7.1    Japanese Trade with Latin America, 1950–1991[a] (in millions of dollars)

| Year | Export Value ($) | Percent[b] | Import Value ($) | Percent[b] | Total Trade[c] ($) | Percent[b] |
|------|------|------|------|------|------|------|
| 1950 | 47 | 5.7 | 67 | 6.9 | 114 | 6.3 |
| 1955 | 186 | 9.2 | 243 | 9 .8 | 429 | 9.5 |
| 1960 | 298 | 7.4 | 310 | 6 .9 | 608 | 7.2 |
| 1965 | 458 | 5.4 | 708 | 8 .7 | 1,166 | 7.1 |
| 1970 | 1,112 | 5.8 | 1,369 | 7.2 | 2,481 | 6.5 |
| 1975 | 4,667 | 8.4 | 2,510 | 4.3 | 7,177 | 6.4 |
| 1980 | 8,572 | 6.6 | 5,702 | 4.0 | 14,274 | 5.3 |
| 1981 | 10,119 | 6.7 | 6,595 | 4.6 | 16,714 | 5.7 |
| 1982 | 8,726 | 6.3 | 6,201 | 4.7 | 14,927 | 5.5 |
| 1983 | 5,902 | 4.0 | 6,368 | 5.0 | 12,270 | 4.5 |
| 1984 | 7,899 | 4.7 | 7,097 | 5.2 | 14,996 | 5.0 |
| 1985 | 7,753 | 4.4 | 6,188 | 4.7 | 13,941 | 4.6 |
| 1986 | 8,716 | 4.1 | 6,087 | 4.8 | 14,803 | 4.5 |
| 1987 | 8,151 | 3.5 | 6,221 | 4.1 | 14,372 | 3.8 |
| 1988 | 8,673 | 3.3 | 8,198 | 4.4 | 16,871 | 3.9 |
| 1989 | 8,837 | 3.2 | 8,639 | 4.1 | 17,476 | 3.7 |
| 1990 | 9,731 | 3.4 | 9,504 | 4.0 | 19,235 | 3.7 |
| 1991 | 12,221 | 3.9 | 9,335 | 3.9 | 21,556 | 3.9 |

[a]Western Hemisphere (IMF definition) plus Cuba; Cuba excluded in 1991.
[b]Percent of total (worldwide) Japanese exports/imports.
[c]Exports plus imports.

SOURCE: International Monetary Fund, *Direction of Trade Statistics* (Washington, D.C.: International Monetary Fund), various issues.

The move into direct investment was closely related to trade through the desire to control an important source of imports and assure a market for exports. In addition, many Latin American countries, but especially Brazil, were providing incentives for foreign companies to invest there as a way to promote the new strategy of import-substitution industrialization. The big Japanese investments began in the late 1950s and flourished in the 1960s and 1970s. Total investment during the two decades amounted to around $6 billion. Projects mainly focused on natural resources, but they also included some industrial investments, for example, in steel and automobiles. Nonetheless, direct investment in other regions meant that Latin America's share of Japanese DFI fell from nearly 30 percent in the 1950s and early 1960s to 16 percent in the 1960s and 1970s and only 4 percent in the 1980s (if the Panamanian shipping registries and Caribbean financial havens are excluded).[14] These trends are shown in Table 7.2.

A major new activity in the 1970s involved private bank loans for Latin American governments. Japanese banks started with participation in syndicates (consortia) formed by U.S. or European institutions. They gradually acquired financial know-how, until, early in the 1980s, some of them began to

TABLE 7.2    Japanese Direct Foreign Investment in Latin America, 1951–1991[a]
(in millions of dollars)

| Fiscal Year | Latin America ($) | Total ($) | Latin American Share (percent) |
|---|---|---|---|
| 1951–1960[b] | 9 | 29 | 29.3 |
| | (9)[c] | | (28.5) |
| 1961–1965[b] | 38 | 134 | 28.5 |
| | (37) | | (27.9) |
| 1966–1970[b] | 57 | 526 | 10.9 |
| | (56) | | (10.6) |
| 1971–1975[b] | 463 | 2,473 | 18.7 |
| | (380) | | (15.4) |
| 1976–1980[b] | 657 | 4,111 | 16.0 |
| | (472) | | (11.5) |
| 1981–1985[b] | 1,894 | 9,431 | 20.1 |
| | (521) | | (5.5) |
| 1986 | 4,737 | 22,319 | 21.2 |
| | (533) | | (2.4) |
| 1987 | 4,816 | 33,364 | 14.4 |
| | (344) | | (1.0) |
| 1988 | 6,428 | 47,022 | 13.7 |
| | (801) | | (1.7) |
| 1989 | 5,238 | 67,540 | 7.8 |
| | (650) | | (1.0) |
| 1990 | 3,628 | 56,911 | 6.4 |
| | (1,193) | | (2.1) |
| 1991 | 3,337 | 41,584 | 8.0 |
| | (673) | | (1.6) |

[a]Investment intentions as reported to Ministry of Finance.
[b]Annual averages for fiscal years (ending March 31 of following year).
[c]Figures in parentheses are on-shore investments (i.e., Panama and Caribbean Island tax havens excluded).

SOURCE: Japanese Ministry of Finance, unpublished data, available from authors.

manage loans on their own. Although no official data are available on Japanese loans by region and year before 1983, some unofficial information suggests that bank loans exceeded direct investment by substantial amounts during the 1970s. Between 1972 and 1982, Japanese banks accumulated more than $18 billion of Latin American debt, meaning that gross lending was much higher.[15]

The impact of Mexico's debt crisis in August 1982 was at least as dramatic in Japanese financial circles as in the United States and Europe. Japanese banks promptly joined debt rescheduling processes. Here too, Japanese banks followed U.S. initiatives. Once an agreement on rescheduling was concluded between a bank advisory committee and a debtor country, Japanese banks as a group were the most faithful in implementing it. Although U.S. banks began

TABLE 7.3   Latin American Medium- and Long-Term Debt Outstanding to Japanese Banks, 1982–1991[a] (in billions of dollars)

| Calendar Year | Latin America ($) | Total ($) | Latin American Share (percent) |
|---|---|---|---|
| 1982[b] | 21.3 | 67.1 | 31.7 |
| 1983 | 23.9 | 77.5 | 30.8 |
| 1984 | 28.6 | 94.4 | 30.3 |
| 1985 | 30.1 | 107.9 | 27.9 |
| 1986 | 36.8 | 152.2 | 24.2 |
| 1987 | 40.9 | 213.5 | 19.2 |
| 1988 | 45.5 | 282.5 | 16.1 |
| 1989 | 44.7 | 336.9 | 13.3 |
| 1990 | 31.2 | 360.5 | 8.7 |
| 1991 | 31.6 | 381.1 | 8.3 |

[a]Includes yen-based lending, which is converted into dollars at end-of-year exchange rate.
[b]As of December 31 of each year.

SOURCE: Japanese Ministry of Finance, unpublished data, available from authors.

to look for ways to withdraw, no Japanese bank did so. Consequently, though the weight of Latin American loans within the Japanese banks' portfolios decreased from 32 percent in 1982 to 13 percent in 1989, total outstandings increased from $21 to $45 billion in the same period (Table 7.3).

In 1991, Japanese banks shifted their policy on Latin American debt. Stimulated by changes in the Ministry of Finance guidelines, the decline in the Tokyo stock market, and resulting difficulties in meeting Bank for International Settlements (BIS) capital/asset ratios, the banks finally began to follow their U.S. counterparts out of the market. Discount bonds have been selected in the Brady negotiations rather than new money, and sales in the secondary market have combined to cut Japanese holdings of Latin American debt for the first time since the crisis began in 1982; the effect can be seen in Table 7.3.[16]

## Japan and Latin America: Recent Developments

As the 1980s drew to a close, several new developments began to emerge with respect to Japanese–Latin American relations. First, insofar as the Japanese private sector maintained an interest in the region, a new geographical concentration became evident. Second, the Japanese government began to take a more active role, acting on its own, rather than as part of public-private consortia. Third, Japanese activities in Latin America were more carefully coordinated with the United States and with the international financial institutions. Nevertheless, certain basic continuities underlay Japan's role in the region.

## Geographical Shifts

Initial Japanese interests in Latin America were heavily centered in Brazil; this pattern continued until the early 1980s. The reasons are fairly obvious. Brazil is the largest country in the continent (with a larger population than Japan) and rich in natural resources. In addition, it has the largest ethnic Japanese population outside Japan itself. Brazil also had a military government from the mid-1960s, with the declared aim of promoting economic growth and development and a need for foreign capital and technology.

The vast majority of Japanese DFI in Latin America went to Brazil. As of 1980, $2.9 billion, representing 8 percent of Japan's worldwide direct investment, was in Brazil. The country was also one of the two leading recipients of Japanese bank loans and Japan's main trade partner in the Latin American region. The two economies were considered highly complementary, and Brazil's rapid growth both stimulated and benefitted from Japanese capital. By the early 1980s, however, Brazil began a period of economic and political instability that still shows no sign of turning around. Growth plummeted while inflation and budget deficits soared; the return to democracy was not going smoothly either.

The Japanese response was predictable. Investment fell off, and private bank loans (other than involuntary loans connected with debt rescheduling) ceased. Brazil's inability to implement any of the multiple agreements signed with the IMF and its various moratoria on debt service meant that the country received no money under the recycling program; other government loan facilities were also closed because of arrears. The privatization of Japanese-Brazilian government joint ventures, such as the Usiminas and Tubarao steel complexes, generated further complaints about inconsistent industrial policy. Overall, the Japanese attitude toward Brazil became extremely pessimistic.[17]

After pulling back from Latin America for several years, Japanese firms began to make some cautious ventures at the end of the decade. Significantly, these involved new countries. Brazil was largely ignored in favor of Mexico, Chile, and Venezuela—the three nations that are widely considered in Japan to have the most stable economic policies and most positive attitudes toward trade and foreign investment.

Indeed, Chile has nearly two decades of experience in implementing a liberal economic model—although punctured by a traumatic crisis in the early 1980s. Most of the public-sector firms were sold, and tariffs were lowered to a uniform 10 percent. Debt service was rescheduled, but payments were always made on time. Over the last several years, a strong growth pattern has developed, with low inflation and an expanded and diversified export sector. Even the transition from authoritarian military rule to democracy did not threaten the economic policy, which the civilian government continued.

Mexico has a shorter history in this regard. Only since 1982 has its government shown support for economic liberalization, and it was not until 1986 that serious steps were taken to extend stabilization policies into the realm of structural reform. Although Mexico has been portrayed as a "model debtor" since its near default in 1982, the Japanese are not unduly impressed with the multiple reschedulings and eventual write-down; they are especially concerned about the large volume of flight capital. Nevertheless, Mexico is perceived as more promising than other Latin American countries except Chile, and it has obvious advantages over the latter—petroleum, a much larger market, and proximity to the United States.

Venezuela is a more curious case. Many Japanese businesspeople mention Venezuela before Mexico as a potential investment site. When asked why, the answer is that, because nothing was expected of the government of President Carlos Andrés Pérez given his populist record in the 1970s, Venezuela's unanticipated turn toward liberalization was all the more appreciated. When Shoichiro Toyoda, then president of Toyota Motor Corporation, was persuaded to act as an informal adviser to President Pérez, this gave further comfort to the Japanese.[18] Other than the first Pérez administration itself, of course, Venezuela also has had a history of fairly conservative economic management, although the recent political instability is troublesome to the Japanese, as it is to others.

Most of the new investment activity in the last few years has been directed toward these three countries. A large percentage of Japanese government loans have also gone to the same three, although the reaction of the private banks has been less enthusiastic. In the Brady Plan negotiations for both Mexico and Venezuela, Japanese banks pointedly refused to put up new money, opting instead for discount bonds. Chile, which did not enter Brady negotiation but elected to reschedule and issue $320 million of par bonds, did not have much better luck. Only two Japanese banks, Bank of Tokyo and Tokai Bank, participated, despite a campaign by the former to enlist support.[19]

The largest new Japanese investment in Latin America is an expansion of the Nissan plant in Mexico. Nissan is investing a total of $1 billion to double the capacity of its engine plant and increase production of vans and compact cars. Of the 100,000 new units that will be produced annually, about one-third will be exported to Japan, and another one-fifth will be shipped to the United States and Canada. The remainder will be sold in Mexico or elsewhere in Latin America. In return for its new investment, Nissan is hoping to receive favorable treatment in the rules governing NAFTA.[20]

Other auto-related investments have seen Honda set up a motorcycle assembly plant in Guadalajara in 1985 and auto parts maker Yazaki open production facilities in Monterrey and Chihuahua to supply the Japanese firms.

The two major electronics firms in Mexico—Matsushita and Sanyo—significantly expanded their operations during the 1980s. In the service sector, Nikko built a large hotel in Mexico City; two other hotels are under construction in Cancún. Major breakthroughs, however, must await the final NAFTA treaty and especially the rules-of-origin provisions.[21]

The Japanese government has also taken a special interest in Mexico during the last half dozen years. Loans totaling $1 billion were provided in connection with the 1986 debt rescheduling, another $2 billion went to support the Brady Plan negotiations in 1989, and Mexico City pollution projects were beneficiaries of $1 billion.[22] As a reflection of increasing Japanese-Mexican ties, a commission was set up by the two governments to consider relations in the next century. The commission issued its report in March 1992 and recommended increased dialogue plus investment and technological assistance for Mexico.[23]

In contrast to the industrial and service focus in Mexico, recent Japanese investments in Chile have been in natural resources: copper and forestry and fishing products. The largest investment to have been completed is the La Escondida copper mine, a $1.1-billion project. Japanese sources provided nearly half of the financing, and 50 percent of the output will be exported to Japan. The forestry sector is also of great interest to the Japanese because they lack an adequate supply of raw materials for their paper industry. Several companies are already exporting wood chips back to Japan; they have recently begun reforesting projects to keep ahead of growing environmental concerns in Chile. The largest project currently planned is by Daio Paper, which will invest up to $600 million to purchase land, engage in reforesting, and eventually construct a pulp and/or paper plant.[24]

The fishing industry is a third main attraction for the Japanese. Two types of activities have been pursued by three large Japanese companies. One is the cultivation of salmon in the southern part of the country; the other is fishing in Chilean waters and processing in so-called factory boats off the coast. The latter has become an extremely contentious issue in Chile because the Japanese companies fish with large nets that sweep up all marine life. The Chilean congress is debating new legislation to restrict net fishing, and two of the three Japanese companies have therefore decided to leave.[25]

Although the Japanese government has tried to be helpful to the new civilian government, all has not gone smoothly. A large loan on soft terms was offered soon after the transition, but no agreement was reached on how to spend the money. Thus, the main government loans have been three credits under the recycling program provided to the previous regime: $120 million for a hydroelectric plant, $150 million for a road project, and $200 million in connection with the third World Bank structural adjustment loan. During President Aylwin's trip to Japan in November 1992, another $190 million was provided for water, railway, and sanitation works.[26]

Venezuela fits between Mexico and Chile with respect to the types of Japanese interests in the country. Aluminum is the longtime principal export to Japan, and various new projects featuring Japanese participation are being discussed. Some petroleum derivative projects are also under consideration, although almost no Venezuelan oil is currently exported to Japan because transportation costs make the price prohibitive. In addition to natural resource projects, two new knockdown automobile assembly projects are under way.[27] Behind only Mexico and Chile, Venezuela has received the third largest amount of loans from the recycling program: over $400 million for bauxite and aluminum projects and for telecommunications. In addition, the Eximbank provided $600 million in conjunction with the Brady Plan debt negotiations.[28]

A final country of interest to Japan—more for political and cultural, rather than economic, reasons—is Peru. Like Brazil, Peru received disproportionate attention from Japan in the early postwar period, with a special emphasis on mining. Petroleum also was important, and Japan helped construct a pipeline to move Peruvian oil to the coast. In the 1980s, however, Peru encountered hard times. It began to fall behind on debt payments, and a major controversy arose over the pipeline repayments. When President Alan García severed Peru's relations with the international financial community, Japanese activity in Peru ceased.

A new era began with the 1990 election of Alberto Fujimori—the first person of Japanese descent to become president of any country outside Japan. Public opinion in Japan strongly favored providing assistance to Peru, but the government's fear of international criticism for aiding a fellow Japanese kept Tokyo waiting for Washington to take the lead. In particular, Peru needed to find a way to repay the large volume of arrears it had accumulated on its debt to the World Bank and IMF. The plan was to establish a "support group" of industrial countries to provide a bridge loan, which would be repaid once new money was flowing from the international financial institutions (IFIs). U.S. determination to enlist Peru's participation in a drug eradication program delayed the support group for nearly a year, exacerbating Peru's already critical economic problems. Indeed, Peru had still not been able to resume borrowing when Fujimori gave up on the country's fragile democracy and assumed dictatorial powers in April 1992.[29]

Fujimori's auto-coup put Tokyo in an awkward position. The United States immediately suspended aid and pressed the Japanese to follow suit. Moreover, Japan had recently declared that it would take democracy into account when allocating economic assistance. But Japanese officials sympathized with Fujimori's difficult situation in trying to deal with acute economic problems, as well as a guerrilla insurgency. Therefore, it did not suspend aid and took the initiative in trying to help resolve the political crisis. The Japanese ambassador in Lima consulted extensively with Fujimori, and ultimately, a top Foreign

Ministry official went to Lima with a letter from Prime Minister Kiichi Miyazawa. The aid was to get Fujimori to attend an emergency OAS meeting and to announce steps to restore democracy. With these goals accomplished and the situation somewhat calmed, Tokyo authorized several new loans.[30]

## Public-Private Shift

Beyond the particularities of the Latin American geographical shift and symptomatic of more fundamental political-economic changes is the loosening of ties between the public and private sectors within Japan. This means the government is now less able to influence private business than it once was, but the government itself can act more independently. Indeed, most Japanese activity in Latin America in the last several years has been initiated and carried out by the government. This includes the doubling of official development assistance, the recycling program, and the proposal for the Miyazawa Plan that eventually became the Brady Plan.

ODA is the main vehicle by which the Japanese have responded to U.S. demands for "burden-sharing." Given the population's hesitation about military expansion, the government has chosen to put increasing amounts of money into economic assistance to developing countries. At the Toronto Summit in 1988, then Prime Minister Noboru Takeshita announced the fourth medium-term ODA target, aimed to again double the dollar amount and disburse at least $50 billion in new funds between 1988 and 1992. In the years immediately ahead, a target as high as $75 billion may be set.[31]

Japanese ODA (grants, soft loans, and technical assistance) to Latin America has never been quantitatively significant. Total net disbursements for fiscal year 1991 were $846 million. Over the past twenty years, less than 8 percent of Japan's ODA has gone to Latin America, compared to 70 to 80 percent for Asia. The main reason is that more attention has been paid to neighboring countries, but in addition, Japan has a per capita income ceiling on loans from the Overseas Economic Cooperation Fund (OECF), the soft-loan institution, that has excluded the majority of Latin American nations until recently. Thus, most Japanese ODA to the Latin American region has gone to the poorest countries, including Bolivia, Paraguay, Honduras, and Peru.[32]

Between 1989 and 1991, there were large increases in OECF's commitments to Latin America. The commitment share rose from 4.9 percent (1989) to 10.7 percent (1990) to 14.6 percent (1991). Major recipients were Mexico (an antipollution loan), Peru (a trade-sector adjustment loan), and Brazil (several infrastructure projects, whose funding had been held up for several years until Brazil finally cleared its OECF arrears). It is not expected that the Latin American share will continue to be this high in coming years, but the increased total will bring a rise in absolute amounts, even if not in percentage terms.[33]

More important than ODA from the Latin American perspective is another government initiative: the recycling program. Announced in 1987, the program was to provide $30 billion over three years to the largest debtor countries. Much attention and fanfare surrounded the announcement, and initial indications were that most of the money would go to Latin America. In reality, the package was somewhat less generous than it first appeared. The $30-billion figure included $10 billion that had already been committed, mostly to the international financial institutions, and a substantial amount of the remaining $20 billion was similarly earmarked. The breakdown of the $20-billion package was: (1) $8 billion directly to the World Bank and regional development banks, (2) $9 billion as cofinancing with the World Bank, and (3) $3 billion in direct credits from the Export-Import Bank.[34] In July 1989, the Japanese government announced an additional $35 billion would be provided over the two years from April 1990 to March 1992. Although no new target had been set by mid-1993 after completion of commitments for the $65 billion, government sources indicated that lending will continue.[35]

The distribution of the recycling scheme has disappointed Latin America. The commitment figures for the geographically specific portion of the $65 billion show that 27 percent from the Export-Import Bank and 22 percent from OECF will go to Latin America, compared to 57 and 52 percent, respectively, to Asia. Although Latin America received nearly $9 billion from the recycling fund between 1988 and 1992, the $3.3 billion from the OECF duplicate the ODA loans already discussed.[36] Data on the recycling program are shown in Tables 7.4 and 7.5.

A third Japanese government initiative of importance to Latin America was the effort to chart a new path on debt policy. By the late 1980s, Japanese public and private officials became increasingly willing to criticize U.S. handling of the debt crisis. The Baker Plan had failed, they said, because it did not manage to restore growth in Latin America. Restoring growth required a mechanism for eliminating the negative transfers of foreign exchange. The basic outline of a new Japanese plan emerged in early 1988, and a public announcement was made at the IMF/World Bank annual meeting in September 1988. To cut down on service payments, a part of the Latin American debt would be "securitized." The idea was to trade old loans for new, long-term bonds with lower interest rates. Although earning less, the new bonds would arguably be safer assets because they would be guaranteed by reserves of the debtor countries, deposited with the IMF. The remainder of the debt would be rescheduled, and new loans would be provided by the international institutions and Japan itself. The essential context for the scheme would be a structural adjustment program for the debtor countries, worked out with the IMF, to ensure that the resulting funds would, indeed, lead to renewed growth.[37]

TABLE 7.4   Progress of the Japanese Recycling Program, as of the End of June 1992 (in billions of dollars)

| Institution | Goal ($) | Commitments ($) | Percent |
|---|---|---|---|
| Export-Import Bank | 23.5 | 23.5 | 100.9 |
| OECF | 12.5 | 15.0 | 120.0 |
| Contributions/subscriptions to multilateral development banks | 29.0 | 28.5 | 98.3 |
| TOTAL | 65.0 | 67.0 | 103.4 |

SOURCE: Export-Import Bank of Japan, unpublished data, available from authors.

TABLE 7.5   Geographical Distribution of Commitments of Japanese Recycling Program, as of the end of June 1992 (in billions of dollars)

| Region | Export-Import Bank of Japan Amount ($) | Share (percent) | OECF Amount ($) | Share (percent) | Total Amount ($) | Share (percent) |
|---|---|---|---|---|---|---|
| Asia | 11.75 | 57.4 | 7.95 | 5 2.3 | 19.6 | 55.1 |
| Latin America | 5.6 | 27.5 | 3.4 | 22.5 | 9.0 | 25.3 |
| Africa, Europe, Middle East | 3.1 | 15.2 | 3.9 | 25. 2 | 7.0 | 19.7 |
| TOTAL | 20.5 | 100.0 | 15.0 | 100.0 | 35.5 | 100.0 |
| IMF(ESAF) | 3.0 | | | | 3.0 | |
| TOTAL | 23.5 | | 15.0 | | 38.5 | |

SOURCE: Export-Import Bank of Japan, unpublished data, available from author.

Although the Miyazawa Plan was presented as complementary to the Baker Plan, with its voluntary, case-by-case nature stressed, it was not welcomed by the U.S. government. At the IMF-World Bank meeting, it was openly attacked by Treasury Secretary Nicholas Brady. Six months later, as treasury secretary for President Bush rather than President Reagan, Brady adopted the main elements of the Miyazawa Plan and labeled them the Brady Plan. The latter, however, included more options for the banks than the former had. In particular, Brady suggested that debt could be reduced through a discounting of loans when they were exchanged for bonds. The Japanese endorsed the Brady Plan and promised money to back it up. Initially, the amount was set at $4.5 billion; as part of the expanded recycling facility, it was raised to $10 billion. The funds were to be used to guarantee payments on the new bonds. The hope was that the plan would finally put an end to the crisis and restore Latin America to a growth pattern that would attract autonomous business support.[38]

### Coordination of Plans

With the exception of the Miyazawa Plan, all the Japanese government initiatives just discussed were carefully coordinated with the U.S. government and/or the international financial institutions. Through such coordination, the Japanese hoped to obtain both recognition that they were assuming responsibilities consistent with their international economic position and relief from attacks by U.S. politicians and business leaders.

Coordination with the United States in the Latin American context has centered on debt policy and on other types of economic assistance. From 1982 until 1988, the Japanese government and banks simply went along with all the U.S. initiatives on debt, contributing their share of additional funds. For a brief period in 1988, there were some independent initiatives around the Miyazawa Plan, although the Japanese apparently thought their proposals were in the spirit of the U.S. debt strategy. And as soon as the Bush administration and Secretary Brady changed their stance and incorporated the Miyazawa proposals, the Japanese hastened to line up behind the Brady Plan and pledge part of the money necessary to make it function. In fact, they seemed quite relieved to be back in a supportive, rather than a leadership, role.[39]

Another type of coordination with the United States centers on countries that are assisted primarily for political reasons. These are countries that, in other times, would have received large sums of money from the U.S. Agency for International Development (USAID) because they were considered friends of the United States; most are in Central America and the Caribbean. The U.S. government requested assistance for Jamaica, Guatemala, Honduras, Nicaragua, and Panama. For the last three on the list, the request was to help provide a bridge loan to clear the countries' arrears to the IMF and World Bank and make them eligible for additional loans. The Japanese agreed to participate as long as the United States took the lead and other countries also contributed.[40]

The Japanese have also been working closely with the international financial institutions. Japan has traditionally placed a higher value on working through multilateral channels than has the United States. After the Japanese trade surplus burgeoned, Tokyo increased its contributions to the IFIs. Initially, the additional contributions were made though special funds to avoid the conflictive issue of voting rights, but eventually, the Japanese decided that they wanted to obtain formal recognition of their economic power as represented in votes. For Japan to obtain more votes, however, the U.S. share had to fall. In 1988, an agreement was finally reached in the World Bank to increase the Japanese share to second place; a corollary was to lower the percentage necessary for a veto so that the United States would not lose that privilege. Similar negotiations in the IMF led to Japan and Germany sharing second place.[41]

The Japanese usually cofinance their loans with the IMF, the World Bank, or the regional development banks. Cofinancing resolves various problems from the Japanese point of view. First, it helps compensate for their lack of operational capacity due to the small number of economic assistance personnel they have relative to their rapidly increasing budgets. Second, cofinancing is helpful in light of Japan's limited experience in developing countries outside Asia. Third, it enables Japan to leave the controversial job of imposing economic conditionality to the IFIs. Fourth, cofinancing offers some modicum of evidence that the recycling loans are "untied," i.e., they can be spent anywhere, rather than restricting them to purchases in Japan.

### Continuities amid Changes

Despite these changes—new geographical patterns, a stronger public-sector role, and more international coordination—Japan's style of relating to developing countries has exhibited certain underlying continuities. Three in particular deserve mention: the requirement of stability, the alliance with the United States, and the separation of economics and politics.

Stability, both economic and political, is a prerequisite for investment or lending. In economic terms, this has meant macroeconomic stability; in political terms, it means maintenance or order. Previously, authoritarian governments were seen as the best mechanism for achieving order. But more recently, Japan, like the United States, has decided that democracy may be a better long-term guarantor of stability. This requirement for stability has been a major reason for the new emphasis on Mexico, Chile, and Venezuela for they have been the most successful Latin American countries in terms of providing both economic and political order.

Another continuity involves trying to stay in the good graces of the United States. Early in the postwar period, this was a less complex process because the U.S.-Japanese relationship was more one-sided. As Japan has become stronger in economic terms, tensions have increased substantially, especially regarding Japan's trade surplus. The increase in aid, including the recycling fund, was stimulated, in large part, by the desire to appease the United States. Indeed, one view of Japan's relationship with Latin America suggests that it exists almost exclusively for this purpose—that Japan has no real interests in the region.[42] It is not necessary to take such an extreme view, of course, to agree that attempts at coordination have their roots in the U.S.-Japanese relationship.

Finally, the Japanese continue to prefer a separation of politics and economics in their international dealings. Intervening in the domestic affairs of their economic partners has never had the attraction that it holds for the United States, although the Japanese have recently announced that they will take account of such trends as the movement toward democracy and away from high military spending when determining foreign aid allocations. Working through the international agencies is clearly a way of avoiding political involvement.

## Conclusions

To summarize, Japan has become the major capital exporter in the world, but the vast majority of its funds go to Asia and the United States. Japan has become a technological leader, but one consequence of this is that its products use fewer raw materials per unit of output. Although Japan has also become an increasing importer of industrial goods, the only Third World area able to break into its market has been East Asia. Latin America has lost the favorable rating it had in the 1970s as a site for Japanese investments and a source of supply for Japanese markets. Trade with that region is now insignificant from the Japanese perspective (although some important raw materials are still obtained there), "real" investment has declined precipitously, and the banks have begun to sell off their Latin American portfolios.

At the same time, some new direct investment projects have been announced and have even begun to materialize in countries with relative political stability and satisfactory economic policies (especially Mexico, Chile, and Venezuela). These investments have the potential to increase trade, exports as well as imports, with Japan. In addition, the Japanese government has opened or reinforced several channels through which a different but overlapping group of countries can obtain funds. Capital disbursed through the recycling fund tends to favor those countries just mentioned because they must have economic programs approved by the IMF in order to qualify for the Japanese loans. There is also another group of countries—smaller and poorer than the previously mentioned set—that have access to ODA funds. These include some of Japan's own choosing (e.g., Bolivia, Paraguay, Peru) and others of particular interest to the United States (e.g., Panama, Nicaragua, Honduras, Jamaica). Finally, Japan is providing significant amounts of indirect funding through the IMF, the World Bank, and the Inter-American Development Bank.

Assuming these trends will continue for the rest of the 1990s, there are two different kinds of implications: policy prescriptions for any actors wishing to expand the existing relationships between Japan and Latin America and analytical projections about the likely impact of doing so.

For Latin America, two policy prescriptions are relevant. First, to gain access to Japanese capital, public or private, Latin American governments must "get their own houses in order." The "order" has specific characteristics: bringing inflation and budget deficits under control; promoting exports and perhaps liberalizing imports; and providing a welcoming attitude toward foreign investment. More generally, the Japanese want clear rules to be established for the operation of foreign capital, rules that will be maintained over time and across changes of government. It will also be necessary to build a record of compliance with agreements undertaken.

Second, beyond implementing acceptable policies and maintaining them, Latin Americans will need to obtain specialized knowledge of how the Japanese system operates, both culturally and in political-economic terms.[43] This implies producing specialists who speak Japanese and have spent time in the country. In keeping with Japanese style, there is also a need for Latin America to take greater initiative. The Japanese system, unlike that of the United States, operates on a "request basis." Another aspect of Japanese style that differs significantly from that of the United States is the time horizon; it must be expected that nothing will happen quickly, especially given the reputation that the region currently must overcome.

Two probable consequences of the trends stand out. First, Latin American countries will have little room for maneuver because they face a unified set of creditors in the 1990s as they did in the 1980s. The "carrot" may increasingly be investment funds, rather than debt rescheduling, but the "stick" remains the need for a particular set of economic policies. The current Japanese insistence on cofinancing their loans with the World Bank or IMF or at least having bank and fund programs in place as a prerequisite for independent loans considerably tightens the conditionality of Japan's own loans in comparison with those of the past. Although coordination with the United States and the international institutions puts Japan in the odd position of requiring policies inconsistent with those it used itself with great success, policies such as import liberalization and the sale of state firms are nonetheless being stressed.

Second, because some countries will be unwilling or unable to adopt the type of policies required by the creditor cartel, an increasing differentiation within the Latin American region will probably emerge in the coming decade. The few countries that have already implemented liberal economic policies and begun to resume growth will get disproportionate access to additional funds and perhaps markets. Those countries—even a large, rich one like Brazil—that cannot or will not implement favorable policies will fall even further behind. A few small countries may be able to hold their own because special U.S. interests win them favors, but this process is less likely to occur after the Cold War.

For the United States, the implications of all these trends are both positive and negative. If the government continues to be the main Japanese actor in Latin America and if it continues the strategy of using cooperation in Latin America as a means to defuse bilateral tensions with the United States, the benefits of an increased Japanese presence should outweigh the costs. The Japanese government's determination to coordinate policies with the United States and to follow U.S. initiatives should forestall potential conflicts. Insofar as the United States can induce Japan to provide capital to restore economic growth in at least some Latin American countries, U.S. export and investment possibilities should increase.

Even with a basically friendly Japanese government, however, Washington must make some gestures to maintain Japanese support. In particular, the United States—not just Japan—must show a willingness to discuss and coordinate policies and perhaps also to allow some significant Japanese input into policy formulation. The increased visibility of Japanese aid policies is arousing opposition at home, and the idea of continuing to provide money with no say over how it is spent will not be viable for too much longer. The United States must accept that burden-sharing ultimately requires power-sharing.

Because U.S. and Japanese firms have their eyes on the same countries, competition for both trade and investment opportunities is likely to increase in Mexico, Chile, and Venezuela. Furthermore, the increased separation between the public and private sectors in Japan means that the government will be less able to restrain corporations and bring them into line with foreign policy in the future. But there is little indication of sufficient Japanese interest in Latin America to provide U.S. firms with serious competition in the short run. Indeed, Japanese companies have closed some of their assembly operations because lower tariffs in Latin America have made supplying Latin markets from Japan more profitable.

These trends also suggest that Japan needs to bolster its knowledge of Latin America. Reliance on the United States and the multilateral agencies will be insufficient if significant amounts of Japanese public money are to be committed to the region. In the past, the Japanese government relied on consulting firms and the trading companies to provide expertise, but the untied nature of the new funds makes this strategy less viable. The common observation about the small number of administrators for the very large and growing Japanese aid program pertains to Latin America with special force.

As a corollary, Japan must develop more bilateral contacts with Latin America, rather than relying on U.S., IMF, or IDB intermediaries. If Latin America is to be more than a pawn on the U.S.-Japanese chess board, the Japanese must make more independent and nuanced judgments about the region. They also need to know how their money is being used and something about the impact. To give one example, the Japanese often talk about the problem of great inequality in Latin America as an important cause of economic, as well as social and political, problems. It should then be of some interest to them to determine whether their activities in the region are alleviating or exacerbating this problem.

Overall, the 1990s promise to be another difficult decade in Latin America. Although most of the effort to get out of the current problems will involve internal decisions and actions, the external environment will not be inconsequential. Japan will not be the major external actor, but it will be one of the few sources of capital, and it could potentially be a new market for Latin

American goods, as well. Making use of this potential is mainly up to the Latin Americans, but the United States can help by encouraging the Japanese to become more involved in the region. And to make intelligent choices about how to get involved, the Japanese must make investments in their own expertise, as well as in Latin American economies.[44]

## Notes

1. This statement pertains to the international role of the Japanese military; according to the Japanese constitution, Japan cannot send troops beyond its borders. Nonetheless, Japan has the third-largest military budget in the world, behind those of the United States and the former Soviet Union. On Japanese security issues, see Mike M. Mochizuki, "To Change or to Contain: Dilemmas of American Policy Toward Japan," in Kenneth Oye, Robert Lieber, and Donald Rothchild, eds., *Eagle in a New World* (New York: Harper Collins, 1991).

2. The figures on current share of world output are from International Monetary Fund, *World Economic Outlook* (Washington, D.C.: IMF, October 1992); the 1965 estimate is from the IMF, as reported in *Financial Times,* September 29, 1989 (Survey on the World Economy). The two are not completely comparable because the former includes all countries and the latter only IMF members. In other words, the increase in the Japanese share of world output is underestimated.

3. OECD, *Economic Outlook, Historical Statistics* (various issues).

4. On Japanese science policy, see Steven Vogel, *Japanese High Technology, Politics, and Power,* Berkeley Roundtable on the International Economy, Research Paper no. 2, Berkeley, Calif., March 1989. For discussion of patent receipts by U.S. and Japanese inventors, see William J. Broad, "In the Realm of Technology, Japan Seizes a Greater Role," *New York Times,* May 28, 1991. A discussion of dual-use military technology is found in John Dower, "Japan's New Military Edge," *The Nation,* July 3, 1989.

5. On the 1970s, see CEPAL, *La evolución económica del Japón y su impacto en América Latina* (Santiago: CEPAL, 1988), especially pp. 9–18. An update on the 1980s is found in Kotaro Horisaka, "La nueva situación japonesa y América Latina y el Caribe," *Integración latinoamericana,* 15, no. 153 (January–February 1990).

6. Data on capital flows are from Bank of Japan, Tokyo, Research and Statistics Department, *Economic Statistics Annual,* 1990. For data on international assets of major industrial countries, see International Monetary Fund, *World Economic Outlook* (Washington, D.C.: IMF, April 1988).

7. On the composition of Japanese capital flows, see Bank of Japan, Tokyo, *Economic Statistics Annual.*

8. Recently, Japan has begun to take a more active role in the IFIs. Tokyo has insisted, for example, that the World Bank conduct a study of the Asian development model. It has also critiqued some World Bank policies; see OECF, "Issues Related to the World Bank's Approach to Structural Adjustment—Proposal from a Major Partner," OECF Occasional Paper no. 1, Tokyo, October 1991.

9. David E. Sanger, "On Tokyo's International Shopping List: More Clout," *New York Times,* July 8, 1990; Steve Lohr, "At Summit Talks, Japan Displays Confidence Based on Economic Power," *New York Times,* July 11, 1990.

10. For a summary discussion of Japanese emigration to Latin America, see Iyo Kunimoto, "Japanese Migration to Latin America," in Barbara Stallings and Gabriel Szekely, eds., *Japan, the United States and Latin America: Toward a Trilateral Relationship in the Western Hemisphere?* (Baltimore, Md.: Johns Hopkins University Press, 1993).

11. Barbara Stallings, "Japanese Trade Relations with Latin America: New Opportunities in the 1990s?" in Mark Rosenberg, ed., *The Changing Hemispheric Trade Environment: Opportunities and Obstacles* (Miami: Florida International University, 1991).

12. Japan External Trade Organization, *White Paper on International Trade: Japan 1990* (Tokyo: JETRO, 1990).

13. International Monetary Fund, *Direction of Trade Statistics* (Washington, D.C.: IMF, various issues).

14. The Japanese government does not keep figures on actual foreign investment by Japanese firms except at the most aggregated level, as shown in the balance of payments. Investments by region or country are merely *intentions* to invest as reported to the Ministry of Finance. Reinvestment figures are not available either.

15. Barbara Stallings, "The Reluctant Giant: Japan and the Latin American Debt Crisis," *Journal of Latin American Studies,* 22, no. 1 (February 1990), p. 7. See also Kotaro Horisaka, "Japanese Banks and Latin American Debt Problems," *Latin American Studies Occasional Papers,* no. 4, Georgetown University, Washington D.C., 1990.

16. Interviews with Japanese bankers. See also Steven Murphy, "The Purge Is On," *Latin Finance* 25 (March 1991).

17. On Japanese economic relations with Brazil, see Erani T. Torres, "Brazil-Japan Relations: From Fever to Chill," in Stallings and Szekely, *Japan, the United States and Latin America;* Mitsuhiro Kagami, "Japanese Business Activities in Brazil" (Santiago: ECLAC, March 1989); and Riordan Roett, "Japan and Brazil in the 1990s: On the Road to Nowhere?" in Susan K. Purcell and Robert Immerman, eds., *Japan and Latin America in the New Global Order* (Boulder, Colo.: Lynne Rienner, 1992). Despite the outpouring of criticism and pessimism, Brazil continues to receive the largest amount of Japanese DFI because of the huge number of firms already located there.

18. Interviews with Japanese business officials, Tokyo, February 1991.

19. Interviews with Japanese bankers, New York, June 1991.

20. Interviews with Nissan officials, Tokyo, February 1991. See also "Nissan to Up Mexico Output as Part of Global Strategy," *Japan Times,* November 28, 1990.

21. On Mexican-Japanese relations, see Gabriel Szekely, "Mexico's New International Strategy: Looking to the Far East While Pursuing Integration with the North," in Stallings and Szekely, *Japan, the United States and Latin America;* Gabriel Szekely, ed., *Manufacturing Across Borders and Oceans: Japan, the United States, and Mexico* (San Diego: Center for U.S.-Mexican Studies, University of California-San Diego, 1991); and Luis Rubio, "Japan in Mexico: A Changing Pattern," in Purcell and Immerman, *Japan and Latin America.*

22. Interviews with officials of the Export-Import Bank of Japan and the Overseas Economic Cooperation Fund, Tokyo, December 1990.

23. Japan-Mexico Commission for the 21st Century, *Final Report,* Tokyo, March 1992.

24. Interview with Chilean embassy official, Tokyo, November 1990. On environmental problems with Japanese forestry investments, see Leslie Crawford, "Too Much

of a Chip Feast," *Financial Times,* December 19, 1990. On Chilean-Japanese relations more generally, see Neantro Saavedra-Rivano, "Chile and Japan: Opening Doors Through Trade," in Stallings and Szekely, *Japan, the United States and Latin America.*

25. Interviews with Japanese businesspeople in Santiago, May 1991.

26. Unpublished data from the Export-Import Bank of Japan, Tokyo. On Aylwin's Asian trip, see *Latin American Weekly Report,* November 26, 1992.

27. Interviews with Japanese businesspeople, Tokyo, February 1991.

28. Unpublished data from the Export-Import Bank of Japan.

29. On Japan and Peru, see Pablo de la Flor Belaúnde, "Peruvian-Japanese Relations: The Decline of Resource Diplomacy," in Stallings and Szekely, *Japan, the United States, and Latin America; Toward a Trilateral Relationship in the Western Hemisphere* (Baltimore, Md.: Johns Hopkins University Press, 1993); *Japón en la escena internacional: Relaciones con América Latina y el Perú* (Lima: CEPEI, 1991).

30. *Nikkei Weekly,* August 1, 1992. On Japanese loans to Peru, see Ministry of Foreign Affairs, *Japan's ODA, 1992* (Tokyo: Ministry of Foreign Affairs, 1993).

31. *JEI Report,* January 8, 1993.

32. Toru Yanagihara and Anne Emig, "An Overview of Japan's Foreign Aid," in Shafiqul Islam, ed., *Yen for Development: Japanese Foreign Aid and the Politics of Burden-Sharing* (New York: Council on Foreign Relations, 1991).

33. Interviews with officials of the Overseas Economic Cooperation Fund, Tokyo, February 1991. See also various issues of the OECF *Annual Report,* Tokyo.

34. On the recycling fund, see Toshihiko Kinoshita, "Developments in the International Debt Survey and Japan's Response," *EXIM Review,* 10, no. 2 (1991).

35. Interviews with Japanese officials, Tokyo, October 1992.

36. Toshihiko Kinoshita, "End of the Cold War and Japan's New Role in International Development," ms., 1992.

37. For an authoritative account of the origins of the Miyazawa Plan by one of the economists who helped write it, see Haruhiko Kuroda, "Miyazawa Initiative: Attacking Debt," *Tokyo Business Today* (December 1988). For details on the final version of the Miyazawa Plan, see *JEI Report,* October 7, 1988, and *Japan Economic Journal,* October 1 and 8, 1988.

38. On the various debt plans and their implications for Latin America, see Economic Commission for Latin America and the Caribbean, *Latin America and the Caribbean: Options to Reduce the Debt Burden* (Santiago: ECLAC, 1990).

39. Interviews with Japanese government officials, Tokyo, June 1989.

40. Interviews with Japanese government officials, Tokyo, February 1991.

41. Julia Chang Bloch, "A U.S.-Japan Aid Alliance?" in Islam, ed., *Yen for Development.*

42. For this argument, see Susan Kaufman Purcell and Robert Immerman, "The U.S., Japan, and Latin America: Prospects for Cooperation and Conflict," in Purcell and Immerman, *Japan and Latin America.* A similar argument is made in Peter Smith, *Japan, Latin America, and the New International Order,* Institute of Developing Economies, VRS Series, no. 179, Tokyo, 1990.

43. A recent study of Latin Americans' current image of Japan and Japanese people was conducted by the Ibero-American Institute of Sophia University in Tokyo. For a summary of the results, see Kotaro Horisaka, "Japan's Image in Latin America and the

Future of Japanese–Latin American Relations," *Iberoamericana,* 13, no. 2 (1st semester 1991).

44. A possible indication of growing Japanese interest in Latin America is the recent publication in Japan of Kotaro Horisaka, Barbara Stallings, and Gabriel Szekely, eds., *Raten Amerika Tono Kyouzon: Atarashii Kokusai Kankyou No Nakada* (Tokyo: Doubunkan, 1991), a volume on Japan, the United States, and Latin America.

# 8

# China and Latin America After the Cold War's End

## *Feng Xu*

China began to show some interest, albeit limited, in Latin America during the early 1960s—immediately after and as a result of the Cuban Revolution. By the 1970s, it had established diplomatic ties with a number of countries in the region, including Argentina, Brazil, Chile, Mexico, and Peru. But Chinese–Latin American relations have expanded slowly and still remain slight. China's trade with Latin America, for example, accounts for only 3 percent of the total Chinese trade and 1 percent of Latin America's.[1] For Chinese policy, Latin American nations have ranked a distant third in priority, after those in Asia and Africa—and relations with all Third World countries have been of lower priority than relations with the industrial world.

Of the many factors that have inhibited the development of Chinese–Latin American relations, the most important are Latin America's geographic remoteness, U.S. dominance of the region, and, lately, China's preoccupation with enhancing its relations with industrial countries in the hope of acquiring the capital and technology necessary for its economic modernization program. Although some of these factors will continue to be significant, it is unlikely that Chinese–Latin American relations will remain the same in the future because the international environment has changed so drastically.

I am deeply indebted to Abraham F. Lowenthal, who encouraged me throughout my work on the chapter and commented constructively on all the earlier versions. I also wish to thank an anonymous reviewer for helpful comments.

This chapter examines how recent international changes have affected Chinese–Latin American relations. It concentrates on China's relations with five Latin American countries—Mexico, Brazil, Argentina, Chile, and Cuba—that are the current foci of Chinese policy toward the region. I will argue that future relations with these countries are likely to be shaped mainly by the residual effect of other policies and primarily depend on each party's relations with the industrial North. There are some incentives on both sides for strengthening bilateral relations, but these may change if either side develops closer ties to the North (in the case of Mexico, Brazil, Argentina, and Chile) or becomes less externally constrained (in the cases of China and Cuba).[2]

## Chinese Policy Toward Latin America in Retrospect

In the 1960s, the impetus for the Chinese leadership to include Latin America in its foreign policy was mainly *ideological*. In the face of economic blockade and political hostility from the United States, China had formulated a strong anti-U.S. foreign policy. All Latin American governments except the Castro regime seemed to collaborate with the United States, and because they denied Beijing a seat in the United Nations, they were seen as pawns of U.S. imperialism and therefore worthy targets of future revolutions. Inspired by the Cuban Revolution, China hoped to see the Cuba model (characterized by social transformation through armed struggle from below) extend to other corners of the region. As a result, China was more interested in establishing ties with radical parties, organizations, and groups according to their ideology, rather than activating close relations with established governments. In this regard, Chinese policy toward Latin America was quite different from its policies toward Asia and Africa. Unlike countries in Latin America, most Asian and African nations were newly independent from European powers and less influenced by the United States, so they were generally regarded as potential allies in a prospective united front against U.S. imperialism.

A major change occurred in Chinese policy toward Latin America in the late 1960s and early 1970s, however, largely due to the worsening of Chinese-Soviet relations and the improvement of Chinese-U.S. relations.

China's split with the Soviet Union began as early as the 1950s, but it was not until the late 1960s that this split developed into a full-scale political and military confrontation. Coming on top of poor relations with the United States, Soviet hostility placed China in a position of simultaneously facing two major enemies. It also forced China to rethink its place in world politics and its desired relationship with the Third World in general, specifically its policy toward Latin America.

China's worldview at that time was partially reflected in Mao Zedong's Three-Worlds Theory—a simplified model for defining and assessing the main contradictions in the international system. In accordance with the theory, China chose to cast its lot with that of the Third World, but, because of the changing world context, it found it difficult to put theory into practice.

Following the Sino-Soviet schism and the resulting change in the international balance of power, China began to discard ideological biases, distance itself from radical movements and guerrilla bands, and develop relations with established national governments in Latin America. China's relationship with the United States also improved, paving the way for warmer Chinese–Latin American relations. After the Kissinger and Nixon trips to China in 1971–1972, China was finally accepted in Latin America. Most Latin governments voted for its entry into the United Nations, and in return, China supported their claims for 200-mile territorial sea limits in the Law of the Sea negotiations. By the late 1970s, China had established diplomatic relations with a number of major Latin American countries, which represented the majority of the region's territory and population.[3]

If China's Latin American policy in the 1960s was ideologically motivated, it was more *politically* motivated thereafter. The change in Chinese–Latin American policy was nominally triggered by the Soviet threat and the need to win more friends. But for the most part, Chinese diplomacy in Latin America had little to do with the Soviet Union. Because of Beijing's long exclusion and isolation from the postwar international system and the still unsettled nature of the Taiwan issue, the search for legitimacy became the concrete goal of new Chinese–Latin American policy. China realized that its search could not succeed without Third World support. Compared with Asia and Africa, Latin America had more countries that still maintained diplomatic relations with Taiwan; thus, it became the last political frontier for China.

Nevertheless, Latin America was still far from a top priority for China. After the early 1970s, the Chinese pursued a dual-track foreign policy, with the relations with the Third World on one track and the relations with Western countries on the other. The first track was normative but necessary for identity and political reasons. The second track was substantive and necessary for strategic and economic reasons.

Despite the rhetoric exemplified by the Three-World Theory, China soon became preoccupied with aligning itself with the United States against the Soviet Union. When Chinese-Soviet relations improved in the early 1980s, this anti-Soviet alliance with the United States was conveniently converted into a policy oriented toward enhancing relations with Western countries in the hope of maximizing the credits, loans, investment, entrepreneurship, and science and technology needed for economic modernization.

Two overlapping patterns are thus evident in Chinese foreign policy between 1950 and the 1980s:

1. When China is concerned with system transformation, ideology matters (as in Latin America in the 1960s); when it is not concerned with system transformation but seeks to take advantage of the existing system, pragmatism holds sway (as happened from the early 1970s until recently).
2. When China is isolated or externally constrained in the international system, solidarity with the Third World is valued (as in the 1960s, through alliance with Third World countries in Asia and Africa); when China is not isolated or externally constrained, the Third World tends to be relegated to a peripheral role (as happened from the early 1970s until recently).

## China After the Cold War

The end of the Cold War, combined with the international reaction to the "Tiananmen incident" in June 1989, created new conditions for Chinese foreign policy.

First, with the end of the Cold War, the strategic importance China had earlier derived from the perception that it could influence the competition between Washington and Moscow suddenly declined. Due to its size, autonomy, and geographical location, China had been viewed by both the United States and the Soviet Union as a trump card that would give them the upper hand in their competition. Because both superpowers tried to play the "China card," China could lean toward either and benefit from both. This strategic leverage came to an end with the disintegration of the Soviet Union.

Second, the transformation taking place in Eastern Europe and the former Soviet Union has left China ideologically isolated. The only countries besides China that still claim to believe in the Marxist doctrine are North Korea, Vietnam, and Cuba, all of which have serious domestic problems.

Third, the Tiananmen incident cost China most of the sympathy it had previously enjoyed in the West. After Tiananmen, a chill developed in Chinese relations with Western countries, as one after another imposed economic sanctions against China. Although most of these countries, with Japan taking the lead, lifted the economic sanctions in mid-1990 and though Chinese relations with most Western countries seem to be improving, the memory lingers. Especially in the United States, China has been criticized for human rights abuses ever since Tiananmen, and its human rights record comes under scrutiny every time its most-favored-nation (MFN) status needs renewal. With the election of President Clinton, China feared that its MFN status could be lost or at least made conditional on improvements in human rights.[4] Today, China still has a long way to go to rebuild its international image, and thus its relations with Western countries remain uncertain.

Fourth, in sharp contrast to the international reaction to the Tiananmen incident, the transformation in Eastern Europe (especially in Hungary and Poland) and the former Soviet Union has been applauded and encouraged by Western countries. Emerging opportunities for trade and investment elsewhere in this former Socialist bloc, in addition to political and ideological reasons, are likely to make China less attractive and thus distract Western business from the mainland.

China therefore faces more external constraints than it did in the 1970s and most of the 1980s. According to the second pattern, China is likely to reidentify itself with the Third World in order to offset the effects of recent international change, but it is unlikely to completely break with the system. If China seeks to maximize its national interests within the existing system, it will take a pragmatic attitude toward its relations with the Third World (second pattern). That is, while strengthening its relations with the Third World, China will cultivate its relations with Western countries because only they can contribute to its drive for economic modernization.

Both tendencies—the efforts to identify itself with the Third World and an emphasis on improving relations with the West—seem contradictory, but they are nevertheless observable in Chinese post–Cold War foreign policy.

After 1989, China sent high-level emissaries throughout the Third World. It exchanged trade liaison offices with Israel and South Korea, and by August 1992, it had established or reestablished diplomatic relations with Indonesia, Singapore, Saudi Arabia, Israel, and South Korea. At the multilateral level, China hosted the forty-eighth meeting of the UN Economic and Social Commission in Beijing, gained observer status in the nonaligned movement and attended its 1992 summit, and participated in the 1992 consultation of the Group of 77, the organized caucus of developing countries in the United Nations.

Despite the economic sanctions, China showed that it was willing to cooperate with the United States and its Western allies on issues of common concern. It participated constructively, for example, in the negotiations over Cambodia. And during the crisis in the Persian Gulf, it actively joined the consultations within the UN Security Council and supported Resolution 660 to make the Iraqis withdraw from Kuwait. Although China eventually abstained from voting on Resolution 678, which sanctioned the use of military operations against Iraq, the fact that it did not use its veto power against the resolution indicates that it did not want to take any risk that would have led to a further deterioration in its relations with the West.

In its bilateral relations with the United States, China has also demonstrated its flexibility and readiness to compromise. On October 10, 1992, just before the final deadline, China signed a memorandum of understanding on market access with the United States, which marked the termination of the year-long 301 investigation and will allow the entry of more U.S. exports. In return, China received a U.S. commitment to support its contracting-party status in the GATT. On the issue of the Bush administration's decision to sell 150 F-16 fighter jets to Taiwan, China displayed self-restraint, and it is unlikely to take any concrete step to retaliate against the United States, despite its verbal attacks on the decision.

Nevertheless, the constraints on Chinese foreign policy persist, and consequently, China may well adopt a more active policy toward Latin America, in pursuit of its own evolving interests. China's chief interests lie in the development of its economy. Its leaders have strongly expressed their commitment to economic development since 1978, when they began a shift away from a policy of economic self-reliance and self-sufficiency to an open-door policy.[5] The new economic policy has emphasized external trade, foreign investment, and the introduction of advanced science and technology, and a closer relationship with Latin America could prove helpful in these sectors.

China's political interests lie in two areas: (1) the maintenance of its territorial integrity, and (2) the establishment of a just and equitable new international order. The ongoing Taiwan issue is the most important topic in the first area. As Taiwan became economically strong, Beijing became more sensitive to the issue than ever before. In almost every joint communiqué issued by the Chinese and foreign governments, Beijing has been determined to include a clause explicitly indicating that "the People's Republic of China is the only legitimate representative of China." To achieve national reunification, Beijing not only opposes the independence of Taiwan but also seeks a diplomatic presence in as many countries as possible.

In the post–Cold War era, China has renewed its call for a more just and equitable international order, different from George Bush's "new world order." Although Bush's vision hinged on transnational activities, changes in polarity, and the role of international institutions (e.g., the United Nations), China's version of a new order has explicit North-South content. It pragmatically aims to rally support from Third World countries at a time when China is externally constrained.

The new international order, according to Beijing, should be based on "the universal observance of the five principles of mutual respect for sovereignty and territorial integrity, mutual non-aggression, non-interference in each other's internal affairs, equality and mutual benefit, and peaceful coexistence."[6] The new order would also include international economic relations. Efforts would be made to strengthen North-South dialogue and cooperation, "with a view to necessary adjustment and reform in commodity, trade, fund, debt, monetary, financial and other important fields of international economy."[7] In terms of human rights, Beijing argues that "equal importance should be attached to civil and political rights, and also economic, social, cultural and development rights." For Beijing, "the right to subsistence and the right to development are undoubtedly the fundamental and most important human rights of all."[8]

Two specific Chinese foreign policy goals exemplifying these political interests are the resumption of China's status in the GATT and its participation in the UN reform process, which is conceived as a step toward establishing a just and equitable new international order.[9]

Beijing's ideological interests increasingly lie in the international legitimation of its Communist rule. Because communism has been discredited, Communist regimes must now turn to each other. Former Soviet clients like Vietnam, Cuba, and North Korea have looked to China for help, and for both psychological and symbolic reasons, Beijing needs their support to legitimize its rule. In late 1991, just a few months after the failed coup in Moscow, both General Secretary of the Central Committee of the Korean Workers' Party and President of North Korea Kim Il-Sung and General Secretary of the Vietnamese Communist Party Do Muoi paid visits to China. High-level contacts between Chinese and Cuban officials are also increasing.

In terms of its overall capabilities (economic, political, and military), China is *not* a global power. Rather, it is a regional power, and as such, its interests are most tangible in Southeast Asia. But if and when China intends to extend its relations with the Third World beyond Southeast Asia, Latin America is likely to be the most appropriate candidate for several reasons.

First, most Latin American countries are at a higher level of economic development than countries in South Asia, the Middle East, and Africa. Their economies experienced rapid growth during the 1960s and the 1970s, and as a result, there is potential for closer economic cooperation between China and these countries.

Second, most Latin American countries are now in a process of historical transition from authoritarian or oligarchical rule to democracy, which, in the long run, allows broad political participation and therefore reduces political instability. If China intends to maximize its national interests within the existing system, political stability and predictability will be important factors affecting its foreign policy options.

Third, with the development of their economies, most Latin American countries, especially major ones like Brazil and Mexico, have become far more active and influential in world politics. They are important international actors that China cannot afford to overlook if it is to achieve many of its foreign policy goals.

Specifically, Chinese interests lie in trade, joint venture enterprises, cooperation in science and technology, foreign policy coordination in certain issue-specific areas, and mutual legitimation, all of which lend themselves to closer ties with Latin America. In contrast to the period before the 1980s, China's Latin American policy in the post–Cold War period is both *economically* and *politically* motivated, though the economic motivation now seems more potent than the political one.

## Mexico, Brazil, Argentina, Chile, and Cuba After the Cold War

In Latin America, the countries that most interest China are Mexico, Brazil, Argentina, Chile, and Cuba. The first four are China's largest Latin American trade partners; Cuba's importance to China is more political and ideological than commercial.

With the end of the Cold War, some of these countries have been caught in a situation quite similar to that facing China. Brazil, Argentina, and, to a certain extent, Chile are now likely to be neglected by the United States. During the Cold War, U.S. policy toward Latin America was designed to prevent the spread of communism, and with its proximity, Latin America naturally fell into the U.S. sphere of influence. Although Latin countries, more concerned with economic development than containing communism, often resented their northern neighbor, they did sometimes benefit from their close relations with the United States. For example, the Alliance for Progress allowed a massive transfer of resources to Latin America for both socioeconomic reform and development purposes. But after the Cold War and the disintegration of the Soviet Union, the impetus for giving a high priority to Latin America in U.S. foreign policy disappeared overnight. The recent developments in Eastern Europe and the former Soviet Union have further switched U.S. attention away from Latin America. Domestic problems such as economic recession, unemployment, and huge budget deficits may also encourage a more inward-looking view.

Benign neglect by the United States would be extremely detrimental to Latin America, especially if it is accompanied by a continuing debt problem in these countries and by trade protectionism in the United States.

Of all debtor countries in the Third World, the three largest are Brazil, Mexico, and Argentina. By 1989, total external debt was $111.3 billion for Brazil, $95.6 billion for Mexico, and $64.7 billion for Argentina.[10] Although there have been negotiations on debt rescheduling and reduction, the measures taken so far are hardly sufficient to solve the problem.

To service their debts, these countries need to generate export surpluses from their external trade. But unfortunately, there has been a tendency toward trade protectionism in the United States since the early 1980s, largely due to the decline of overall U.S. economic competitiveness and increasing U.S. trade deficits. Although Japan and Southeast Asia's newly industrialized countries are said to be responsible for most of the U.S. trade deficit, trade protectionism often targets any country intending to penetrate the U.S. market. In the 1980s, the percentage of Latin American exports to the United

States showed a constant decline.[11] And though countries like Brazil, Argentina, Mexico, and Chile have been told to liberalize their trade and have actually made efforts toward this end, their exports are still being discriminated against in the U.S. market.

Meanwhile, the Castro regime in Cuba is experiencing its hardest times since 1959. Economic aid and oil supplies from the former Soviet Union have been substantially cut, and Soviet troops are being withdrawn. Without economic, political, and military support from the outside world, the Castro regime will find it hard to survive unless it locates another patron or makes major changes in its domestic and foreign policies.

All these Latin American countries, be they neglected or externally constrained, must find ways out of their predicaments. Whether it is possible for them to develop their relations with China depends on what their interests are and whether these interests are identical or overlapping with those of China. Economically, the interests of Mexico, Brazil, Argentina, and Chile center on debt rescheduling and reduction, the expansion of external trade to generate trade surpluses needed to service debts, the inflow of new money for productive activities, and the acquisition of advanced technology that can facilitate economic growth.

Although China cannot help these countries resolve their debt problems, it can contribute a certain amount of capital in the form of joint venture enterprises, and it can be of some help in the fields of technological cooperation. Most important, China is a huge potential consumer market, with an industrial economy badly in need of raw materials and modern equipment.

Politically, the interests of these four countries include the preservation of their independence and national sovereignty. But beyond that, it is not easy to identify what their specific political interests are in international relations and how they are pursued. These countries do not always speak in one voice as they did in the 1970s, and sometimes they are in competition for multilateral and bilateral financial aid and preferential trade arrangements. Nevertheless, the idea of equal development opportunities is by no means dead. As Third World countries, they are concerned with issues like the transfer of resources from rich to poor countries, the improvement of conditions for their exports, debt reduction, and, more generally, the obligation on the part of the rich countries to take practical measures to narrow the gap between them and the South. In other words, their political interests also lie in seeking ways to improve their situation in North-South economic relations.

These countries may not necessarily echo China's call for the establishment of a just and equitable new international order or its views on human rights. But the economic aspect of China's grand scheme seems to match many of their demands for fair and favorable treatment in North-South economic relations and thus to serve their interests in international negotiations on issues like resource transfer, trade, debt, and money. In this sense, it is development issues that are most likely to unite these countries with China vis-à-vis the United States and other northern industrial countries.

Cuba's present interests, which center on maintaining the crumbling Castro regime, entail ideological legitimation, political support, and economic assistance. Obviously, Cuba needs China more than the other four Latin American countries do, and for ideological and political reasons, China is unlikely to dump Cuba at a time when the latter desperately needs help. However, due to the recent drive for economic modernization, China's support for the Castro regime tends to be confined to exchanging visits of high-level officials and making political statements. Where economics is involved, China insists on the principle and practice of reciprocity.

## More Opportunities for Cooperation?

Some steps have been taken both by China and by Latin American countries to enhance their relations. During May–June 1990, Chinese president Yang Shangkun visited five Latin American countries—Mexico, Brazil, Uruguay, Argentina, and Chile. The visit was ignored in the United States and other Western nations, but it received prominent attention from the Chinese media. It was hailed as "a new chapter in Sino–Latin American friendship," "an important milestone in the history of Sino–Latin American friendly relations," and "a major event in Sino–Latin American history."[12] Although one should not take such rhetoric too seriously, this was nevertheless the first visit by a Chinese head of state to Latin America since the founding of the People's Republic of China.

During President Yang's visit, China and the five Latin countries exchanged views on major international issues and signed a number of cooperation accords and agreements on economics, trade, and science and technology. The accords involve seventeen major joint venture projects in forestry, fishing, mining, textiles, and oil exploration, with a total investment of $36 million, $22 million of which is Chinese capital.[13] The agreements include an economic and technological arrangement with Brazil and a memorandum defining China's purchase of Brazilian iron ore over a period of three years.[14]

The period after President Yang's trip to Latin America saw an increasing number of Latin leaders visiting China, from Brazilian Foreign Minister Francisco Rezek (August 1991) to Chilean President Patricio Aylwin (November 1992). Most of these visits resulted in agreements on economic cooperation and foreign policy coordination. China's economic ties with Mexico, Brazil, Argentina, and Chile are also strengthening.

### Trade

In 1989, the total Chinese–Latin American bilateral trade volume was $2.97 billion, of which China managed a total trade value of $1.2 billion with Brazil,

$576 million with Argentina, $240 million with Chile, and $190 million with Mexico.[15] In 1990, China's trade with Mexico for the first time exceeded $200 million,[16] and according to one source, this figure increased to about $300 million in 1991.[17] In the first six months of 1992, China's trade with Chile reached $174 million, making up almost 73 percent of the total trade value in 1989.[18] Its trade with Argentina and Brazil is also on the increase.[19]

There are two reasons why China's trade with these four countries may expand further. First, China's economy and those of Latin America are mutually complementary. China's major exports to these countries include textiles, garments, light industrial goods, chemicals, petroleum, machinery, and equipment. Its major imports from Latin America are basically raw materials, such as iron ore, copper products, nitrokilite, wheat, wool, sugar, paper pulp, urea, fish meal, chemical fertilizer, and chemical fiber, most of which are not available from its Southeast Asian trade partners.[20]

Second, Latin American countries have had a notable trade surplus with China. Of the 1989 figure, China's exports were $550 million, and its imports were as high as $2.42 billion.[21] This has already forced China to export more to Latin America (rather than import less) in order to reduce its trade deficits, as happened in its trade with Chile. But the favorable balance of trade may also induce Latin American countries to further develop their trade relations with China.

## Joint Venture Enterprises

China has set up joint venture enterprises, mostly in textiles, in certain Caribbean countries (e.g., Jamaica) as a way of penetrating the U.S. market. The new joint venture projects that were formalized during President Yang's visit are no longer confined to textiles, and they extend to Mexico and South America.

With the increase of its investment in Latin America, China has also signed agreements to protect bilateral investments, avoid double taxation, and prevent tax evasion on income with Brazil, Argentina, and Chile.[22] If NAFTA is ratified, China will be very interested in setting up more joint venture enterprises in Mexico to take advantage of U.S.-Mexican free trade. When commenting on NAFTA, a Chinese official said that "potential Chinese investors are looking at the climate in Mexico for future development in textiles, light industry and electronics."[23]

In November 1992, China bought Peru's largest iron ore mine (also the largest in South America) for $120 million and has become its sole owner. This is, thus far, China's largest investment in Latin America.[24]

## Cooperation in Science and Technology

Of all Latin American countries, Brazil has developed the closest ties with China in science and technological cooperation. The two countries have initiated a number of accords in this area in agriculture, hydroelectric power, aviation, and astronautics.[25] The two nations have also agreed to cooperate in an aerospace program for the production and launching of two satellites, slated to be put into orbit before the end of 1994 and 1995, respectively.[26] Argentina and China are also expecting to carry out a long-term program of technical cooperation in the fields of geology and mineral resources.[27]

Coupled with closer economic ties between China and these four countries are their efforts to coordinate foreign policies on major issues in international politics. Among the most recent of these major international issues are the resumption of China's membership in the GATT and environmental protection.

In China's search for backing on its membership in the GATT, these four countries have rendered their unequivocal support. At the UN Conference on Environment and Development, held in Rio de Janeiro in June 1992, Brazil, China, and other Third World countries stood together in insisting that developed nations should contribute more to environmental protection by transferring technologies, rather than profiting from their sale; they also pressed for the passage of the biodiversity treaty, which the Bush administration refused to sign.

Both China and Cuba have quickened their steps to improve their relations in response to the recent international changes. In July 1991, Vice President of the Council of State and Vice President of the Council of the Ministers of Cuba Carlos Rafael Rodríguez visited China at the invitation of the Chinese government. During his visit, both General Secretary of the Chinese Communist Party (CPC) Jiang Zemin and President Yang Shangkun met with him. A few days before his visit, Fidel Castro had sent a telegram to Jiang Zemin, congratulating the CPC on its seventieth birthday. Two months later, a CPC delegation headed by Yang Rudai, a member of the CPC Central Committee Political Bureau, arrived in Havana. During their stay, Castro met with the delegation several times, and in a farewell visit at the delegation's guesthouse, he expressed appreciation for Yang's visit at a time "when Cuba was faced with great difficulties."[28]

But China is unlikely to take over the Cuban burden from the former Soviet Union. Aside from mutual political support and ideological legitimation, it will give priority to bilateral trade, instead of unilateral aid. As Yang Rudai made quite clear during his recent visit to Cuba, China will "promote bilateral economic relations and trade according to the principles of equality and mutual benefit."[29] In early 1992, a protocol on bilateral trade was signed between China and Cuba, and Havana has also decided to send personnel to China's special economic zones to study and run joint ventures there.[30]

## Conclusion

Now that the Cold War is over, China may seek to reidentify itself to some extent with the Third World. But because it still chooses to maximize its national interests within the existing international system, rather than to break with it,

China will still value its relations with Western countries more than its relations with the Third World: Only the former can substantially help the drive for economic modernization.

Opportunities for Chinese cooperation with Mexico, Brazil, Argentina, Chile, and Cuba are now greater than ever before. As Third World countries, the two sides have compatible or overlapping interests, and they share similar views on many international issues. To the extent that either or both sides are neglected or externally constrained, China and Latin America are likely to develop closer relations.

If relations with Western industrial countries improve for either China or the Latin American nations, however, then incentives will turn into disincentives. In this respect, Mexico is the prime example for NAFTA will tend to discourage it from developing closer relations, especially economic ones, with other Third World countries. And to the extent that U.S.–Latin American relations become more integrated, further development of Chinese relations with Latin America will be problematic.

## Notes

1. Oxford Analytica, *Latin America in Perspective* (Boston: Houghton Mifflin, 1991), p. 296.

2. The Mexico case is illustrative. If the North American Free Trade Agreement, signed by the United States, Mexico, and Canada on December 17, 1992, is ratified by the congresses of the three countries, Mexico will be less interested in promoting its relations with China.

3. Now China maintains diplomatic relations with seventeen of the thirty-three independent Latin American countries, which account for more than 80 percent of the region's total population.

4. In his acceptance speech at the Democratic Convention in New York, Clinton commented that the United States needed a government that "does not coddle tyrants from Baghdad to Beijing," thereby convincing China that he would be a tough customer to deal with.

5. See Deng Xiaoping, *Dent Xiaoping wenxuan, 1975–1982* (Beijing: Renmin Chubanshe, 1983).

6. Chinese Foreign Minister Qian Qichen's speech at the 47th UN General Assembly, in *U.S. FBIS Daily Report, China,* September 24, 1992, p. 2.

7. Han Xu, "New World Order: A Chinese Perspective," in *Beijing Review,* September 9–15, 1991), p. 34.

8. Qian Qichen, "Establishing a Just and Equitable New International Order," in *Beijing Review* (October 7–13, 1991), p. 15; Qian Qichen's speech at the 47th UN General Assembly, in *U.S. FBIS Daily Report, China,* September 24, 1992, p. 3.

9. During a general debate at the 47th UN General Assembly, Chinese Foreign Minister Qian Qichen outlined China's four-point proposal on UN reform: (1) The United Nations should contribute to maintaining the sovereignty of its member states; (2) it should encourage the peaceful resolution of international conflicts; (3) it should devote

the same attention to the issue of development as it does in approaching international conflicts and crises; and (4) it should promote a new international order that is peaceful, stable, fair, and rational.

10. The World Bank, *World Development Report, 1991* (Washington, D.C.: World Bank, 1991), pp. 244–245.

11. Oxford Analytica, *Latin America*, p. 212.

12. *U.S. FBIS Daily Report, China*, May 14, 1990, p. 23; May 22, 1990, p. 15; June 4, 1990, p. 19.

13. *U.S. FBIS Daily Report, China*, May 16, 1990, p. 13; May 29, 1990, p. 30.

14. *U.S. FBIS Daily Report, China*, May 21, 1990, p. 23.

15. *U.S. FBIS Daily Report, China*, May 1, 1990, p. 11.

16. *Renmin ribao, haiwaiban* (Beijing), June 15, 1991, p. 4.

17. *U.S. FBIS Daily Report, China*, February 19, 1992, p. 15.

18. *U.S. FBIS Daily Report, China*, August 31, 1992, p. 11.

19. *U.S. FBIS Daily Report, China*, June 1, 1992, p. 16

20. *China Daily* (Beijing), May 1, 1990, p. 2; *U.S. FBIS Daily Report, China*, June 1, 1992, p. 16, and August 31, 1992, p. 11.

21. *China Daily* (Beijing), May 1, 1990, p. 2.

22. *U.S. FBIS Daily Report, China*, August 6, 1991, p. 14: September 23, 1992, p. 18.

23. *U.S. FBIS Daily Report, China*, April 2, 1992, p. 14.

24. *Renmin ribao, haiwaiban* (Beijing), November 11, 1992, p. 1.

25. *Liaowang, haiwaiban* (Beijing), May 14, 1990, p. 7.

26. *U.S. FBIS Daily Report, China*, July 27, 1992, p. 12.

27. *U.S. FBIS Daily Report, China*, May 12, 1992, p. 24.

28. *U.S. FBIS Daily Report, China*, September 25, 1991, p. 18.

29. *U.S. FBIS Daily Report, China*, September 20, 1991, p. 20.

30. *U.S. FBIS Daily Report, China*, February 19, 1992, p. 16.

# PART THREE

*Framing Policy Responses*

# 9

# Regionalism in the Americas

## *Andrew Hurrell*

The dramatic reconfiguration of the international system has given a new impetus to regionalism and to the growth of regional awareness. For many commentators, increased regionalism and strengthened regional cooperation are viewed as central elements of the post–Cold War international order.[1] The end of the Cold War and the decline of the Soviet Union are, it is argued, encouraging the emergence of regionalism by reducing the incentives for superpower intervention, by eliminating the pattern of global Cold War alliances that cut across regions, and by creating more autonomous "regional spaces" freed from the distorting impact of the East-West confrontation.

The relative decline of U.S. hegemony and the reduced capacity and willingness of the United States to play a global role are both stimulating and providing space for the development of regional power systems constructed around the European Community in Europe and Japan in Asia. Economic pressures are also seen to be working toward regionalism: the European Community; the current difficulties of the Uruguay Round; the impact of structural changes in the global economy pressing both states and firms toward expanded collaboration; and changed understandings of economic development in many parts of the developing world and the widespread adoption of market-liberal development strategies. Although the relationship between rhetoric and reality has varied widely, few parts of the world have been immune from the revival of interest in regionalist options.

The new wave of regionalist activity ranges from discussion of a world of regional trading blocs, on the one hand, to increased emphasis on subregional cooperation and integration, on the other. Indeed, one of the most important features of the new regionalism concerns the relationship between bloc regionalism, often built around a hegemonic or potentially hegemonic power (the United States, Japan, and Germany), and subregional groupings, between what might be called macroregionalism and microregionalism. In many parts of the world, the relationship between these different regionalist options has become a central question, defining the broader pattern of international relationships.

This is nowhere more true than in the Americas. For Latin America, regionalism has historically meant two quite different things. In the first place, it has meant regional cooperation between the countries of Latin America itself. After more than a decade of disillusionments, the 1980s saw a significant resurgence of this form of regionalism. The first wave was essentially political in nature. It involved regional attempts to promote peace in Central America in the form of the Contadora Group and the Contadora Support Group. It also involved moves toward increased political consultation and coordination through such forums as the Group of 8 and its successor, the Rio Group. And it could be seen in the improved political and strategic relationship between Brazil and Argentina that began in 1980 and gathered pace in the period after 1985.

More recently, the focus has shifted back to proposals for increased regional economic cooperation or even integration. Most prominent has been the evolution of relations between Brazil and Argentina. Building on the political rapprochement of the early 1980s, the two countries signed the Argentina-Brazil Integration Program in July 1986, followed by other formal agreements in November 1988 and August 1989. In March 1991, Argentina, Brazil, Uruguay, and Paraguay signed the Treaty of Asunción, which created Mercosur and which foresaw a Southern Cone Common Market by 1995. In July 1991, the members of the Central American Common Market (CACM) sought to extend and revitalize the organization, and free trade agreements have been signed between CACM and Mexico and Venezuela. The year 1991 also saw efforts to relaunch the Andean Pact, with the adoption of a timetable for moves toward a full common market by 1995. A free trade agreement has been negotiated between the Group of 3 (Mexico, Colombia, and Venezuela). Finally, the early 1990s witnessed an outpouring of regionalist rhetoric and discussions on regional cooperation involving, in one form or another, almost all the countries of the region.

The second form of regionalism covers the entire Western Hemisphere. Inter-American regionalism has, of course, a long history, again going back to the nineteenth century. In the course of the century, it was given an elaborate, formal, institutional structure in the Organization of American States and its related bodies. Moreover, this brand of regionalism has also acquired a new momentum over the past few years, primarily in terms of economic relations.

The decision to make a North American Free Trade Area an objective of U.S. trade policy goes back to the Trade Agreements Act of 1979. One notable step was the successful negotiation of the U.S.-Canadian free trade agreement, which went into effect in January 1989. A further crucial development has been the reversal of Mexican policy that, for most of the 1980s, had resisted the Reagan administration's offers to negotiate a free trade agreement. In 1985, however, the United States and Mexico signed an agreement on countervailing duties and subsidies. In November 1987, they signed a framework agreement that provided mechanisms both for the resolution of trade disputes and for the process of bilateral trade liberalization. In June 1990, President Salinas formally requested negotiations on a free trade agreement; in August 1992, a draft treaty was agreed and initialed; and in December 1992, it was signed by the presidents of Mexico and the United States and the prime minister of Canada.

The idea that the North American Free Trade Area might extend further south was given prominence by Bush's Enterprise for the Americas Initiative speech of June 27, 1990. This pointed to a hemispheric free trade area as a long-term objective, one that would include both bilateral negotiations and agreements with the various subregional trade groupings within Latin America in a process that would begin with the negotiation of loose framework agreements.[2] The initiative spoke of the importance of debt reduction and rescheduling, but it placed heavy emphasis on encouraging foreign investment, both by continuing economic reforms within the countries of Latin America and by creating a multilateral investment fund.

The relationship between these two forms of regionalism has become the dominant issue on Latin America's foreign policy agenda. Although relations with the United States have dramatically altered throughout the region (with the exception of Cuba), attitudes toward hemispheric regionalism vary. Mexico has, of course, already moved decisively toward integration with North America. Chile was the first South American state to request membership in NAFTA, and it has made no secret of its coolness toward subregional integration. The Mercosur countries have, in general, adopted a wait-and-see approach, looking to subregional cooperation as a bargaining tool vis-à-vis Washington and as a fallback alternative. This chapter explores the logic of these varying positions and is divided into two sections. The first analyzes the sources and strengths of the factors that explain the revival of Latin American interest in some form of inter-American hemispheric bloc. The second considers the factors that are likely to limit the growth of inter-American regionalism: On what issues does an inter-American regional focus make sense? How are Latin American perceptions and needs likely to be reflected in U.S. policies? And, if the prospects for inter-American regionalism are limited, where does this leave the future of subregional cooperation?

# The Pressures on Latin America

## *Power Political and Systemic Pressures*

One approach to the emergence of regionalism stresses the importance of external configurations of power and the dynamics of power political and mercantilist competition. It is certainly true that changes in the international configuration of power have been very relevant to the emergence of regionalism in the Americas. To a significant extent, the "return to the region" and the revival of Latin American interest in hemispheric cooperation has reflected the perceived relative absence of foreign policy and foreign economic policy alternatives. This process is by no means new, although it has been strengthened by recent developments.

By the early 1980s, the idea that the Third World movement might serve as a platform for the projection and promotion of Latin American interests had all but evaporated, and *tercermundismo* ("Third World Movement") has everywhere been on the retreat. Although Latin America placed great hopes during the 1980s on the expansion of ties with Western Europe, progress was limited: European political involvement did increase significantly in Central America and has, indeed, become institutionalized, but elsewhere, European professions of political support were undercut by the stagnation of economic relations and a European willingness to follow the U.S. lead on the management of the debt crisis. Although Japanese involvement in the region grew through the 1980s, it, too, fell far short of Latin American expectations.

Moreover, for many in Latin America, this pattern has been reinforced by the dramatic developments of the period since 1989. Though publicly applauded, the collapse of communism in Eastern and Central Europe has led to an acute fear of marginalization. Latin American governments have tended to see themselves competing with the newly democratic states of Eastern and Central Europe for a limited pool of aid, loans, foreign investment, and technology. They fear that the developing world will lose out in this competition and that, within the developing world, Latin America will find itself at the bottom of the list of priorities, unable to match either the geopolitical importance of the Middle East or the humanitarian pull of Africa and South Asia. There is fear, too, that events in Eastern and Central Europe—coinciding with the movement of the European Community toward completion of the internal market, with the European Economic Area agreement between the EC and the European Free Trade Area countries, and with renewed discussion of (and dissension over) monetary and political union—will lead to a period of sustained introspection in Europe. Even if it does not mean an increase in trade barriers, Latin Americans fear that it will certainly lead to a general European lack of interest in the problems of their region. And there is particular concern that Germany, preoccupied and burdened by the demands of reunification, will no longer be able to play its central role at the heart of the EC–Latin American economic relationship.

The logic of seeking to balance the power of the United States through an active policy of diversification reached its limits in the late 1970s and was reversed through the 1980s. As the counterpoint to this, the 1980s witnessed the renewed centrality of the United States. Its position as the region's major trading partner was firmly reestablished. The U.S. share of Latin American exports rose from 32.2 percent in 1980 to 38.2 percent in 1987. For Brazil, the U.S. share increased from 17.4 percent in 1980 to 29.2 percent in 1987, for Chile from 12.1 percent to 21.5 percent, and for Mexico from 63.2 percent to 69.6 percent. Critical decisions on the management of the foreign debt lay in the United States—with the administration itself, with U.S.-based multilateral agencies, or with U.S.-chaired committees of private banks. Indeed, the mutual recognition of regional "spheres of influence" (the United States in Latin America, Japan in Asia, West Germany in Eastern Europe) was one of the most notable features of the debt crisis in the 1980s. In addition, Latin America faced a U.S. administration that put a good deal of emphasis on recovering its power and authority in the region after what it saw as the weakness and vacillation of the Carter years. It is true that some of this "reassertion of hegemony" remained rhetorical and that practical implementation was mostly concentrated in Central America. But its impact was not entirely absent further south, most notably in terms of the increasingly forceful trend in U.S. trade policy and, in a negative sense, in the unwillingness to make concessions on debt management.

As in the case of diversification, U.S. hegemony has, in many ways, been entrenched by the broader international developments of the past two or three years. In contrast to other parts of the developing world, in Latin America, the end of the Cold War has certainly not opened up an autonomous "regional space." In fact, the invasion of Panama pointed to the ease with which Cold War rationales for intervention could be replaced by historically far more deep-rooted ones: the need to maintain "order," to promote democracy, and to safeguard U.S. property and economic interests. If the central structural feature of the new world order is its unipolar distribution of political and military power, then the problems to which this gives rise are nowhere more apparent than in Latin America. Alternatives to the United States are hard to discern, and to many in Latin America, the lessons of the 1980s suggest that direct opposition to Washington is both costly and counterproductive. Proponents of this view cite, for example, the dismal record of dissenting strategies on debt or the extent to which the Brazilian refusal to fall into line on trade and investment issues only served to provoke expensive and ultimately fruitless conflict with Washington.

The need to find a new basis for relations with Washington has led to a recasting of policy across a wide range of issues. From support for U.S. action against Iraq to policies on arms production and nuclear proliferation to the promotion of democracy, Latin American and U.S. policies have moved far more closely into line. Although the debate on hemispheric regionalism is, on the surface, mostly concerned with trade and economic issues, such issues form only one part of a broader rethinking of relations with the United States that has important strategic and geopolitical implications and whose institutional consolidation would amount to the creation of a new hemispheric order. The close links between economic and noneconomic issues is well illustrated by the ease with which the Latin American debate slips between discussion of free trade blocs, on the one hand, and the much broader subjects of "international insertion" or "alliances within a new international order," on the other.[3]

The renewed centrality of the United States provided a significant stimulus to subregional cooperation. Certainly, the growth of political coordination in the 1980s reflected a common rejection of U.S policies, above all over Central America and the debt crisis. Equally, the consolidation of Brazilian-Argentinian cooperation and the decision to create Mercosur was at least partially a defensive reaction to the prospective creation of NAFTA. As in earlier periods, one option was to seek to balance the power of the United States through renewed subregional cooperation. But as the perceived limits to subregional options have grown more apparent, the states of Latin America have shifted from a strategy of "balancing" the United States to one of "bandwagoning," that is, of seeking as productive and positive an accommodation as the constraints of radical inequality allow.

On this view, the viability of subregional cooperation built around Mercosur was undercut by Mexico's "defection." Not only did this weaken the collective power of Latin America, but the consolidation of NAFTA threatened countries like Brazil with substantial economic costs. Brazil's exports to the United States would suffer from Mexican competition, just as its trade to Latin America (especially in manufactured goods) would suffer from increased U.S. competition. And without the advantages of proximity and zero tariffs, Brazil would see a significant diversion of foreign investment to Mexico.[4]

Faced with these pressures, it is significant that the character of Argentina-Brazil economic "integration" shifted significantly under Menem and Collor, moving away from the earlier emphasis on intraindustrial specialization (especially in the capital goods sector) and toward a more orthodox approach that could be more easily integrated with possible future free trade arrangements with the United States.[5]

However crude this kind of argument is, it has the virtue of drawing attention to the continued importance of U.S. power. Given the undoubted improvements in U.S.–Latin American relations, the dominant political discourse has tended to jettison the language of hegemony in favor of "partnership" and "cooperation." But neither partnership nor cooperation is incompatible with the continued U.S. hegemony.[6] Preponderance and inequality among states can take many forms. At one extreme, inequality is manifested through the exercise of raw power and recurrent coercion. At the other, preponderance derives from leadership freely chosen from a group of otherwise equal states, a true primus inter pares.[7] Between the two lie the many varieties of hegemony.

By most indexes of crude power, U.S. preponderance over the hemisphere is still overwhelming, and the possibility of any resort to the use of force remains in the background of U.S.–Latin American relations. But more important is the fact that hegemonic powers have sought to avoid direct coercive force: first, through the creation and maintenance of regimes and institutions that both set the agenda and decide which issues are to be accorded importance and how they are to be treated; second, through the provision of benefits to weaker partners; and third, through the conscious cultivation of common values designed to legitimize authority. Hegemony therefore involves a sharing of benefits and a degree of active consensus on the part of the weaker states. From this perspective, we might even say that the renewed U.S. interest in regional institutions and the pursuit of common values presages a further attempt to rebuild U.S. regional hegemony after the crude reliance on coercion of the Reagan years.[8]

At a broad level of abstraction, then, this kind of geopolitical logic explains much about the dynamics of regionalism in the Americas. But on its own, it overlooks the crucial ways in which both the competitive dynamics of interstate relations and the definition of state interests have been affected by changes in the global economic system. Changes in technology, in communications, in the operation of global markets, and in the growth of global systems of production have had a profound impact on the ways in which Latin American governments have defined the two most important goals of foreign policy—economic development and political autonomy—and the range of acceptable trade-offs between them. Latin American leaders have increasingly lost faith with the kinds of inwardly oriented development policies and the schemes for self-reliance and autonomy that characterized so much earlier Third World thinking. Indeed, one of the most striking changes of the past five years has been the move away from development strategies based on import substitution industrialization (ISI), high tariffs, and a large role for the state. More and more governments have embraced economic liberalism—placing greater reliance on market mechanisms, seeking to restructure and reduce the role of the state, and putting greater emphasis on integration in world markets.

In part, this shift has been the result of direct external pressure from multilateral agencies and governments, as well as the increasing tendency to make economic assistance conditional upon moves toward economic and political liberalization. But recent shifts in economic policy have not simply been imposed from outside; they have significant domestic roots—in the discrediting and failure of previous development policies built around import substitution, in which wide-ranging subsidy programs and extensive direct state involvement in industry played a major role; in the increased recognition of the need for effective stabilization; and, most importantly, in the analytically distinct but temporally interconnected fiscal, political, and institutional crises of the state. Moreover, as illustrated by Mexico and Argentina, the implementation of neoliberal economic policies has proved—unexpectedly to many—to be electorally popular.

But these shifts in economic policy are impossible to understand without reference to the impact of structural changes in the global economy, and especially the increased pace of the globalization of markets and production and the dramatically increased rate of technological change.[9] This has led to a powerful Latin American perception that dynamic economies are internationalized economies; that growth depends on successful participation in the world economy; that increased foreign investment is central to the effective transfer of modern technology; and that the increased rate of technological change has undermined projects that aim at nationally based and autonomous technological development. The failures and limits of Brazilian policies designed to create nationally based industries in computers, arms production, and the nuclear sector provide a graphic illustration of the way in which new international constraints have undermined early notions of autonomous development. Structural changes in the global economy have also reinforced the common Latin American fear that economic interdependence is rapidly growing on a North-North axis and that Latin America and other parts of the developing world are becoming increasingly marginalized. Indications of this trend toward marginalization can be seen in the steady decline in Latin America's share of world exports (down from 10.9 percent in 1950 to 5.43 percent in 1985 and to around 3 percent in 1990), in Latin America's share of total direct foreign investment (down from 15.3 percent in 1975 to 9.1 percent in 1985), and in the fall of Latin America's share of both European and Japanese trade and investment.

How do these changes affect patterns of regional cooperation? Their most important impact has been to make the region more outward-looking and more dependent on the international economy precisely when the overall pattern of international relations is in a state of great flux. They have increased Latin American interests in the continued existence of a more or less open, multilateral world economy. But they also increase the stakes and alter the options when global multilateralism appears to be under threat. One option has been to look toward subregional economic integration, especially in order to attract increased levels of foreign investment. Indeed, the fact that Latin American countries having been moving together (if still unequally) toward economic liberalization suggests a far more promising basis for subregional economic cooperation than old-style UN Economic Commission for Latin America (ECLA) prescriptions. But the importance of increased integration in the global economy also means that subregional integration is, on its own, too limited in scope and potential and too easily undercut by the emergence of larger and more powerful economic blocs.

Thus, in a world where the outcome of the Uruguay Round has been in continual doubt, maintaining access to the United States has been of dominant importance, reinforcing the attraction of bilateral free trade agreements (FTAs) with the United States. FTAs offer the prospect of maintaining and guaranteeing access to the region's most important market and escaping the growth of U.S. protectionist measures (both countervailing duties, anti-dumping investigations on regional exports to the United States, and Section 301 investigations on Latin America's own trade and investment regimes).

This is significant given the obvious importance of the U.S. market and the contribution the United States makes to the region's trade surplus. It is even more important because so much of the success of recent export expansion in Latin America has been in manufacturing products and because the United States has been far more open to these products than either the EC or Japan. The U.S. share of total Latin American manufactured exports increased from 21.8 percent in 1980 to 49.5 percent in 1987. Mexican manufactured exports to the United States doubled between 1985 and 1987 and now account for around half of the total Mexican exports, replacing oil as the most important export sector. By 1990, manufactured goods made up 76 percent of Brazilian exports to the United States (as compared to 29 percent in 1972 and 43 percent for the EC and 17 percent for Japan). These increases in manufactured exports raised obvious questions about long-term market access, precisely because these kinds of products have been most susceptible to U.S. protectionism. In addition, the consolidation of such market access increases the attractiveness of countries for foreign investors, especially when combined (as in the Mexican case) with geographical proximity.

The changed character of Latin American foreign economic policy goals therefore explains *why* the United States has become so important and also why there is a strong incentive to prevent friction on noneconomic issues from disrupting economic relations. But these changes also help explain *how* many previous sources of friction have been overcome. The gradual implementation of market-liberal policies has removed many of the sources of friction that existed between the United States and Latin America.

Thus, much of the bitterness in U.S.-Brazilian relations in the 1980s focused on economic friction and, in particular, on attempts by the United States to alter Brazilian polices over trade and investment issues and over intellectual property rights (most notably in the pharmaceutical and informatics sectors). Brazil's (still lagging) program of tariff reform, the virtual abandonment of the protectionist informatics regime, and the decision to place intellectual property rights legislation before congress led, under President Collor, to a significant shift in the tone and character of relations with the United States.[10]

For Mexico, the perceived costs of failing to modernize its economy gradually came to outweigh long-standing fears that freer trade with the United States would impose unacceptable adjustment costs, especially in manufacturing, and would undermine the traditional quest to preserve national autonomy. Both Brazil and Mexico illustrate the close linkage visible in many parts of the developing world between the adoption of more outwardly oriented economic policies and a more general redefinition of national autonomy on issues as varied as nuclear proliferation and environmental management.

### Regionalism and Interdependence

A second approach to the emergence of regionalist groupings views regionalism in terms of the functional response by states to the problems created by interdependence. Such ideas have some purchase as an explanation of the new regionalism in Latin America but principally in terms of U.S.-Mexican relations. It is certainly true that systemic pressures of the kind described earlier have played an important role in shaping both Mexican and U.S. policy toward NAFTA. But it is also true that the U.S.-Mexican relationship conforms quite closely to the image of complex interdependence and that the density of cross-border interdependence has created problems that demand common management.

Economic interdependence is already at a high level. Around 70 percent of Mexican trade is with the United States, and Mexico is the third most important trading partner of the United States. Mexico's policy of unilateral trade and investment liberalization preceded moves to create formal economic regional arrangements. Tariffs have already fallen significantly (the average Mexican tariff is 10 percent, compared to 30 percent in 1985), and there is already a high degree of integration of cross-border production arrangements. In addition, migration has led to a high degree of human interdependence, which dramatically increases Washington's stake in the continued economic development and political stability of Mexico; it has also begun to have an impact on identity and social and economic values in Mexico. Ecological interdependence, in particular in the border regions, is well established, and the process of negotiating NAFTA illustrated the difficulty of preventing discussions of economic integration from spilling over into the environmental field.

Thus, the asymmetry of the overall relationship is at least partially balanced by the U.S. need to find solutions to such nontraditional security concerns as drugs, migration, and the environment. Here, at least, interdependence is more than an empty slogan. Finally, the powers to be accorded to the commission charged with implementing the wide-ranging and often highly technical provisions of NAFTA offer some possibility of seeing the kinds of social and political processes that have been so central to thinking about European integration: a process of institutional growth and spillover across different sectors; a leading role for technical elites and international bureaucracies; and the extent to which the institutionalized structure of the complex negotiating process can become the focus in mobilizing transnational interest groups.

Further south, however, the picture is far more mixed. Certainly, elements of interdependence have played a role in pressing Latin American governments to rethink their attitudes about the United States. The growing perception that narcotics are not simply a problem for the United States but also something that threaten both producing and consuming countries provides a good example. But in general, there is a striking contrast between the reality of complex interdependence between the United States and Mexico and the relatively low levels of interdependence between the United States and much of South America. Although still important, South America is not a major economic partner, and the relations that matter will continue to be those with the major industrialized countries. Indeed, Latin America's share of U.S. trade has been on the decline. In 1989, its share of U.S. exports was 13.46 percent (compared to 17.5 percent in 1980), and the region supplied 12.2 percent of U.S. imports (as against 15.5 percent in 1979). In 1989, Latin America represented only 10.6 percent of the total U.S. foreign investment and 13.5 percent of its foreign investment in manufacturing. In addition, the buildup of bank reserves and the process of debt rescheduling has drastically reduced the threat to U.S. banks posed by a Latin American default. Consequently, what is most striking is the way in which the scramble for inclusion in bloc regionalism by South America is a political response to the relatively low and, in some cases, declining levels of interdependence between North and South America.[11]

## Domestic-Level Factors

A third approach to regionalism stresses domestic-level factors. One common theme, for example, has been to highlight the importance of linguistic, cultural, historical, and political homogeneity in providing the basis for closer ties between the states of a given region and in fostering a new regional identity. Although, by most measures, such homogeneity is still far higher between the countries of South America than between North and South America, it is important to remember that, just as with nations, regions are "imagined communities," whose identities are artificially constructed and promoted for a specific set of political ends. There are no "natural" regions, any more than there are "natural" nations. But though it is not inconceivable that a dynamic process of region-building could eventually foster a stronger sense of inter-American identity, such developments belong to the future.

The impact of the process of democratization in Latin America is more important, albeit still ambiguous.

A good case can be made that democratization was an important factor in the growth of subregional cooperation, particularly between Brazil and Argentina.[12] However, even though it is certainly relevant to the possible extension of hemispheric regionalism (see the related discussion that follows), it is difficult to view democratization itself as a factor in explaining the renewed interest in such regional arrangements. The most important domestic-level explanation for the Latin American interest in hemispheric regionalism does not rest on some general similarity of regime type, on some putative solidarity between democratic countries, nor on transnational coalition formation between elite groups. Rather, it rests on the international requisites of specific regimes. Thus, most obviously in the case of Mexico, intensified regional economic integration with the United States provides external reinforcement for the political and economic policies of the Salinas government—on the one hand, securing external support for domestic reforms; on the other, making it far harder for any future government to instigate an alternative economic project.

## The Limits of Hemispheric Regionalism

### *Latin American Dilemmas*

Although the pressures on Latin American governments are very strong, moves toward the acceptance of a more cohesive regionalism involve difficult dilemmas and problematic trade-offs between issues.

**Economic Dilemmas.** The exact costs and benefits of membership in NAFTA for countries such as Brazil and Argentina, whose patterns of trade and investment are highly diversified, are much debated but still uncertain.[13] At best, the positive benefits (as opposed to the costs of exclusion) are unlikely to be substantial, and there is a real fear that inclusion in what is perceived from the outside as an exclusive hemispheric bloc will damage political and economic relations with Europe and Asia. In addition, much will depend on the durability and perceived seriousness of Mercosur as an alternative regionalist project.

Although Mercosur represents a very significant achievement by historical standards, increased strains and tensions have been emerging. Macroeconomic imbalances between Brazil and Argentina have become more pronounced, resulting in a trade gap in Brazil's favor of over $1 billion in the first nine months of 1992. Exchange rate policy, inflation rates, and the process of trade liberalization have moved radically out of line, so that, even in areas of managed trade, Argentine exporters have been unable to achieve their quotas. The continued failure of the Brazilian government to achieve economic policy coherence has certainly increased the number of those in Argentina who argue that greater emphasis should be placed on the negotiation of a free trade agreement with Washington, and it has reinforced Chilean doubts about the viability of joining Mercosur.

But perhaps more important than specific economic costs is the extent to which inclusion in a NAFTA or NAFTA-like agreement with the United States would place significant restrictions on the available range of political or economic policies. What countries like Brazil desire most is an FTA with the United States that preserves market access and acts as an insurance policy (or what John Whalley calls a "safe haven trade arrangement") against negative international economic developments but that otherwise does nothing to restrict freedom of action at home or abroad.[14] Yet such an option is not on the table, and the notion that even large countries like Brazil have the bargaining strength to insist upon it is illusory. The U.S. agenda is already well established, and future agreements would almost certainly cover the full range of "intrusive" trade-related provisions (investment liberalization, intellectual property protection, liberalization of trade in services), as well as further pressure for the broader adoption of market-liberal policies.

Much, therefore, depends on the future progress of economic liberalization within the region. Of all the major countries in the area, Brazil has been, by far, the most ambiguous in its acceptance of the new liberal orthodoxy. Its liberalization of trade has lagged well behind that of its neighbors, and its privatization program has been continually postponed, remaining a source of domestic political controversy. And the impeachment of Collor brought into office an administration under Itamar Franco whose commitment to structural economic reform remains uncertain and whose political support depends on a continued process of delicate coalition-building within congress. Moreover, this ambiguity on domestic policy has its counterpart in terms of international attitudes: in continued Brazilian doubts that the United States could be seriously interested in free trade agreements beyond Mexico and (perhaps) Chile and in the belief that, despite the depth of the crisis, Brazil has options not available to the rest of the region. On this basis, there remain powerful voices arguing that Brazil should continue with its policy of pressing for multilateralism at a global level, while actively promoting Mercosur and other subregional arrangements (such as the Amazon Pact) within South America.

However, the dilemmas facing Latin America are by no means exclusively economic. As discussed earlier, the renewed centrality of the United States and the changed character of Latin American foreign policy goals have led to improved relations across a range of noneconomic issues. How likely is it that this mutually reinforcing relationship between economic and noneconomic issues will continue?

**Democratization.** The promotion of democracy has reappeared as an important theme of the debate on inter-American regionalism. It might be argued that democratization has emerged as a factor that will reengage U.S. interests in the region and serve as a source of common values that will underpin and strengthen the growth of economic ties. Western governments have once more made democratization prominent on the international agenda, and it is noteworthy that the promotion of democracy was an important element in the rhetoric of the Clinton campaign. With the end of the Cold War, the role of democracy as a principle of international legitimacy has grown more salient.[15] Participation in elections and political activity has become a more central element of international human rights law, and the international monitoring of elections has become more widespread and accepted.

Attempts have been made to condemn challenges to democracy (in Haiti, Peru, and the August 1991 coup in the Soviet Union) and to make democracy and respect of human rights an element in recognition policy (especially in the case of EC policy toward the former Yugoslav republics). Furthermore, there is, in the Americas, an extensive inter-American institutional framework around which regional support for democratization might be built. Indeed, as Heraldo Muñoz emphasizes in his chapter, OAS policy toward Haiti and Peru demonstrates the extent to which the formal commitment to democratic government in the OAS Charter has become a catalyst for actual policy.[16] The ability of the OAS to coordinate regional responses to the military coup in Haiti and the "palace coup" in Peru and, more importantly, U.S. willingness to set its own policy within a multilateral framework might be seen, then, to provide solid evidence of a growing convergence of attitudes on democratization.

Moreover, democratization has already emerged as an important issue in the possible expansion of regional arrangements. Although the persistence of pluralist democracy is not an explicit criterion for admission (as in the case of the EC), the growth of U.S. concern with promoting democracy and the steady emergence of institutionalized forms of democratic conditionality would make the extension of economic regionalism to a nondemocratic Latin American state far less likely (and far harder to sell domestically). But there are obvious temptations to move one step further and to make democracy a formal criterion for membership in a hemispheric bloc. Unlike attempts to support democratization at the subregional level (for example, through the Rio Group or the Brazil-Argentina integration agreements), such a linkage would impose real costs on domestic actors and, together with the human rights provisions of the OAS, offer the prospect of effective international action.

However, the problems of finding effective means to support democratization and of integrating democratization into the broader regional agenda remains immense. In the first place, the problematic relationship between consistency and credibility that plagued U.S. human rights policies in the late

1970s is once more complicating international support for democratization. Much international action has been concentrated on weak and dependent states (Zaire, Kenya, Malawi, Haiti) while human rights abuses in large and important states are ignored or overlooked (China and Indonesia, most conspicuously). As in the 1970s, Latin America will have to be integrated into a credible and consistent set of *global* policies.

Second, the ability of external actors to influence specific domestic policies should not be exaggerated. Certainly, the difficulties of supporting Russian democracy are not unexpected. But can the OAS response to Haiti really be seen as a success? Third, the costs of effective international action (both in terms of carrots and sticks) are likely to be extremely high, and, for all the rhetoric, there is little sign of a U.S. (or EC or Japanese) willingness to bear these costs. Fourth, making democracy a high priority can all too often cut across other U.S. interests and objectives. This was, of course, a central feature of the Cold War period, in which fear of radicalization consistently forced the United States into the hands of decidedly undemocratic military regimes. But it remains a potential difficulty—for example, on the question of drugs, where the U.S. belief in militarization may run counter to the needs of democratization (economic development, negotiation, and social reincorporation). Even more critical would be a situation in which the process of political liberalization fails to keep pace with economic reform and in which Washington would be faced with a choice between its economic interests and political preferences.

Fifth, there is a question mark regarding the effectiveness of purely regionally based efforts to support democracy, most obviously in terms of support for economic sanctions. (See, for example, the ambivalence of non-OAS states on supporting sanctions against both Haiti and Cuba.) More generally, however, democratization and regionalism do not neatly coincide. It is not at all obvious that democratic or ideological common interest point Latin America in the direction of the United States. If democracy is to become a central element of international alignments, then political and ideological common interests are, in many fundamental ways, far stronger with Europe than with the United States. This is certainly true of political parties and ideologies, illustrated by the fact that 95 percent of the members of the party internationals consist of groups from Europe and Latin America.

Sixth, as the example of Peru demonstrates, democratic backsliding is not always easy to define and identify, and different elements in the broad definition of "democracy and good governance" may well come into conflict with each other. If there are to be democratic criteria for admission to a hemispheric bloc, of what should they consist and who would decide this? To take one emotive example: The Brazilian government may be democratically elected but still do little to counter widespread violations of human rights, including those committed by its own security forces. Finally, the perceived "naturalness" of democracy could erode very quickly given a successful challenge to democracy in a major Latin American state. Thus, the pursuit of democratization *may* develop as the ideological cement for a strengthened inter-American regionalism. But moves in that direction are beset with difficulties, and it is equally possible that democratization will either be quietly downgraded or else risk emerging as a source of friction and frustration.

**The Environment.** A second important issue concerns the environment.[17] Environmental problems have become a central issue on the inter-American agenda and are particularly important to Latin America for three reasons. The first is their intrinsic importance and the direct damage likely to be suffered by Latin America if problems of deforestation, soil erosion, and the deterioration of the urban environment are not tackled. There are also significant international costs attached to a failure to take the environment seriously, as Brazil discovered with the international campaign against Amazonian deforestation.[18] Moreover, the global environment provides Latin America with potentially significant opportunities because it is the one area where North-South interdependence is based on solid reality, rather than empty rhetoric. The effective management of the global environment is one subject on which the cooperation and active participation of developing countries is likely to prove essential, both in terms of negotiating international agreements and, more importantly, ensuring that those agreements are effectively implemented.

There are clearly some environmental issues that can best be dealt with at a regional or inter-American level. There have been a wide range of regional environmental initiatives (the UN Environment Program [UNEP] regional seas program, the EC environmental regime), and the OAS has recently drawn up its own program for inter-American environmental action in the aftermath of the UN Conference on Environment and Development (UNCED).[19] Cross-border pollution between Mexico and the United States is an obvious example of a fundamentally bilateral environmental issue whose management has already become the subject of detailed negotiations within (but technically separate from) the moves to a free trade agreement. It is also true that UNCED saw no overt confrontation between North and South America. Latin American states were in the forefront of Southern moderation in Rio; partly because of the gains, albeit limited, that were achieved (above all, the acceptance of the link between environment and development), partly because the ongoing sets of negotiations mean that there is still a good deal to play for (negotiations on filling out the framework conventions on global climate change and biodiversity and on the structure of the Commission for Sustainable Development), and partly because of an unwillingness to provoke a confrontation with the North in general and the United States in particular.

However, it is far from clear that inter-American regionalism is the most logical or most politically effective forum for securing Latin American objectives in environmental negotiations. The most obviously important strategic alliances are between Latin American and other parts of the developing world (though the developing world itself is deeply split on the environment and though such alliances would vary greatly from one environmental issue to another). Although easily exaggerated, the potential bargaining power of the developing world is considerable, and Latin America has a fundamental interest in using this both to ensure a fair distribution of the costs and benefits of global environmental management and as lever to force the North to address the broader question of inequality.

Moreover, although the United States has accepted the principle of environmentally related resource transfers since the Houston Summit in July 1990, it has been the least willing of the industrialized countries to make significant moves in this direction. In general, Europe has been consistently more willing to consider mechanisms to provide additional resources. And it is Japan, often pilloried for its environmental record, that has promised the largest amount of foreign aid for environmental projects. Thus, not only does the logic of environmental negotiations point Latin America toward the developing world, it also suggests that the region is more likely to achieve concessions from Europe and Japan and to face the United States as an opponent, rather than an ally. The deep divisions that continue to exist between North and South are mirrored within the Americas: divisions over the distribution of the costs of managing the global environment, over the choice of environmental priorities, over the ways in which sovereignty may need to be curtailed in the interests of environmental management, and over political control of the institutions within which these decisions will be negotiated or imposed.[20]

In addition, translating the ubiquitous rhetoric of sustainability into concrete action may well expose tensions within currently dominant ideas about Latin American development. Taking the environment seriously means giving a far higher priority to questions of distribution and social justice, to definitions of democracy that stress the empowerment of local groups and communities rather than simply regular elections, and to the need to build up stronger and more effective state structures. It will also inevitably mean facing up to the extremely difficult and politically treacherous linkages between the environmental agenda, preferred economic prescriptions, and international economic relations, both global and regional.

**Security.** A further important set of issues concerns security. The consolidation of a regional security order was, after all, the most important element of the hegemonic regionalism of the early postwar period. What are the chances that security might reemerge as a focus for hemispheric regionalism? There are some signs of convergence. The United States has placed considerable emphasis on both nuclear proliferation and controls of conventional arms sales as elements of its proclaimed new world order.

The proliferation issue in Latin America has been transformed by two related factors. The first is the rapprochement that has taken place in the Brazil-

Argentina relationship and the role that nuclear confidence-building measures and low-level cooperation have played in this. The second is the shift in Brazilian nuclear policy, highlighted by Collor's speech to the United Nations in September 1990 and illustrated by the public abandonment of the country's so-called parallel nuclear research program. There has also been progress in resolving disputes with Brazil and Argentina over arms sales to the Middle East and the transfer of missile technology. These changes open the way for the belated but very important consolidation of the Tlatelolco regime. More generally, Latin America's solid, if not wholly unequivocal, support of U.S. and UN policy during the Gulf War was a further sign of convergence in security perspectives.

But it would be wrong to paint too rosy a picture. The transfer of sensitive technology remains a problematic issue (witness the continued differences between the United States and Brazil over the transfer of supercomputer technology). A good deal of the public shift in attitude on these issues has been geared as much to please the United States and in the expectation of future benefits as it has been based on fundamental change in thinking within the political and military establishments of these countries. Latin American nations are distinctly unhappy about the growth of U.S. ideas on economic assistance to controls on military spending and arms sales. And underneath the public support, the idea that the United States had manipulated the UN for its own purposes during the Gulf War and backed only the selective enforcement of international law found an echo in many places in Latin America. The apparent willingness of the Clinton administration to consider reform of the membership in the UN Security Council is likely to expose tensions on this question, especially with Brazil and Mexico.

What of the broader security agenda? Mutual cooperation against extrahemispheric threats has been rendered almost wholly obsolete with the decline in Soviet power. There are certainly numerous instances of potential interstate friction within the region. But, particularly in comparison to other parts of the developing world, the overall pattern of the 1980s was positive, featuring the resolution of a number of long-standing tensions (most notably between Brazil and Argentina and Argentina and Chile). This suggests that whatever tensions continue to exist or reemerge are best dealt with by an increase in the kinds of bilateral confidence-building measures that have been developed by Brazil and Argentina and perhaps later by some form of subregional security arrangement. It is hard to see that there is either a military or a political rationale for U.S. involvement in such an arrangement. As in other parts of the developing world, the most pressing security issues are internal: instability resulting from social tensions, political polarization, drug-related violence, or environmental degradation. Security issues and a flare-up of old border disputes are likely to result from the underlying fragility of domestic social, political, and economic structures. But the very nature of the issues, together with the asymmetry of power between the United States and Latin America, works against the reemergence of an effective inter-American security system. On the one hand, Latin America remains extremely sensitive to anything that might facilitate or legitimize U.S. intervention. On the other, there has been a patterned divergence over the appropriate response to these kinds of threats, with the United States tending to favor counterinsurgency and militarization and Latin America looking more to social and economic reconstruction. There is reason to believe that this kind of divergence will reappear in the future.

These three issues are typical of the "new inter-American agenda" in that tackling them will inevitably impinge very heavily upon domestic affairs. There is no inevitability of conflict, and there are very substantial advantages to be gained from cooperation. But they all pose very serious dilemmas, suggest that a positive and mutually reinforcing relationship across different issues cannot be assumed, and point to patterns of alignment that are by no means destined to coincide with a hemispheric regional system.

## U.S. Interests

Although there is certainly room for creative statesmanship on the part of Latin American governments (particularly at a time when the exact definition of U.S. interests in many areas is uncertain), it is ultimately the response of Washington that will be the most important single factor in determining how far and how fast hemispheric regionalism is likely to proceed.

As discussed in other chapters in this volume, U.S. interest in regionalism in the Americas has grown significantly over the past five years. In part, this has been in response to the perception of growing trends toward exclusive regionalism in other areas of the world. In part, it has followed from increasing disenchantment with the GATT: with its institutional weaknesses, with the problems that it has faced in dealing with the complexities of post–Tokyo Round trade issues, and with the difficulty of securing key U.S. objectives during the Uruguay Round, especially trade in services, intellectual property rights, and agricultural trade. Faced with an erosion of the GATT, structured free trade agreements offer the United States both economic benefits (market access, the ability to ensure compliance with a favorable investment regime and adequate patent protection, and a means to promote microeconomic adjustment and increased international competitiveness) and a political framework for the effective management of other issues (drugs, migration, and environment).[21]

Moreover, even if the GATT system holds together, the prospects for increased economic relations with other regions are not promising. It is becoming ever more clear just how intractable the difficulties of political and economic reform in Eastern Europe are; the Soviet Union remains in economic chaos; and economic relations with China are restricted by political frictions. On this basis, the United States needs Latin America as a market in a world where free trade can no longer be taken for granted. It is, after all, a market in which the United States has an obviously strong historical position. It also has enormous potential (a population of about 430 million in contrast to 110 in Eastern Europe), and it is a market in which the process of economic liberalization has already made significant progress. Moreover, business and investor confidence is slowly returning to this market—witness the return of some flight capital, renewed flows of foreign capital, the revival of some bank lending, and impressive growth rates in several countries (the new confidence being most apparent in Mexico, Chile, and Venezuela but still absent in Brazil).

The regionalist option is strengthened by the fact that it can be deployed, albeit in various ways, by both liberals and conservatives and can readily be accommodated both in the declining hegemony thesis and in the idea of the United States as the world hegemon of the post–Cold War world. For the declining hegemony school, Latin America becomes the refuge from an increasingly hostile world. For the resurgent hegemony school, Latin America is a test of U.S. ability to give concrete embodiment to its still diffuse vision of a new world order, to act decisively in support of its values, and to assert its authority over recalcitrant or delinquent states.

Yet it is also clear that important factors work against U.S. promotion of a cohesive and broadly based regionalism in the Americas. First, U.S. economic interests do not point toward the creation of a close, exclusivist regional bloc. U.S. trading patterns are strongly multilateral (in 1989, 26 percent of total U.S. trade was with Canada and Mexico, 35 percent with Asia, and 20 percent with the EC). There is little hard evidence of a long-term trend toward increased economic regionalism in either the Americas or Asia, and, as Fred Bergsten has pointed out, "Geographical propinquity is no longer central to trading patterns."[22] A move toward regional blocs would risk cutting the United States off from the most dynamic world markets and would favor less efficient Latin American producers in a number of sectors over their more efficient Asian counterparts, thereby eroding the long-range competitiveness of U.S. industry. Moreover, it is difficult to see how an American regional bloc would significantly increase U.S. bargaining power in international trade negotiations.

Second, the rhetoric of regionalism must be set against countervailing trends toward economic globalization, in which the structures of global economic interdependence have followed from the consolidation of global markets and global production—a dense and complex network that could only be altered at extremely high cost. In particular, regional blocs would cut across the emergence of the complex cross-regional production arrangements that have developed both within and between companies and the rapidly expanding volume of foreign trade based upon transnational production.[23]

Third, U.S. economic attention in the Americas has been and is likely to remain firmly fixed on Mexico. Indeed, Mexico has increasingly come to dominate U.S. economic relations with Latin America. Its share of total U.S. exports to Latin America grew from 39.4 percent in 1980 to over 50 percent in 1991, and its share of imports rose from 32.3 percent to nearly 50 percent over the same period. As we have seen, U.S. social, political, economic, and environmental interdependence is far greater with Mexico than with the rest of the region. In addition, the Clinton administration's insistence on the need to negotiate supplementary agreements to the existing draft treaty is likely to complicate and delay the process of ratification.

Beyond Mexico, it is not clear that South American claimants to membership will be in a stronger position than, say, Singapore or New Zealand. NAFTA is misnamed in that future accessions to the agreement are neither politically nor legally limited to the Americas (unlike the geographical limits to the EC).[24] Inter-American regionalism is likely to continue to be used as part of the broader politics of multilateral trade negotiations. However, it is perfectly possible that Washington will believe that it can achieve its political and economic objectives without making regionalism or the construction of new economic arrangements a high priority. If Latin American states are already altering policies in ways that conform to U.S. interests and if deviations from U.S. preferences can be adequately dealt with on a bilateral level, why negotiate a free trade agreement? Hegemony, in other words, may well be seen to make institutionalized regionalism unnecessary.

## Conclusion

The hegemonic character of inter-American relations, together with the power of the political and systemic pressures on Latin America and the widespread recasting of Latin American attitudes toward the United States, creates a situation in which the U.S. *could* push for the emergence of something resembling a cohesive regional bloc. Despite the dilemmas outlined earlier and the range of crosscutting issues, it would be very difficult for even large Latin American states to opt out of such a scheme. Given a firm lead from Washington, the position of laggard countries, even large ones like Brazil, would become increasingly untenable, and bloc regionalism would "trump" and undermine subregional cooperation.

However, the limits to the scope and range of inter-American regionalism remain significant. Hemispheric regionalism is of growing importance to Latin America and, to a lesser extent, to the United States, and it is likely to remain so. There is much to be gained by regional cooperation, and there are some issues, such as migration, transborder pollution, or the drug issue, that can only be effectively addressed on a regionwide basis. But even in the economic field, the southward expansion of free trade arrangements is likely to remain somewhat patchy and ad hoc and to take place over a lengthy period of time. And though hemispheric initiatives are likely to occur, the chances of inter-American regionalism defined in terms of a closed, cohesive, and exclusivist regional bloc are reduced by (1) the balance of U.S. interests and concerns in which both globalism and regionalism will continue to be present; (2) the continuing ambiguities of U.S.–Latin American relations across a range of issues; (3) the range of Latin American interests; (4) the greater pluralism of the international system, even if the full impact of that pluralism has yet to work itself out (particularly in terms of European and Japanese foreign policies); (5) the emergence and consolidation of global markets for production, finance, and technology; and (6) the growth of global issues that cannot be contained within a purely regional framework.

Such a scenario would suggest that there is space for a variety of regional arrangements, some hemispheric, some subregional. These would reflect the differentiation of U.S. interests across diverse issues and with various Latin American states, as well as the heterogeneity of the region and the variation and complexity of Latin American foreign policy concerns. But the current European example suggests that "alphabet soup regionalism," in which many different bodies seek to assume responsibility for various areas of policy, is a source of weakness and potential conflict, not strength, and that the meshing of different regionalisms is, in practice, far from simple. For South America, the worst of all possible worlds would be one in which the United States was unwilling to clearly commit itself to the region, a world in which protracted uncertainty about future U.S. intentions worked to complicate, if not undermine, the recent movement to strengthen subregional integration.

## Notes

1. For a clear argument in favor of regionalism, see W. W. Rostow, "The Coming Age of Regionalism," *Encounter* (June 1990), pp. 3–7. For an overview of the reemergence of regionalism, see Louise Fawcett, "Regionalism Reconsidered," in Louise Fawcett and Andrew Hurrell, eds., *The New Regionalism and International Order* (Oxford University Press, 1993).

2. Some twenty-nine such agreements have been signed with individual Latin American countries, with groupings such as Mercosur, and, significantly, with extrahemispheric states, such as Singapore.

3. Thus, it is profoundly misleading to suggest that there is no strategic or geopolitical dimension to trade arrangements in the region. For such a view, see John Whalley, "CUSTA and NAFTA: Can WHFTA Be Far Behind?" *Journal of Common Market Studies,* 30, no. 2 (June 1992), pp. 125–141.

4. For elaboration, see Roberto Bouzas, "U.S.-Mercosur Free Trade," in Sylvia Saborio et al., *The Premise and the Promise: Free Trade in the Americas* (Washington, D.C.: Overseas Development Council, 1992), especially pp. 262–264.

5. On this shift, see Claudia B. Sánchez Bajo, "Argentine-Brazilian Integration in a Historical Perspective," Working Paper no. 131, Institute of Social Studies, The Hague, August 1992.

6. For an alternative view that sees hegemonic and coercive control giving way to a genuine partnership, see Augusto Varas, "From Coercion to Partnership: A New Paradigm for Security Cooperation in the Western Hemisphere," in Jonathan Hartlyn, Lars Schoultz, and Augusto Varas, eds., *The United States and Latin America in the 1990s* (Chapel Hill: University of North Carolina Press, 1993).

7. See Bull's distinction between dominance, hegemony, and primacy: Hedley Bull, "World Order and the Superpowers," in Carsten Holbraad, ed., *Superpowers and World Order* (Canberra: Australia National University Press, 1971), pp. 140–154.

8. For an argument on the role of socialization and ideological legitimation as central to hegemonic power, see G. John Ikenberry and Charles A. Kupchan, "Socialization and Hegemonic Power," *International Organization*, 44, no. 1 (Summer 1990), pp. 283–315. See also Joseph Nye's discussion of "co-optive power," in his *Bound to Lead: The Changing Nature of American Power* (New York: Basic Books, 1990), especially pp. 31–33, 191–195.

9. On this question, see also Thomas J. Biersteker, "The 'Triumph' of Neoclassical Economics in the Developing World," in James N. Rosenau and Ernst-Otto Czempiel, eds., *Governance Without Government: Order and Change in World Politics* (Cambridge: Cambridge University Press, 1992), pp. 102–131.

10. In 1990, Brazil was removed from the "priority country list" of Section Super 301, and the 301 action against Brazil's informatics regime was canceled. See Bouzas, "U.S.-Mercosur Free Trade," p. 529.

11. As Albert Fishlow argued, "Rather than the culmination of decades of increasing economic integration, [moves to hemispheric cooperation] represent an attempt to reverse a decade of weakening ties and economic depression"; see his "Regionalization: A New Direction for the World Economy" (Paper presented to the Latin American Studies Association, Los Angeles, September 21–25, 1992), pp. 13–14. For a broader review of North-South interdependence, see John Ravenhill, "The North-South Balance of Power," *International Affairs*, 66, no. 4 (October 1990), pp. 731–748.

12. For an elucidation of this argument and its application to Latin American regional cooperation, see Philipe C. Schmitter, "Change in Regime Type and Progress in International Relations," in Emanuel Adler and Beverly Crawford, eds., *Progress in Postwar International Relations* (New York: Columbia University Press, 1991), pp. 89–127.

13. For an analysis of the costs and benefits, see the chapters on Chile, the Andean Pact, and Mercosur in Saborio et al., *The Premise and the Promise*.

14. Whalley, "CUSTA and NAFTA," p. 139.

15. For a recent argument that democratic entitlement is changing from a moral prescription to an international legal obligation, see Thomas Franck, "The Emerging Right to Democratic Governance," *American Journal of International Law*, 86, no. 1 (January 1992), pp. 46–91.

16. Article 5 of the OAS Charter establishes the duty of members to promote "the effective exercise of representative democracy" and the June 5, 1991, resolution on Haiti states that the principles of the organization "require the political representation of [member] states to be based on the effective exercise of representative democracy." See Franck, "The Emerging Right," pp. 65–66, and Tom Farer, "The United States as Guarantor of Democracy in the Caribbean Basin: Is There a Legal Way," *Human Rights Quarterly*, 10 (1988).

17. For a discussion of environmental issues in inter-American relations, see, in particular, Heraldo Muñoz, ed., *Environment and Diplomacy in the Americas* (Boulder, Colo.: Lynne Rienner, 1992), and Steven E. Sanderson, "Policies Without Politics: Environmental Affairs in OCED–Latin American Relations," in Hartlyn, Schoultz, and Varas, eds., *The United States and Latin America,* pp. 235–261.

18. On this point, see Andrew Hurrell, "The International Politics of Amazonian Deforestation," Andrew Hurrell and Benedict Kingsbury, eds., *The International Politics of the Environment* (Oxford: Oxford University Press, 1992), pp. 398–429.

19. OAS, "The Organization of American States and the Issues of Environment and Development," Draft Report, OEA/Ser. G., May 1992, especially Chapter 3. For a review of regionalist options, see Peter H. Sand, "International Cooperation: The Environmental Experience," in Jessica Tuchman Matthews, ed., *Preserving the Global Environment: The Challenge of Shared Leadership* (New York: Norton 1991).

20. For an overview of these divisions, see Andrew Hurrell and Benedict Kingsbury, "The International Politics of the Environment: An Introduction," in Hurrell and Kingsbury, eds., *The International Politics of the Environment.*

21. Paul Krugman has argued that regional FTAs allow neighbors to negotiate at a level of detail and mutual intrusiveness that has become increasingly difficult at a global level. See Krugman, "The Move to Free Trade Zones" (Paper presented to the symposium on "Policy Implications of Trade and Currency Zones," Jackson Hole, Wyo. August 22–24, 1991), p. 35.

22. C. Fred Bergsten, "Policy Implications of Trade and Currency Zones," ms., August 23, 1991, p. 8.

23. For an examination of these trends, see DeAnne Julius, *Global Companies and Public Policy: The Growing Challenge of Foreign Direct Investment* (London: Printer for RIIA, 1990).

24. The accession clause to the NAFTA treaty (Article 2205) does not make reference to the Americas and allows for extracontinental applications for membership. The freedom for the United States to negotiate NAFTA-like agreements with third parties without the consent of Mexico and Canada underscores Washington's predominant voice in determining the ways in which NAFTA might be extended. For a discussion of the problems of accession, see Laurence Whitehead, "Requisites for Admission" (Paper presented to the IRELA conference on "The Politics of Regional Integration: Europe and the Western Hemisphere," October 15–16, 1992).

# 10

# A New OAS for the New Times

## Heraldo Muñoz

The Organization of American States was created in the wake of World War II, but it was soon rendered impotent by the Cold War. For very different reasons, both North Americans and Latin Americans arrived at the conclusion that the organization served very little useful purpose, and for many years they tended to ignore it. Today, somewhat paradoxically, the end of the Cold War has opened new prospects for the organization. And its actions in the areas of democratic governance and human rights, narcotics, environment, and trade have generated significant public attention.

One may ask, however, whether the renewed governmental and media attention regarding the OAS indeed signals its revitalization and whether the organization really serves important purposes in a post–Cold War context in which so many assumptions, arrangements, and institutions born out of World War II either have disappeared or are no longer valid.

This chapter seeks to answer these questions and to examine and evaluate the principal areas of present OAS activity. The central argument is that the OAS agenda is changing to reflect broader world transformations but that independently of the positive contributions the organization may provide in specific areas like drug trafficking or the environment, the promotion and preservation of democracy is the principal issue that defines the public profile of the OAS; it is also the one that will determine its future as a viable hemispheric political organization.

### The End of the Cold War and the New OAS Agenda

The sea changes in the international situation have posed new opportunities for the renewal of the OAS and underlined some of its enduring limitations.

Clearly, the end of the Cold War has tended to remove one of the principal factors behind the stagnation and credibility crisis of the OAS: that is, the perception that the hemispheric organization was an instrument of one of the superpowers in the East-West conflict. Although the OAS still carries the negative historical image of alignment with the United States, it has been able to confront new challenges and crises free of the ideological straitjacket of the Cold War period.

The relative decline of the old military-strategic component of security has been reflected in the OAS. Most significantly, a Working Group on Hemispheric Security, created at the 1991 General Assembly, has begun rethinking the role of the Inter-American Defense Board (IADB) and the Inter-American Defense College (IADC) and redefining their connections to the OAS. There is a strong argument for bringing both military entities under the civilian-diplomatic control of the OAS, to limit their scope of action to technical assistance on specific military or security-related matters, to serve as a meeting ground for civilian and military officials from the Americas, and, in general, to change them to reflect the transformations in regional and world affairs.

In this perspective, the IADB has opened its membership to all member countries of the OAS, not merely to the signatories of the Rio Treaty. Currently, it is undertaking, at the request of the OAS political organs, a project to remove thousands of land mines along the Nicaragua-Honduras border left from the armed conflicts that ravaged the Central American isthmus during the 1980s.

Similarly, although the OAS has a long history of technical cooperation on matters related to natural resources and environmental management, only in 1991 did it bring the environment—viewed as a new "security issue"—to the political level. The Inter-American Program of Action for Environmental Protection was approved, creating a Permanent Committee on the Environment within the Permanent Council, and various activities were initiated—ranging from publications to seminars and training workshops—to comply with the recommended measures of the Inter-American Program of Action.[1]

The international economy also has changed radically in recent years. Interdependence has increased enormously, and so has the degree of globalization of economic affairs. The new technological revolution has prompted us to question the notion of "national" economies and has altered the very nature of production, with "inputs of knowledge" becoming more important than capital, labor, and natural resources. Yet the arguments in favor of managed trade instead of free trade and the formation of regional trade blocs has led some to argue that trade wars could replace the Cold War.[2]

Despite the host of other institutions—public and private—involved in the international economy, the OAS has been playing a role in this area. In 1991, it created a Working Group of the Permanent Council on the Enterprise for the Americas Initiative, which monitors the tendency toward free trade in the

Americas and functions as a clearinghouse for up-to-date information on trade matters. More importantly, a process of reform has begun to radically revamp the old OAS Special Commission on Consultation and Negotiation (CECON), which, during the 1960s and 1970s, was a forum of confrontation on economic issues between, on the one hand, Latin America and the Caribbean and, on the other, the United States, thus leading to its gradual inactivity and political irrelevance.

The OAS and its predecessors have a long history of dealing with the narcotics trafficking problem. But beginning in the mid-1980s, as the problem intensified, it introduced new programs and initiatives. In 1986, the Inter-American Drug Abuse Control Commission (CICAD) was established to develop, coordinate, evaluate, and monitor the Program of Action of Rio de Janeiro Against the Illicit Use, Production and Trafficking of Narcotic Drugs and Psychotropic Substances. CICAD's main objective is the elimination of illicit drug trafficking and drug abuse in the inter-American region through hemispheric cooperation. One interesting feature is that CICAD has an executive secretariat with considerable autonomy. Although it is not an enforcement agency, CICAD has defined five main areas of action: legal development, education for prevention, community mobilization, harmonization of statistical systems, and access to information.

With the end of the Cold War has come a worldwide validation of free elections, democratic politics, and open markets.[3] This is evident from South Africa to Poland and from the final collapse and disappearance of the Soviet Union to the growing demands for democracy in various African and Asian countries. The appeal of centrally planned economies and the very notion of dictatorship (of either the Right or the Left) has become highly questionable.

Latin America has hardly been immune to this tendency. For the first time in decades, freely elected governments prevail throughout the region. And not surprisingly, the promotion and defense of representative democracy has become the centerpiece of OAS actions in the post–Cold War era.

Most of the critical issues today (such as free trade and drug trafficking) are, indeed, transnational and regional problems that cannot be addressed successfully except through cooperative, hemispherewide efforts. The OAS is therefore seen by many countries as a potentially useful forum to discuss and attempt to solve such matters.

This perceived new role and opportunity for the organization has been strengthened by the recent addition of Canada, Guyana, and Belize as full members. Similarly, the heightened importance of multilateral diplomacy[4] and—in the view of UN Secretary General Boutros Boutros-Ghali—of regional organizations in particular[5] in the post–Cold War period have underlined even further the new possibilities for the hemispheric organization.

Some countries may prefer a low-profile and weak OAS in order to deal directly, at the bilateral level, with the United States. But in the present world context of undisputed U.S. supremacy, at least in conventional terms, or "unipolarity," as some have called it, most nation-states of the Americas seem to want to preserve a hemispheric forum. This would permit a collective dialogue between Latin America, the Caribbean, and the United States, in addressing the common inter-American agenda of the 1990s.

A tacit agreement on this new common agenda has already emerged in the OAS, as seen in the new committees, programs, and activities dealing with issues from drug trafficking and the environment to democracy promotion and the Enterprise for the Americas Initiative. However, the OAS as an eminently *political* organization will be judged by governments and public opinion on the basis of what it does or does not do regarding the promotion and preservation of democracy in the Americas. In fact, the organization has been attracting renewed public attention to the extent that it has decisively reasserted its doctrinal commitment to promote and defend the exercise of representative democracy,[6] a fundamental component of the OAS Charter that was barely mentioned just a few years ago.

## The OAS and the Promotion and Defense of Democracy: Recent Actions and Some Suggestions

The end of the Cold War has furthered the promotion and defense of democracy in the region by removing the ideological and strategic connotations attached to democracy for many years. In other words, the perception today is that representative democracy can be defended in the Western Hemisphere without running the risk of being trapped in the logic of the East-West confrontation.

In the past, navigating between the claims of sovereignty and nonintervention, on the one hand, and of respect for human rights and representative democracy, on the other, hemispheric leaders and the OAS were obviously influenced by the tempo of the Cold War. Sometimes, it pushed them off course, even to the point of undermining, rather than reinforcing, democratic regimes, as in Guatemala in 1954. In the name of democracy, the OAS also became involved in the internal crisis of the Dominican Republic, and later, as the Cold War eroded, it firmly favored the ouster of Anastasio Somoza's regime in Nicaragua. In the early 1990s, by monitoring elections and promoting internal dialogue in Nicaragua, Paraguay, Suriname, Haiti, and El Salvador, the hemispheric organization expanded its role on behalf of democracy.

At the twenty-first regular session of the OAS General Assembly—held in Santiago, Chile, in June 1991—the organization took an important step toward codifying the abundant precedents for international action in the interest of democracy and human rights. In a formal declaration entitled the "Santiago Commitment to Democracy and the Renewal of the International System," the foreign ministers, after recognizing the need for the organization's renewal in the light of new international challenges and demands, expanded the hemispheric commitment to the promotion and defense of representative democracy. The following day, they adopted a resolution creating an automatic mechanism to react to coups d'état in any member country of the hemisphere.[7]

In a clause stating the rationale for creating the mechanism against coups, the member states invoked the preamble to the OAS Charter. They cited the charter's premise "that representative democracy is an indispensable condition for the stability, peace, and development of the region" and affirmed the necessity, in light of the widespread existence of democratic governments in the region, to make that premise operative.

Why did the OAS countries decide to take this major initiative to protect representative democracy? Surely, as suggested earlier, it had something to do with the end of the Cold War. The passing of that conflict sharply reduced the risk that resolutions endorsing hemispheric action on behalf of democracy would be treated as licenses for the pursuit of political ends related loosely, if at all, to the consolidation and preservation of representative government.

When, on September 30, 1991, the military forces of Haiti ousted President Jean-Bertrand Aristide, they triggered the mechanism created in Santiago. Within a few days, the foreign ministers assembled in Washington and resolved to recognize President Aristide and his appointees as Haiti's only legitimate government; they would also recommend that all member states take specific steps to economically and diplomatically isolate the group that had seized control. In addition, they dispatched a special mission to Haiti, composed of foreign ministers and the secretary general, with a mandate to press for the restoration of the democratically elected government. When that mission failed to achieve its objective, the ministers reconvened and stiffened their recommendations to include the immediate freezing of all assets of the Haitian state held in any OAS member state. They also outlined cooperation plans to implement once President Aristide's administration was restored and explored means for strengthening constitutional democracy in Haiti.

Well over one year after the military coup, no solution had yet been found to the Haitian crisis. But though the OAS efforts—joined by the United Nations in late 1992—had failed, the de facto government was unable to avoid diplomatic and financial isolation. The lack of real progress was linked by some to Haiti's history of undemocratic rule and the absence of a credible threat of force to restore the status quo. Nevertheless, seen against the hemisphere's traditional pattern of acquiescence (however grudging) in military coups d'état, the Haitian case at least signaled a crystallized will in the Americas to resist the enemies of democratic government.

The Santiago mechanism was activated a second time when, on April 5, 1992, democratically elected President Alberto Fujimori of Peru illegally closed congress, intervened in the judiciary, arrested several congressmen and political and labor union leaders, and suspended various civil rights, including that of free expression. A few days later, the foreign ministers met and stated that they "deeply deplored" President Fujimori's actions; they urged the restoration of democratic rule in Peru and called on the Peruvian authorities to fully respect human rights. At the same time, the ministers appointed a special diplomatic mission to travel to Peru to promote negotiations between the government and opposition forces for reestablishing full democracy.

Some countries, including the United States, cut economic aid to Peru, and the Rio Group prohibited Peru from attending its meetings. In this context, the presence of Fujimori at the OAS meeting of foreign ministers, held in Nassau, the Bahamas, in May 1992, was unexpected; reversing his earlier statements, he committed himself to democratic restoration in his country through a process culminating in the election of a democratic constitutional congress.

The elections for the constitutional congress took place in late November 1992. Some opposition forces participated, while others abstained, alleging a lack of sufficient guarantees for free and fair elections. The Organization of American States oversaw the electoral process. Clearly, the elections represented a step in the direction of democratic restoration but by no means ensured the full return to democratic rule in Peru.

The meager results of the organization's actions regarding Haiti and Peru suggest that, in order to make the democratic premise of the charter and the Santiago declarations operative, the OAS may need to adopt additional instruments and measures.[8] To be sure, it can be argued that legal theory does not demand them and that what is required is an addition not of language but of will.

However, that would be an oversimplification. In the first place, will must not only be felt, it must also be demonstrated if it is to have the desired deterrent effect. The Santiago resolution does not enumerate the measures that the organization is prepared to employ, although the resolutions on Haiti approved by the ad hoc meeting of foreign ministers list a whole range of steps recommended for application against the Haitian dictatorship. A systematization of such measures for future cases may now be needed.

In the second place, enumeration of measures in conjunction with operational plans for implementing them stiffens the commitment of member states, transmits a deterring message, and, if deterrence fails, enhances the efficiency of member state action. For example, all member states should have domestic legislation in place to enable executive enforcement action when authorized by the political organs of the OAS. And they should draw up plans for the scrupulous enforcement of sanctions. In some cases, for instance, it may be more efficacious to target the economic resources of delinquent individuals, like the domestic financiers of the Haitian soldiers' coup. Of course, targeting requires knowledge or the means to rapidly acquire knowledge about the location of the delinquents' assets.

Is consensus on the threat or the use of force as a last resort likely to form in any scenario now imaginable? The collective response to the overthrow of democracy in Haiti offers grounds for doubt.

Economic sanctions—particularly the trade embargo—have not been adhered to by countries outside the hemisphere; moreover, they have apparently hurt the average citizen without threatening the putschists' control. And to be sure, the mixed outcome of economic sanctions in the Haitian case do not guarantee that such measures would not be effective in other cases. Sanctions probably work least well when directed against economies in which a subsistence agriculture predominates. Countries with large urban populations and a substantial middle class will generally prove more vulnerable. Nevertheless, as the situation in Panama demonstrated, a de facto military government may be able to sustain control even in the face of sanctions that inflict injury broadly on the civilian population.

That the member states should feel great reluctance about employing arms for the defense of democracy is not without basis. Leaving aside important international law objections,[9] even when it achieves its immediate objective, military action can result in serious collateral injury to innocent people and their property. Furthermore, if democratic institutions are precarious in the country where force has been applied, their reconsolidation may require time and protection. Thus, if collective action is to achieve its broader objective, the organization may have to sustain its presence beyond the time required simply to displace an illegal regime. The cost and complications of sustained involvement are very real disincentives to direct action against antidemocratic governments.

On the other hand, if forceful measures undertaken at the request of displaced elected officials are ruled out, the OAS may have lost a significant instrument of deterrence and leverage. But using force to displace a de facto government will probably continue to be unacceptable to a substantial number of hemispheric governments and nongovernmental entities. The problem of who will exercise and control the use of force in an asymmetrical hemispheric context is one reason. The peril of selective application due to motivations tied to power politics is clearly another.

No consensus exists within the OAS on the use of military action against a dictatorial government. And there is probably no consensus regarding the value of peacekeeping to assist in restoring democracy. Yet some countries, particularly the smaller members in the Caribbean, are concerned by the prospect of power being seized by a handful of thugs who may be surreptitiously armed, trained, and influenced by foreign elements, not necessarily governmental ones. One way of reconciling doubts among certain members about OAS-authorized military actions with the legitimate concerns of others may be a pact among states willing to assist each other in guaranteeing the survival of democracy. Of course, the more states that participate in such pacts, the less the danger of intervention for ulterior motives.

A more solid foundation for peaceful collective action to support democracy and deter coups d'état was provided by the important OAS Charter reform approved in December 1992. That reform—the Washington Protocol—introduced the temporary suspension of member states in which the democratic process is illegally interrupted through the use of force.[10]

Still, identifying and implementing an appropriate response to the overthrow of a democratically elected government (or the imminent threat thereof) is difficult and demanding work. At this point, the OAS has no choice but to improvise a response. That will not do for the mission is far too complex and demanding. One complexity stems from the fact that threats to democratic government do not always originate in the cantonments of the armed forces.

It follows that the organization requires a cadre of persons on whom it can draw to assemble the relevant facts. It also needs an internal capacity to formulate a total strategy for meeting an imminent threat to any democratic government or restoring the government if the threat has matured.

The Unit for Democracy Promotion within the OAS might assume such a responsibility. The unit, created by a decision of the 1990 General Assembly, could add this to the tasks already identified, including providing governments with technical assistance on election monitoring and facilitating the exchange of ideas and experiences in strengthening democratic institutions. As a further step toward implementing the Santiago Commitment, the OAS member states could elevate the unit to the under secretariat level and, in any event, provide it with material resources proportional to its tasks. The same kind of support is needed for the Inter-American Commission on Human Rights, an OAS organ that continues to play an important role in the defense of liberty and human dignity.

A serious commitment to strengthening democracy must encompass positive measures in the economic sphere. Prominent among those that have been widely discussed in recent years is the alleviation of Latin America's debilitating debt. Although no longer as dramatic an issue in the regional agenda as it was in the 1980s, the debt's huge burden (in excess of $420 billion) and interest payments of roughly $35 billion a year have crippled economic growth in many countries. They have also forced the adoption of austerity measures that have degraded long-term potential for growth, dragged millions into the depths of extreme poverty, associated democratic governments with deprivation, and inhibited their efforts to deepen democracy through the transformation of rigid and deeply inequitable social and economic structures. In the name of consolidating democracy, an OECD-led coalition of countries orchestrated a 50 percent cut in Poland's foreign debt. That debt-reduction rationale is equally applicable to the countries of Latin America, which could benefit from a "debt for democracy" scheme extending beyond existing programs. Such a scheme could even include the purchase of small amounts of privately owed debt and their exchange for democracy promotion projects in the pertinent countries.

Democracies in the region also confront the reluctance of the great industrial states—states that champion the uninhibited play of market forces—to match rhetoric with practice. Under extraordinarily difficult circumstances, Latin American states have reduced the size of their public sectors, slashed economic regulations, and generally oriented themselves toward participation in the global economy. Protectionism mocks their efforts to compete and threatens their economic and political stability.

In launching the NAFTA negotiations and the Enterprise for the Americas Initiative, the first steps were taken toward establishing a hemisphere-wide free trade community. When the European Community expanded from its original core, democracy was an indispensable criteria for membership, affecting Spain and Portugal until they became democratic and Greece until it returned to democratic rule. Likewise, in 1986, when Argentina and Brazil signed the far-reaching economic agreement that led to the Mercosur integration arrangement, they emphasized that their purpose was "to consolidate democracy as a way of life and a system of government," and their respective presidents declared that a "basic requirement" for the participation of third parties would be that they be democratic countries. As the North American free trade zone moves south, it could serve a similar purpose. Both governmental leaders and nongovernmental organizations throughout the hemisphere could identify criteria that might stimulate the maintenance and consolidation of democracy as economic integration proceeds.

Still, despite the fact that there is a vital role for the international community in fostering and safeguarding democratic governance, we must keep in mind that democracy in any country ultimately rests in the hands of its people and on the existence of a civil society that can effectively use the instruments that democracy provides.

## Conclusions

Having partly reemerged from a long period of stagnation and political irrelevance, the Organization of American States is engaged in a process of renewal to adapt itself to the new times of the post–Cold War era.

Most analysts and government officials seem to agree on the convenience of maintaining a revitalized hemispheric organization to confront the challenges of the new inter-American agenda; by their regional nature, most such challenges demand a collective effort. Moreover, there seems to be a continuing need to have a hemispheric forum where Latin America and the Caribbean can collectively dialogue and negotiate with the United States and Canada on ways to confront the most salient problems that affect them. The resurgence of multilateral diplomacy in the post–Cold War further underlines the positive role that a strengthened OAS can play.

A new common agenda of relevant themes may already be perceived in the present work of the OAS, ranging from democracy promotion and human rights to the control of drug trafficking and environmental protection. But given the convergence of a long-standing tradition of support for representative democracy in the inter-American system, the global ascendancy of democratic politics, and the predominance of democratic regimes in the region, the renewal of the OAS has been characterized by an overriding concern for democratic governance in the Americas. The widely recognized facts that democracies are still very frail in the region and that democratic rule cannot be taken for granted have led to an unprecedented collective action to deepen and consolidate democratic gains and to discourage and oppose democracy reversals.

The crises in Haiti and Peru have demonstrated how difficult it is for an international organization to reverse coups d'état or illegal interruptions of democratic rule in sovereign countries. This, in turn, may also threaten the process of renewing the OAS by re-recreating an image of incompetence or paralysis. Still, the actions already taken in both instances by the organization in line with the Santiago Commitment, as well as the recent charter reforms to suspend undemocratic governments, suggest that most countries of the region agree that forceful reaction to overthrows of democratic rule is worth pursuing, even if the desired democratic restoration is not achieved. Such actions could represent something of a deterrent for the future, and, at the very least, they would signal a crystallized collective will within the Americas to resist the enemies of democracy.

Although it is important to recognize the great potential of a renovated OAS, one must also be conscious of its limitations. As with any international organization, the decisions of the OAS will be most effective when the countries affected by its actions are willing to accept its assistance or mediation. Beyond that, the OAS is essentially a *political* institution that operates best when it is guided by the consensus of its member states. Hence, for example, to expect the OAS—an organization still plagued by a controversial past and constituted by members equal in juridical terms but unequal in size and power— to use force to solve a given problem is simply unrealistic. The same can be said of the excessive expectations of some observers regarding the OAS potential in economic development and technical cooperation: It cannot and should not compete with other specialized regional or subregional organizations like the Economic Commission for Latin America and the Caribbean (ECLAC) or the Inter-American Development Bank (IDB).

Regarding the controversial question of the use of force (as well as in other matters), the OAS must work closely with the United Nations, which has the expertise and the mandate to engage in peacekeeping operations. Following the categories outlined by UN Secretary General Boutros-Ghali, it would be preferable for the OAS to act in situations that involve electoral observation, preventive diplomacy, and consolidation of peace, leaving peacemaking and peacekeeping operations to the United Nations.[11]

The achievement of relatively modest tasks and well-focused efforts may be the recommended road for the OAS as it continues its renewal process. The organization should, therefore, concentrate its political attention, energies, and financial resources only on a few policy areas of the highest political significance for the member states, setting aside obsolete or secondary matters.

This will require the strengthening of the general secretariat so that it may have a larger, politically experienced, and highly qualified staff. At the same time, some streamlining will be needed in other areas of the organization, such as technical cooperation. The existing Inter-American Economic and Social Council and the Inter-American Council for Education, Science and Culture, which saw their best times during the Alliance for Progress era, could well be combined into a single Inter-American Council for Integral Development. This would conserve resources, eliminate possible duplications, and perhaps also improve the volume and efficiency of technical cooperation.

To emphasize, it must be reiterated that the Organization of American States is, in essence, a political organization that serves as the principal forum for dialogue and negotiation on the most relevant issues of common interest to the member states. Some years ago, neither the United States nor the Latin American and Caribbean countries assigned much importance to this hemispheric forum. Each country, for its own specific reasons, had arrived at the conclusion that the OAS and the inter-American system in general should be disregarded when it came to critical matters like the Central American conflict or the external debt problem. This situation has changed in the 1990s. Crises like those in Haiti and Peru have been taken to the OAS; new instruments have been created to deal with breakdowns of democratic regimes; OAS electoral observation is requested regularly by governments of the region; new member states have joined the organization; the OAS organized the process of internal disarmament and reconciliation agreement in Suriname; and issues like the Enterprise for the Americas Initiative have been brought to and discussed in the OAS.

The process of renovating the hemispheric organization is still uncertain and far from completed. Many positive changes have occurred, but many more are needed. The new international context has helped the process of change, but, inevitably, the transformations of international organizations tend to lag behind the new realities. If expectations are not unreasonable about its potential, we may, indeed, see a new OAS emerge for the new times—an organization that serves the purposes and principles of its charter and the fundamental aspirations of the peoples of the Americas.

## Notes

1. See Heraldo Muñoz, ed., *Environment and Diplomacy in the Americas* (Boulder, Colo., and London: Lynne Rienner, 1992). Also see "The Organization of American States and the Issues of Environment and Development," AG/DOC.2834–92 (Washington, D.C., OAS, May 11, 1992).

2. C. Fred Bergsten, "From Cold War to Trade War?" *International Economic Insights*, 1 (July–August 1990).

3. See Inter-American Dialogue, "A World in Ferment," *The Americas in a New World* (Washington, D.C.: The Inter-American Dialogue Report, 1990), pp. 7–8.

4. According to a 1992 report prepared by the School of Foreign Service of Georgetown University, "Multilateral diplomacy will increasingly eclipse bilateral diplomacy." See *The Foreign Service in 2001*, Institute for the Study of Diplomacy Report, Georgetown University, Washington, D.C., August, 1992, p. 2.

5. See Report of the Secretary General, "A Program for Peace," A/47/277-S/24111 (New York: UN General Assembly/Security Council, June 17, 1992).

6. See, for example, the long report entitled "OAS Displays New Vitality in Bid to Restore Haiti's Ousted Leader," *Christian Science Monitor,* November 20, 1991, pp. 1–2.

7. See "The Santiago Commitment to Democracy and the Renewal of the Inter-American System," AG/DOC.2734–91 (Washington, D.C.: OAS, June 4, 1991), and Resolution 1080, "Representative Democracy," June 5, 1991. The resolution instructs the OAS secretary general to immediately convoke a meeting of the Permanent Council in the event of any irregular or illegal interruption of the democratic institutional process in any member state and, if necessary, to convene an ad hoc meeting of foreign ministers or a special session of the General Assembly that can adopt "any decisions deemed appropriate" under the charter and international law.

8. Some of the suggestions outlined in this chapter were presented originally in Tom Farer and Heraldo Muñoz, "Reinforcing the Collective Defense of Democracy" (Paper presented at the Inter-American Dialogue's 1992 Plenary Session, Washington, D.C., April 1992).

9. See Heraldo Muñoz, "Haiti and Beyond," *Miami Herald,* March 1, 1992.

10. See "Texts Approved by the O.A.S. General Assembly in Its Sixteenth Special Session in Reference to Charter Reforms of the Organization," AG/DOC.11 (XVI-E/92) (Washington, D.C.; OAS, December 14, 1992). The new articles recommend negotiations prior to the eventual suspension, a decision that must be made by a two-thirds vote.

11. Report of the Secretary General, "A Program for Peace," pp. 6–17.

# 11

# Cuba in a New World

## Jorge I. Domínguez

During the Cold War, Cuba was a significant actor on the world stage. But by the early 1990s, its international role had been reduced to that of a small and unusually isolated country struggling for survival. To face up to these new circumstances, the Cuban government has repositioned its foreign policy. Except for the continuing adversarial relationship with the United States and residual aspects of its relations with Russia, Cuba's current foreign policy is not markedly different from that of other Caribbean islands.

## The Good Ol' Cold War and Its End

The Reagans and the Gorbachevs danced in the White House in December 1987 to celebrate the end of the Cold War in Europe, but at that very moment, thousands of Cuban troops were crossing the Atlantic Ocean on a mission to lift the South African military's siege of Cuito Cuanavale in southern Angola. This episode captures well several features of Cuba's role in the international system from the consolidation of its domestic communist regime in the early 1960s until the end of the 1980s.

1. The Cuban leadership made the decision on its own and, for the most part, even implemented it independent of the Soviet Union. Cuba could not have acted, however, without the Soviets' long-standing military, economic, and political support.
2. Cuba's actions had important repercussions for U.S.-Soviet relations, although in this particular case, it led to collaboration to settle a southern African conflict.
3. Cuba's military deployment achieved the ends for which it was intended, namely, to repel the South African invasion of Angola. But the

deployment had other unanticipated benefits, such as the subsequent independence of Namibia and the accelerated unraveling of South Africa's apartheid regime. Force worked.

4. Cuba's successes reaffirmed its place as a significant international actor, demonstrating its self-confidence and prowess.
5. The U.S. government was irritated and unhappy with Cuba's international success even though there were, in this case, significant benefits for U.S. foreign policy: After Cuban troops bloodied South Africa's armed forces, the South African government became much more responsive to U.S. efforts to settle this conflict.[1]

These five themes recurred often from the early 1960s to the late 1980s, but they have changed in some important ways since 1989. Cuba is still, no doubt, independent from the Russian federation, but it has also lost essential Russian support for its ambitious foreign and domestic policies. Cuban actions continue to impinge on U.S.-Russian relations, although this is now mainly because the U.S. government wishes to erase all traces of external support for the Cuban government. Havana, meanwhile, remains as convinced as ever of the necessity and utility of military force to achieve important ends. But Cuba can no longer replenish its weapons inventories free of charge, nor does it have enough funds to purchase sufficient armaments in the world markets to keep its military capacity up to the levels that it deems prudent. The resulting insecurity fosters the Cuban government's sense that the country is a besieged fortress. Absent the Cold War and the resources that the USSR had made available, Cuba is no longer a major actor on the international stage. Indeed, the only constant remaining from the Cold War period is Washington's continued hostility toward Havana.

The end of the Cold War and the disappearance of the Soviet Union, therefore, have deprived Cuba of most of the opportunities and resources that had enabled it to conduct a global foreign policy. Without U.S.-Soviet competition, Cuba lacks the protection and the resources to deploy its forces abroad. And without civil wars connected to that Cold War competition, there are fewer insurgencies to support and fewer revolutionary states that might dare seek the assistance of Cuban troops to pursue their own ends.

As a result, the hundreds of thousands of Cuban troops that had fought bravely and often effectively on the battlefields of the horn of Africa and Angola have been repatriated. The tens of thousands of Cuban students and guest workers once posted in the former Soviet Union and the former Communist countries of Eastern Europe have also returned home.[2] Cuban military advisory missions have been brought back from countries near and far, and civilian assistance to many Third World countries has also been scaled back. Cuban support for insurgencies throughout the world has virtually come to an end.[3]

Some of Cuba's former assets have turned into liabilities. For example, were Cuba to increase its aid to certain of the remaining insurgencies in Latin America, it would lose even the modest level of support that it receives from various Latin American governments. Were it unilaterally to deploy its armed forces overseas to assist one of its allies in distress (from international enemies or domestic insurrection), it would risk U.S. military interposition or retaliation. Nonetheless, the Cuban government feels compelled to retain a large military establishment, now supported entirely by its own much diminished resources, for fear of the United States.

Beyond these important international political and military changes, the disappearance of the Soviet Union and of Eastern European communism has had a major adverse effect on Cuba's economy. In the mid-1980s, Soviet subsidies just for Cuban sugar and for financing the Cuban-Soviet bilateral trade deficit amounted to about one-sixth of Cuba's gross product (the most important other subsidy was the continuous transfer of large amounts of weaponry free of charge); the subsidy on sugar exports and the trade deficit from the European Communist countries amounted to an additional 2 to 3 percent of gross product.[4]

In early September 1992, Fidel Castro reported to the Cuban people that their nation had lost about 70 percent of its international purchasing power (in 1992 current dollars) as a result of the loss of all subsidies, that is, those just mentioned plus other lesser forms of assistance. Cuban imports declined from $8.139 billion in 1989 to an estimated $2.2 billion in 1992.[5] Castro went on to explain the catastrophic consequences of this import contraction for nearly every kind of economic activity. This economic implosion sharply reduced the supplies of imported foodstuffs, clothing, and gasoline for public and private transportation, thus directly affecting the people's standard of living.

Today, Cuba remains virtually as dependent on the export of sugar as it has been throughout its modern history: More than 70 percent of its exports come from this crop. Without Soviet and other subsidies for these sugar exports, however, the residual world market price determines most of Cuba's international sugar sales prices. Since 1982, the world market price has averaged about $0.08 to $0.09 per pound, though it fell to about half that level in 1985 and rose to about twice that level in 1989. Just as the Soviet sugar price subsidy was being cut in 1990 and 1991, so, too, was the world market price of sugar falling from its peak in 1989.[6]

In sum, once the Cold War ended, Cuba had lost much of the basis for its foreign policy. Its main international allies had been defeated or even disappeared, and its main international enemy seemed to have triumphed. Its economic foundations were in shambles; for the most part, its industrial products were internationally uncompetitive. Its role in the world had shrunk, and it became, once again, merely a small country in the Caribbean.

## The Transition to a New International Role

Heir to a social revolution, Cuba's political regime entered the 1990s battered and weakened but not bowed. As Communist regimes tumbled everywhere and some people in the United States even bet on the timing of Fidel Castro's fall, the pace of political change within Cuba—despite some innovations—remained slow. Only in Cuba and in East Asia have Communist regimes survived, and only Cuba and North Korea have attempted to retain political structures nearly intact. Nonetheless, to adjust to the new world, Havana adopted fairly significant changes in its foreign economic policy.

Before describing those changes, however, it is necessary to note some important continuities: On the whole, Cuba's exports to its previous market-economy partners have continued, even as its exports to previous Communist partners plummeted. I will use 1988 as a baseline (the year before the collapse of Eastern European Communist regimes) and focus on countries to which Cuba exported not less than $50 million or from which Cuba imported not less than that amount. Between 1988 and 1991, Cuban exports to the Netherlands, Spain, and Japan increased, and those to Canada doubled; exports to France and Italy declined slightly, and those to Germany fell markedly. Taken as a whole, Cuban exports to these countries increased slightly. On the import side, the same thing happened. Imports from France, the Netherlands, and the United Kingdom fell slightly, and imports from Canada and Japan and perhaps from Germany fell sharply.[7] On the other hand, there were substantially increased imports from Italy, Spain, Mexico, and Brazil, and Cuban-Soviet arrangements for petroleum swaps through a Venezuela held firm. On balance, Cuban imports from these market-economy countries also probably increased slightly.[8]

Cuba's capacity to trade with countries other than those once governed by Communist regimes was not, therefore, much impaired in the early 1990s. Interestingly, Cuban foreign trade patterns began to look more "more normal" for a Caribbean country: Most Caribbean countries, after all, do not trade much with Romania, but they do trade with Canada. The decline in Cuba's trade with Communist countries has given it a trade partner profile closer to that of its Caribbean neighbors—with the obvious but important exception that there is very little commerce with the United States.

In May 1990, at Varadero Beach, President Fidel Castro inaugurated two new hotels: "[For] the first time during the Revolution ... we have opened a project with ... foreign capitalists. It's quite an experience." The reason for his enthusiasm was straightforward; the only news was that it had taken him thirty years to conclude that "we don't know how to run a hotel, how to handle tourism and ... how to make money from tourism."[9] The number of foreign tourists that Cuba was receiving had, in fact, increased each year during the 1980s, rising from about 100,000 in 1980 to just over 200,000 in 1987,

270,000 in 1989, and 380,000 in 1991. In 1991, gross income from tourism amounted to about $400 million.[10]

The Cuban government's promotion of the tourist industry by means of joint ventures with foreign firms represented a double about-face: the welcome to tourism and the welcome to private foreign investment. Shortly after the revolutionary victory in 1959, Havana consciously turned its back on many aspects of the tourist industry that it described as repulsive and unacceptable, including gambling connected to organized crime, prostitution, and a servile mentality. The decision to search for the country's economic salvation in the tourism sector during the 1980s was, therefore, surprising. And even though organized crime plays no role and gambling is not legalized, some aspects of tourism that the government once found disturbing have returned. Prostitution, for example, has reappeared. Interestingly, the Cuban government decided to permit *Playboy*'s staff to enter Cuba; government officials also identified and persuaded some local women to pose naked for the magazine.[11] This new version of central planning represents quite a change from fighting heroic wars.

To mitigate some of the possible adverse effects of tourist development, Havana has sought to create tourist enclaves and to limit the contact between Cubans and foreigners. Nonetheless, as evident especially in May 1992 during the discussions of the Sixth Congress of the Communist Youth Union, some young people have engaged in what the Report to the Congress called "inappropriate behavior" (e.g., "black" markets in currency and goods, prostitution, and so on). More worrisome was the fact that even Communist party members engaged in such behavior. The barriers to contact between foreigners and tourists turned out to be permeable. Equally troubling to the regime's leaders was the public unhappiness with arrangements that discriminated against Cubans within the tourist sector: Some facilities and services were not available to Cubans unless they were invited by a foreigner.[12]

The regime was risking its political support as it sought to address some of its economic problems. As Political Bureau member Carlos Lage put it, "There are people who, when confronted with the country's need to give priority to tourism services for foreigners, become angry and upset." Nonetheless, for the sake of earning foreign currency and creating jobs domestically, Lage argued that Cuba had to accept tourism's "social and political cost."[13]

The second important change was the welcome extended to private foreign direct investment. In October 1991, President Castro explained to the Fourth Communist Party Congress that his motivation was entirely "pragmatic," adding: "Would that all the hotels could be ours! But, where could we get the money?" He insisted that he did not intend to change the overall political-economic framework of central planning and ownership of the means of production. But in fact, this same speech highlighted the magnitude of the policy shift.

By the end of 1991, the Cuban government welcomed foreign investment in virtually all sectors of the economy, not just tourism, provided there was a hard-currency gain to Cuba. Foreign investment was now welcomed in agriculture and industry and even in deep-sea drilling for petroleum under risk contracts. President Castro noted that the typical joint venture was a 50–50 split but that his government was willing to permit more than 50 percent equity ownership of a project. To lure foreign capital, he noted that the entire investment could be recovered in about three years—a high rate of profitability, though investors admittedly face a high political risk from hostile U.S. action.[14] For a Communist regime founded, in part, on the expropriation of foreign property, this was a significant policy innovation.

In early 1992, Cuban economist José Luis Rodríguez estimated that about sixty private foreign investment projects were in operation, half of them in tourism and the remainder in various other sectors. The total worth of the investments was $400 to $500 million (excluding a possible Canadian investment in a nickel project).[15] As things went with tourism, so, too, more generally did they proceed with private foreign investment. But some Cubans came to believe that the regime was "selling out the country."[16]

The net effect of these policy changes with regard to tourism and private foreign investment has been, again, to make Cuba's foreign policy look much more like that of a Caribbean country. Most of those countries do not send troops to battle in the Ogaden, nor do they dispatch military advisers to Brazzaville, but they do recruit multinational firms to run their hotels and to promote the export of industrial, agricultural, and mineral products. Cuba's new economic development strategy is not unique to a Socialist regime. It may either enable the current regime to survive or become an embryonic policy that is followed more relentlessly by a successor regime.

The next step in turning Cuba into a "normal" Caribbean country has been the process of Soviet military withdrawal from the island. In the fall of 1991, Soviet President Mikhail Gorbachev unilaterally announced the withdrawal of Soviet military personnel from Cuba. Negotiations proceeded for a year. Cuba at first objected that it had not been consulted about the troop withdrawal, and it indicated that only a simultaneous U.S. withdrawal from the Guantanamo Naval Base would fully warrant the Russian troop repatriation; in the end, however, those objections were shelved. In September 1992, Russia and Cuba agreed that all remaining Soviet troops would be withdrawn by mid-1993.

Despite all these developments, however, Cuba is not yet truly a normal Caribbean country. This is so for various reasons, of which two stand out: residual relations with Russia and the nature of U.S.-Cuban relations. The Russian-Cuban agreement on troop withdrawals broke a logjam in negotiations, coinciding also with the strengthening of Cuba's political allies within Russia itself. The two countries followed up with negotiations, parts of which were made public in October 1993, for a new trade agreement based on the stated rationale that they share many economic interests after thirty years of intimate collaboration. Cuba would resume exports of sugar, nickel, and citrus fruits to Russia at prevailing market prices (in contrast to the subsidized prices that had once been a central feature of Cuban-Soviet relations).[17]

More notably, Russia announced that, for its national defense, it would hold onto its military installations at Cienfuegos Bay and to its electronic intelligence facilities at Lourdes. Russia and Cuba also entered into detailed negotiations to complete the construction of Cuba's nuclear power installations, also in Cienfuegos. (In December 1992, Aeroflot's successor, Russian International Airlines, announced that it would resume flights to Havana and Managua and that Havana would be its Latin American hub.) Although the Russian government's position paper emphasized the "normality" of its proposed relations with Cuba, likening them to those of many Western European countries, none of the latter nations have military or espionage installations in Cuba. And as long as these remain, the Cuban-Russian bond will still make Cuba considerably different from its Caribbean neighbors.

For those and other reasons, U.S.-Cuban relations remain quite hostile. In the early 1990s, the rhetoric of U.S. policy toward Cuba returned to its origins: The very nature of Cuba's political regime was unacceptable. The principal difficulty was how to implement that policy. In 1992, the principal U.S. policy innovation with regard to Cuba was the adoption of the so-called Cuban Democracy Act, sponsored by U.S. Rep. Robert Torricelli and signed into law by President George Bush. The act imposed penalties on U.S. firms whose subsidiaries based in third countries traded with Cuba.

For the Cuban government, the Torricelli Act was a bonanza. Before its people and the world, Havana could present the act as palpable evidence that the United States was truly an enemy. Most of the trade to be cut off was in foodstuffs, enabling the Cuban government to describe the United States as an agent of hunger. Because Cuba could proceed to buy the same products from other companies, however, the net impact on Cuban consumption should be negligible.

The act's main outcome was to rally U.S. trade partners to protest the extraterritorial extension of U.S. legislation. Most of those protests were made bilaterally. In addition, on November 24, 1992, the United Nations General Assembly approved a resolution introduced by the Cuban government, entitled "The Need to Terminate the U.S. Economic, Trade and Financial Blockade Against Cuba." The resolution expressed concern over laws and regulations whose extraterritorial impacts affect the sovereignty of other states, and it called on member countries not to cooperate with U.S. policies toward Cuba. It carried with fifty-nine yeas, three nays, and seventy-one abstentions. Only Israel and Romania joined the United States in voting no. Russia and all but two members of the European Community abstained; France and Spain voted yes, as did Canada, China, and all the larger Latin American countries except Argentina and Peru, which also abstained.

This international victory recalls the continuing support given to the Cuban government by much of the international community, especially in the nonaligned movement (over which Cuba once presided) and in Latin America. It underlines the skill that Havana's diplomats have shown, time and again, in international forums. But it probably could not have happened without Washington's assistance.

The Cuban government's principal response to the United States is to resist Washington and whatever demands it might make. Coupled with this insistent and often reiterated view is the assertion that Cuba is willing to discuss all matters with the United States on the basis of sovereign equality, which would mean the early dismantling of U.S. economic embargo policies. The Cuban government does not state, however, what it might be willing to do to accommodate the United States. President Castro has often said that Cuba should not yield an inch because the U.S. government will simply escalate its demands; this observation would suggest that the Cuban government expects Washington to make unilateral changes in its policies toward Cuba.

The leaders in Havana could reasonably argue that all but one of the important issues in dispute between the United States and Cuba are now settled to Washington's satisfaction. There are no longer any Cuban troops in Angola or in Ethiopia; there are no Cuban military personnel and few Cuban civilians in Nicaragua (most of those still there are health personnel). The Salvadoran civil war has come to an end, and the U.S.-backed regime remains. Cuban support for insurgencies has dwindled. The Russian-Cuban entente is but a pale shadow of the former Soviet-Cuban alliance. And Cuba's terms for private foreign investment are quite acceptable to many businesses.

Thus, only the very nature of the Cuban regime remains a problem. President Castro has repeatedly stated his willingness to die fighting before yielding—standing alone, defiant still—now as in decades past, as he claims Cubans have done over the centuries in confronting foreign empires. The difficulty with the current U.S.-Cuban impasse is that it is just that: an impasse that prevents either party from achieving its goals.

## Policy Responses

For Cuba, a strategy of survival and resistance may steel the spirit and preserve national dignity, but it surely promises a grim future unless it can be accompanied by major changes in national politics and economics. Mere resistance offers no hope except tears, sweat, and perhaps blood. The prospects in tourism and other economic activities on which Cuban government places its hopes seem poor unless U.S.-Cuban relations improve, thereby removing the obstacles that such hostility poses to economic collaboration or to Cuba's reengagement in the world economy.

Cuba's international political space will remain very narrow for the foreseeable future. The major Latin American governments, constituted as the Rio Group, have, since 1991, sought to protect Cuba's sovereignty but also to edge Havana toward domestic political reforms. Its relations with those Latin American countries will not improve much unless there is a wider political opening in Cuba. And though Cuba's trade relations with European countries, Canada, and Japan may remain at the levels of the early 1990s, that will not rescue the nation from either economic stagnation or international isolation.

Cuba's political and economic relations with China have improved greatly. Sino-Cuban relations had soured in the mid-1960s, in part for bilateral reasons and in part because Havana cast its lot with the Soviet government in the midst of the Sino-Soviet disputes of those years. In the late 1970s, Cuba also opposed China's turn toward market-based economic policies. As the 1980s progressed, Sino-Cuban relations improved again, especially as Gorbachev's perestroika gathered force; Cuba came to see China as the more politically resilient Communist regime.[18]

Cuban exports to and imports from China increased by a factor of 2.5 from 1987 to 1989, when, by either measure, China had become Cuba's third most important trading partner (after the USSR and East Germany). By 1991, Cuba's exports to China had fallen slightly, but China had become Cuba's most important export market after the Russian federation; at the same time, Cuba's imports from China had grown somewhat, ranking third behind Russia and Spain. Nonetheless, China was neither willing nor able to subsidize the Cuban economy, nor does it wish to confront the United States on behalf of Cuba. Sino-Cuban trade proceeds at market prices.[19] By the end of 1992, Political Bureau member Carlos Lage publicly cited China as the one other country whose "experience" Cuban leaders seek "to study, analyze, and keep … in mind."[20]

For the leaders in Havana, most of the changes in the international political and economic systems since the end of the Cold War have been adverse. Cuba's capacity to project power in the world, to resist the United States, and to improve the standard of living of its people have all suffered. Its opportunities to exert international influence have narrowed greatly, as superpower conflicts end and civil wars turn into civil peace. In the days of the Cold War, influence belonged to those who had the guns and the guts; influence in the 1990s goes to those who have economic dynamism. In turn, in the early 1990s, Cuba faced an emboldened and more hostile U.S. government. Moreover, the collapse of the Communist regimes and the evolution of politics in Latin America fostered the widely held conviction that pluralist democracy is the preferred form for the organization of domestic politics: Even Latin America was challenging the Cuban political regime's very legitimacy.

To those adverse trends, Cuban leaders responded with surprising willingness to alter their foreign economic policies but a virtually unyielding resistance to changes in the domestic organization of politics. Although they repatriated their troops and bid adieu to Russians and other former Soviets, they also sought, in the early 1990s, to crush the small human rights and opposition groups that had operated with some limited liberties. Cuba's foreign economic profile began to look more like that of the Caribbean, but its politics once again began to include protests about tourism and about selling out the country.

Curiously, the prospect that leaders in Havana might adjust to becoming merely the governors of a Caribbean country may surprise some who have been writing about Cuba's future. For Susan Kaufman Purcell, for example, the only plausible scenario is collapse, not adjustment, even though adjustment (albeit painful) has been Cuba's pattern for several years.[21] For Edward Gonzalez and David Ronfeldt, the only circumstance in which they foresee Cuba's current regime surviving is in confrontation with the United States, even though Havana's actions in the recent past have removed most of the reasons for any such confrontations.[22] Meanwhile, the recent historical record suggests, on the contrary, that the Cuban regime might continue to linger and, from the perspective of international relations, even become a little boring.

Bereft of its closest allies, who literally disappeared, and saddled with an internationally uncompetitive economy, Cuba's foreseeable future at home is grim. And it will remain so no matter what changes may occur in its domestic politics. The international structural circumstances that had once brought resources to Cuba are gone, and they are not likely to be replaced on the same scale now that the superpower competition is over.

If the Cuban government wishes to make no changes beyond those few that it has already implemented, the scenarios for the future are quite narrow. The regime has adapted its economic policies enough that it could well survive; indeed, the Cuban regime has already been more resilient than that of its erstwhile Communist allies in the Soviet Union and Eastern Europe. But this strategy is unlikely to return the country to a path of economic growth. Rather, it will probably bring a continuation of the extremely austere standard of living, along with the erosion of social policy gains from the past three decades.

If the Cuban government wishes a better future for its people, then it must take some calculated risks. Bold behavior has never been alien to Cuba's leaders, so the following is not an unthinkable strategy: Confident that it retains the support of most Cubans (or at least that it has more support than any alternative government), President Castro's regime chooses to open up domestic politics and free up domestic markets even more. The opening up of domestic markets might resemble that in the People's Republic of China. The opening up of domestic politics could begin primarily in the confines of the existing constitution, provided that the electoral laws were to be liberalized to ease the right of the opposition to run for office and to contest the Communist party's power openly and lawfully. The more of these domestic policy changes that occur, the more Cuba's international circumstances are likely to improve.

To be sure, such a modest political opening would not satisfy the regime's domestic and international opponents, but the Cuban government would have transformed the terms of the debate—a debate that, in the early 1990s, it was losing badly at the international level for Cuba's leadership was seen as recalcitrant, rigid, and out of touch. The risk would be, of course, that such an opening might be the beginning of the end for the regime. Taking the risk would require confidence that the regime still retained support from an effective majority of Cubans—a confidence that could be misplaced. Therefore, this would not be an easy choice for the Cuban government, but it is the only one that offers even a hint of a better future under the current regime.[23]

If Cuba's current leaders were replaced, the nature of its relations with the United States would undoubtedly change; all Russian military and intelligence facilities would also likely be removed. Nonetheless, important features of Cuba's international relations would remain much as they were under Castro. The nation's economy would still be bankrupt, and its exports generally uncompetitive and overwhelmingly dependent on sugar. And the prospects of significant U.S. assistance for a non-Communist Cuba are not good. The United States is likely to have a large budget deficit throughout the 1990s, which will prevent it from committing vast public sums to Cuba. In the early 1990s, the United States had an unimpressive record in terms of providing economic assistance to countries that had replaced governments that, in the 1980s, the United States either sought to overthrow (such as Nicaragua's) or did overthrow (such as Panama's). The U.S. government is not likely to cancel its domestic protectionist policies to permit Cuba to export sugar to the United States; in the 1980s, it had toughened its protection of the domestic sugar industry at the expense of Caribbean and Central American sugar exporters. Russia and several former Communist countries would therefore remain Cuba's main export markets for sugar.

Under a full replacement scenario, the new Cuban government would accelerate the search for private foreign investment, continuing and reinforcing the Castro government's policies of the early 1990s. Cuba would expand its tourism sector, as well. Fleeing from economic hardship, a great many Cubans would seek to emigrate to the United States, just as their neighbors in other Caribbean countries do today. These Cubans would be deemed economic migrants, no longer political refugees, and though this would not stop them from migrating—just as U.S. barriers have not stopped Dominicans—the new would-be Cuban migrants would, by and large, be illegal.

In addition, Cuba sits astride many of the drug traffic routes from northern South America. Some of Cuba's newly freed entrepreneurs and perhaps some of its underpaid government officials might collaborate with traffickers, thereby adding yet another dimension to Cuba's Caribbeanization: Cuba would pose a new problem for U.S. drug interdiction. Were Cuba's new regime to collaborate with the United States by repressing both migration and drug trafficking, it would, in effect, return to the Castro government's policies: The only difference is that Castro's collaboration with the United States over these matters was mostly implicit, and such implicit collaboration broke down from time to time.

The point, of course, is that today, more than at any time in the past thirty years, Cuba's margin of maneuver in the restructured international system has come to be defined by its unchangeable location on the map and by the weakness of its economy. Cuba's current political regime has begun to adapt to these circumstances; a possible successor regime would find itself under parallel constraints and opportunities. Any future government would need to build on the foreign policy that the Castro government formulated and began to implement in the early 1990s, that is, Cuba's return to the Caribbean. Whatever its leadership or prevailing ideology, this nation will certainly be saddled with its geography and the burdens of its recent history.

In the longer term, Cuba's prospects might be better. The normalization of its foreign economic policies builds on some of the nation's comparative advantage in ways that any Cuban government might develop. Ultimately,. Cuba's main resource is its people. Cubans remain a well educated, healthy people, extraordinarily resourceful under extremely adverse circumstances at home and abroad and with a wide and varied international experience. But if the Castro government seeks a brighter future for Cuba—a future less scarred by misery and even violence—it will need to free the people's energies for economic growth, rethink the nature of the nations's domestic politics, and further reshape relations with its neighbors in the Americas. If the present leadership lacks the courage and imagination to make major changes, Cubans will have a very difficult time in the 1990s.

### Notes

1. Cuba's successful military assistance to Ethiopia to repel a Somali invasion in 1977–1978 provided another occasion on which the U.S. government was irritated with a Cuban military success despite the fact that it coincided with U.S. policy objectives: The United States verbally opposed that Somali action.

2. By their own choice, several hundred have not returned to Cuba. Many started careers and families in those countries. Others sought asylum.

3. U.S. government officials assert that some Cuban support continues to certain insurgencies. I have not been able to verify these charges independently. Some residual Cuban support no doubt continues to movements that Havana has supported in the past, in settings where civil peace has not yet been achieved in full—e.g., the Palestine Liberation Organization, the African National Congress, and the former Spanish Sahara's POLISARIO.

4. See the calculations in Jorge I. Domínguez, *To Make a World Safe for Revolution: Cuba's Foreign Policy* (Cambridge, Mass.: Harvard University Press, 1989), pp. 87, 95.

5. *Granma,* September 8, 1992, p. 3. This calculation involves various Cuban government guesses. About one-sixth of the loss (roughly $1 billion) refers to indirect economic costs, such as the unreliability of supplies. This may well be an underestimate. The calculation also includes an estimate of the loss in Soviet sugar subsidies worth just under $2.5 billion. Because the calculation is made with reference to the so-called world market price (a residual market), not to the prices that Cuba had actually been receiving in its international sugar market transactions, this number may somewhat overestimate the magnitude of the subsidy loss. For a technical discussion, see Jorge Pérez López, *The Economics of Cuban Sugar* (Pittsburgh, Pa.: University of Pittsburgh Press, 1991), Chapter 9. On balance, however, the order of magnitude of the loss in purchasing power is probably right.

6. Pérez-López, *The Economics of Cuban Sugar,* pp. 140, 154. U.S. Central Intelligence Agency, Directorate of Intelligence, *Cuba: Handbook of Trade Statistics* (U), ALA 92–10033 (Washington, D.C.: CIA, 1992), p. 59, hereafter cited as CIA.

7. In 1991, the former East Germany and West Germany reported as a single country. There is little doubt that imports from East Germany had fallen. On the other hand, imports from West Germany had increased each year from 1986 through 1990. CIA, *Cuba: Handbook of Trade Statistics* (U), pp. 4–5.

8. Ibid., pp. 4–7.

9. *Granma Weekly Review,* May 27, 1990, p. 2.

10. Comité Estatal de Estadísticas, *Anuario estadístico de Cuba, 1989* (Havana: Cuban government, 1990), p. 397; presentation by Cuban economist José Luis Rodríguez, deputy director of Cuba's Centro de Investigaciones de la Economía Mundial, at the Wilson Center, Washington D.C., April 29, 1992.

11. Jeff Cohen, "Cuba Libre," *Playboy* (March 1991), pp. 69–74, 157–158.

12. *Juventud Rebelde,* March 22, 1992, p. 5.

13. *U.S. FBIS Daily Report, Latin America,* November 19, 1992, p. 2.

14. *Bohemia,* October 25, 1991, pp. 37–38.

15. Conversation with José Luis Rodríguez, April 27, 1992.

16. *Juventud Rebelde,* p. 5.

17. For an interesting and well-informed Russian perspective on these negotiations, see Sergo Mikoyan's chapter in this volume.

18. For a reciprocal perspective, noting China's interest in relations with Cuba, see Feng Xu's chapter in this volume.

19. Gladys Hernández, "Las relaciones comerciales entre Cuba y China 1960–1990: Evolución preliminar," *Boletín de información sobre economía cubana,* 1, no. 4 (April 1992), pp. 2–9; *Anuario estadístico de Cuba, 1989,* pp. 253, 255, 257, 259; CIA, *Cuba: Handbook of Trade Statistics* (U).

20. *U.S. FBIS Daily Report, Latin America*, p. 3.

21. Susan Kaufman Purcell, "Collapsing Cuba," *Foreign Affairs*, 71, no. 1 (1992), pp. 130–145.

22. Edward Gonzalez and David Ronfeldt, *Cuba Adrift in a Postcommunist World*, report no. R-4231-USDP (Santa Monica, Calif.: Rand Corporation, 1992), Chapter 5.

23. For a thoughtful assessment of the harsh choices before Cuba's leaders, see Manuel Pastor, Jr., "External Shocks and Adjustment in Contemporary Cuba," working paper, the International & Public Affairs Center, Occidental College (Los Angeles, 1992).

# 12

# Confronting a New World: Latin American Policy Responses

## The New World Reconsidered
### *José Octavio Bordón*

From the fall of the Berlin Wall in November 1989 to the allied forces' triumph over Iraq early in 1991, a sense of euphoria gripped the West, even in Latin America's southern reaches. Grand talk of the "end of history," the "new world order," and a united Europe was matched in the Western Hemisphere by ardent optimism about consolidating democracy and beginning a new economic boom on the basis of neoliberal reforms. In this upbeat context, President George Bush launched his surprising and attractive Enterprise for the Americas Initiative. For a brief time, it seemed possible to imagine democracy, free trade, and growing prosperity throughout the Americas in a new world at peace.

This buoyant optimism was understandable after so many years of Cold War frustration and after Latin America's devastating "lost decade" of economic stagnation. But the positive enthusiasm was also due, in truth, to intellectual and political laziness, a little wishful thinking, and the bad habit of accepting ideological clichés without confronting pragmatic realities.

With the passage of time and with greater perspective, it is evident that there is no new world order but rather messy and violent disorder; that European unity is still quite far off; that the world economy is slumping; that the United States, although the only remaining "superpower," has had its power reduced by grave internal problems; that Latin American democracy is highly uneven, fragile, and incomplete; that the "Washington consensus" on free market economics and a reduced state role is not likely to alleviate dire poverty; that U.S.–Latin American relations will continue to include abundant conflict and tension—in short, that history is far from over. It is not yet clear at all what Latin America's future will be—whether it will become still more unjust, repressive, and divided or whether it will build stronger civil society, improved equity, and social solidarity. Nor is it by any means clear how the United States will evolve—whether the uprising in Los Angeles is a precursor of others or rather a timely alarm that will lead to effective reforms.

It is in this highly uncertain and insecure new world that countries like Argentina must devise their policies, internal and international. This is not the place for a full discussion of this topic, but from an Argentine perspective, I would call for trying to fashion a new era of cooperation with the United States, based on appreciating and paying attention to shared interests and priorities.

Both the United States and Latin America now need to redress inequities and reduce poverty. Both need to strengthen education and improve the skills of their workers. Both need to confront environmental dangers, to safeguard public health, and to control the danger of narcotics. Both need to strengthen democratic governance, to reduce military spending and influence, and to resist nationalism and racism. Both Latin America and the United States need, above all, to fight protectionism and self-indulgence and to improve competitiveness in an open world economy.

Because of these shared challenges, there is room for much greater cooperation between Latin America and the United States than in the past. But this will be so only if all Americans, North and South, tackle the social, economic, and political agenda with policies that are open, participatory, solidary, and cooperative.

This is today's hope, and it is a reasonable hope to which I am personally committed as a political leader. But this positive future could still be overwhelmed, we must understand, by narrow and selfish impulses—by nationalism, racism, anti-immigrant sentiment, beggar-thy-neighbor international economic policies, and trickle-down domestic approaches.

The direction in which inter-American relations will evolve in the 1990s depends both on Latin America and the United States and on their capacities to rise to the level required by the new international circumstances this book illuminates. Exchanges of ideas and information, like those fostered by the Inter-American Dialogue, can make a positive contribution, helping to build the needed vision and will.

## Latin America: Decline and Responsibility
### *Osvaldo Hurtado*

The dramatic changes in the world are all around us: the end of the Cold War and the possibilities for peace despite the confrontations unleashed by nationalism, the collapse of the Soviet Union and the waning of ideological conflict, and the surging onto the agenda of new issues like migration or the environ-

ment. In these circumstances, the concepts of the Third World or of nonalign-
ment have lost meaning.

Economically, the trends we see are paradoxical. On the one hand, capital
now knows no nationality, and the nations of the world are becoming ever
more interdependent. Yet on the other, the world seems to be developing into
great regional economic blocs—in Europe, East Asia, and North America. Although the United States is much less dominant an economic power than it
used to be, it will continue to play the main role in Latin America.

The reality of economics and of other issues of mutual interest—from migration to narcotics to the environment—will impel the United States and
Latin America to try to find common ground. The United States will not be
able to respond to the challenge presented by Europe and Japan if it does not
form a larger economic unit, a process already begun with NAFTA, joining
the United States with Canada and Mexico. It may also turn out that turbu-
lence in the former Socialist lands of Eastern Europe and the Soviet Union
will limit their economic promise and so turn the eyes of world commerce toward Latin America once again.

If Latin America's popular and middle classes continue to be impoverished,
they will migrate in large numbers to the United States in search of employment. Given current birthrates, the Hispanics in the United States will then
be the second largest ethnic group there by the next century—a fact that will
surely have some impact on U.S. policies.

So, too, as ecology moves up on the international agenda, Latin America
may acquire some negotiating leverage by virtue of possessing the globe's biggest reserves of tropical rain forest. And to the extent that the tragedy of narcotics can be addressed through reducing supplies—as well as restraining demand—the states of Latin America are necessary partners.

In confronting these new realities, moreover, Latin America is less locked
into the old pattern of confrontation or subordination in its relations to the
United States. Both halves of the hemisphere are moving toward more constructive, less confrontational approaches, thus opening possibilities for mutual benefit.

## The Regional Crisis

This is the positive prospect. Reaching it will require overcoming the crises—
of economy, state, and governance—of the 1980s. It will require Latin Americans to take responsibility for their future.

The dimensions of the economic crisis that has gripped the continent for a
decade are well known and do not need to be rehearsed here. Although the
1960s and 1970s were a generation of growth for the region, the debt, stagnation, and inflation of the last decade has left the area as a whole no better off
than it was in the late 1970s, and in Peru, Argentina, and Bolivia, the fall has
been greater still.

*how have standards of living improved in their countries*

All countries of the region have had to put their houses back in order through painful adjustment programs. Except for Colombia, Chile, Mexico, and, to a certain extent, Argentina, none has yet succeeded in correcting its economic disequilibrium and beginning to improve general standards of living.

In the process, hard questions have arisen about the role of the state, which was the main agent of change during the decades of inward-looking, import-substituting growth. Yet with the collapse of the Socialist economies, statist economic policies were discredited, and the debt crisis left Latin American nations bereft of new resources. More to the point, the states that resulted were bloated and inefficient, presiding over protected national industries that were uncompetitive in the increasingly open global marketplace.

All these states of the region have had to shrink and to open their national economies. Yet the state will continue to be important. "Smaller" is not the only answer to the question of what kind of state should evolve in Latin America. "More effective" will also be a critical characteristic.

In some parts of Latin America, pressured by the economic crisis, states have virtually decomposed, losing control of large areas of territory or, even where they retain it, losing their monopoly of force. The virtually ungovernable Peru is the most striking example. If Latin American states relinquish their ability to fulfill the fundamental functions of states, they will be still less able to undertake the more complex policies required in the decade ahead—setting in motion and upholding economic policies to assure that markets remain open and information flows freely.

That task also raises deep questions about the strength of democracy in the region. Until recently, democracy seemed to have taken root almost everywhere in Latin America. Despite the sacrifices of economic austerity, more and more countries turned (or returned) to democracy, and in others, power alternated peacefully between political parties. Yet those democracies found themselves administering scarcity (and perhaps making it worse), rather than stimulating growth. Ideology followed ideology with no solution to the economic problems.

In such circumstance, most visibly in Peru and Brazil, voters turned to a new style of leader above or apart from the perceived evils of professional politicians. But these leaders, too, have failed, not just because of the difficulty of the problems they have confronted but also because of their own weaknesses. They have not been able to build supporting political parties and so have lacked parliamentary majorities, they have been short on democratic experience and vocation, and they have not been able to count on technically strong governing teams.

The coups d'état in Venezuela and Peru—the first a failure, the second a success—stand as testimony to the loss of credibility of political leaders and the loss of faith in democracy and its institutions. In the process, the shallow roots of democracy in Latin America have become apparent. The kinds of political parties that can integrate a government and, in turn, constitute a responsible opposition are lacking. Instead, parties are fleeting, organized around personalities. The culture of negotiation hardly exists; Latin Americans are more likely to debate and litigate than work toward compromise.

Democracy is not ingrained. Legal legitimacy is not enough; it must be buttressed by social legitimacy. And basic political rights are insufficient unless augmented by some promise of achieving the well-being of citizens and families.

## A Basis for Hope

If there is a basis for hope, it rests on the promising economic signs of the early 1990s and, more fundamentally, in the realm of ideas—in a convergence of thinking in the region and on a willingness to take responsibility on the part of Latin Americans themselves.

Growth in the region reached 3 percent in 1991, more still in 1992. Inflation diminished almost everywhere, in particular in most countries where it had become chronic. The burden of debt decreased for the fifth straight year, and for the first time in a decade, Latin America stopped being a net transferrer of resources abroad. Money that was once invested overseas has been returning home.

To be sure, these hopeful signs are no more than that. The successes are confined to a few countries—Chile, Mexico, Argentina, and Colombia—and even there, the tangible fruits of the economic transformation are yet meager. Poverty in the region has increased; some four-fifths of the population now must be labeled poor. If protectionism increased in the industrial world or if the promising path of the region's debt reversed (perhaps through a sharp increase in interest rates), the hopeful beginnings would be snuffed out.

Latin America's on-again, off-again economic performance has reflected the instability of its politics. In Europe after World War II or in Asia's "four tigers" more recently, economic success rested on great continuity in politics and policies. In Latin America, by contrast, there has been little such continuity.

Communist groups were always in the minority in Latin America (Cuba and Chile excepted), but Marxist ideas inspired guerilla groups, student organizations, and labor unions. These groups questioned the democratic system and were radical critics of market economics. At the other end of the political spectrum, if authoritarian regimes were not bluntly repressive, their paternalistic policies ended up converting public money and public institutions into benefactors of particular groups in private society.

Today, however, the convergence toward democracy and market economics is striking. Communism collapsed of its own weight in the Soviet Union and Eastern Europe, and the Cuban model has ceased to inspire Latin Americans. The Sandinistas in Nicaragua were obliged to submit to free and fair elections, and in Columbia and El Salvador, guerrillas opted for national democratic processes. The convergence from the Right has been less visible but no less important; for their part, groups on the Right have moved away from autocratic politics and paternalistic economics.

Perhaps even more important, Latin Americans have realized that their problems are their own responsibility. For a long time, it was common for Latin Americans to blame economic dependence and U.S. imperialism for the majority of the region's troubles. Yet now, though the industrial world has lost interest in Latin America, the region's problems have not gotten better; on the contrary, isolation has made them worse.

It has become ever more clear that Latin America's problems are the responsibility of its leaders—politicians, people of commerce, workers, intellectuals, and technicians. The region's decline originates in the Latin Americans' inability to confront and resolve their problems, and the road to solution therefore must begin with the region's own efforts. A new generation has recognized that fact. What is important now is that Latin America's leaders sustain those efforts and implement policies that make sense in a new world.

## Brazil in a New World
### *Celso Lafer*

For Brazil, as for any other nation, the discussion of its international role must depart from both the realities of a globe in constant transformation and the specifics of its own permanent interests and anxieties as a sovereign nation. Particular objective elements deriving from what might be called the external profile of the country must also be taken into account.

The first of these, plainly, is the nation's dimension, both in terms of territory and people, as well as its politics, economy, and culture. Brazil has an undeniable weight and identity in the global panorama, similar to that of Russia, India, or China, despite differences in culture and level of development.

Geographic location naturally adds another fundamental fact to this analysis. In Brazil's case, elements of this geographical context have become familiar—the large number of neighbors and the variety of forums for national action (ranging from the Treaty of the River Plate to cooperation in the Amazon, as well as the organizations for economic and political integration). Thus, Latin America is, for Brazil, not merely a diplomatic option. It is its circumstance.

---

"Brazil in a New World" is adapted from a speech to Brazil's Escola Superior de Guerra, on August 24, 1992, printed in *Politica externa*, 1, no. 3 (December 1992).

This Latin American circumstance is even more important given the new challenges and new opportunities for dialogue on a new agenda, one driven by the understandable preoccupations of societies about their environment, control of narcotics, protection of indigenous communities, and dislocations of populations. To pursue these themes, a guiding principle of Latin American diplomacy might be the transformation of frontiers of separation into frontiers of cooperation. The former did not, in Brazil's case, derive from conflict. They were the consequence of open spaces in regions where communication was difficult, like the Amazon, and where there were conditions that could lead to tension, as has been the case with miners.

The frontier of cooperation, for its part, is visible in the region of the River Plate, where Brazil's interests are served not only by traditional types of infrastructure (such as roads, bridges, and hydroelectric projects), but also by the added dimension of innovative economic integration. The Mercosur is, in this sense, the best example of frontier cooperation, in a frontier that gradually will lose its primordial significance as a dividing line of sovereignty in order to realize the economic and social advantages of a broader market.

Yet for Brazil, the concept of a frontier of cooperation has a much wider significance. It applies, for example, to its maritime frontier in the South Atlantic, the line to its African neighbors. This Brazilian interest is comparable to those on any other of its borders, and, for this reason, it obliges Brazil to translate the frontier into a great area of peace and international cooperation.

This idea of a frontier of cooperation in a broader sense distinguishes Brazil's international role. In contrast to other countries, Brazil is not conditioned by preponderant influences like the proximity of a superpower or the concentration of a great part of its foreign commerce with a single trading partner. That is the case for Mexico and Canada, whose positions adjacent to the United States determine their options—for example, in the negotiation of NAFTA. A similar circumstance surrounds the entry of the Iberian countries into the European Community; those countries will redefine their international identities in light of the force of continental integration in the new Europe.

In this context, it is usual to invoke the notion of Brazil as a land of contrasts, a country that demonstrates the economic and social patterns of both the First World and the Third World. Indeed, Brazilian diplomacy has been capable of taking advantage of both dimensions. The Rio Conference on the Environment and Development demonstrated this capacity in the sense that Brazilians were interested in both the central aspects of the conference—the environment and development—and those aspects they confront in their daily lives—the problems caused by the double face of the environmental issue. On the one hand, these problems are typical of developed countries, caused principally by patterns of industrial production; on the other, there are problems common to developing countries, primarily resulting from poverty.

As a synthesis, the concept of sustainable development developed at Rio is the driving idea of a more just world order. It might be the basis for an international social contract and a vision of the future for it encompasses not only the idea of efficiency in the production of wealth but also that of environmental sustainability, which is critical to overcoming poverty. Poverty is, in its essence, an unsustainable condition.

The external commerce of Brazil is just as diverse as the society and the nation's diplomacy. Annually, Brazil exports something like $32 billion and imports $21 billion, numbers that represent about a fifth of Latin America's total international trade. The profile of Brazil's external commerce has come a long way from the model, still typical of a majority of developing countries, that is based on exporting primary products. Today, more than 70 percent of Brazil's sales abroad involve industrial products—54 percent manufactured goods and 17 percent semimanufactured.

The diversification of trade is particularly evident in the fact that the EC and the United States account for, respectively, 31 and 20 percent of Brazil's exports and 22 and 23 percent of its imports. Thus, Brazil strikes a balance between two of the principal international markets. The other countries of Latin America account for 15 percent of exports and 17 percent of imports. At the same time, Asia's role in Brazil's international trade has grown significantly from less than 10 percent in 1980 to nearly 17 percent in 1990, of which Japan counted for 7.5 percent. The numbers confirm, in the commercial field, that Brazil's interests are global—an aspect that I have already underlined as a general feature of the Brazilian international presence.

At the same time, despite Brazil's commercial push outward, its participation in the international economy remains relatively modest, all the more so when the absorption of investment and technology is taken into account. Thus, a paradox exists in Brazil's international position: Today, the world is much more important strategically for Brazil than Brazil is for the world. From that paradox derives the challenge of adjusting expectations to possibilities.

## Democracy and Diplomacy

Needless to say, Brazil's return to democracy has had a positive impact on its foreign policy, especially given the international order that is emerging. The constitution of 1988 makes democracy the driving idea and accelerates the constitutionalization of foreign relations.

Brazil's highest law establishes as principles human rights, the defense of peace, the solution of conflicts, and the repudiation of terrorism and racism. In terms of limits, the constitution gives legal force to restricting nuclear energy to peaceful purposes. At the level of incentives, the integration of Latin American peoples is established as a fundamental objective of Brazilian foreign policy.

Democracy has a rich range of effects in the international realm, effects that already benefit Brazilian foreign policy and that can be deepened. Looking outward, democracy increases the backing of a nation's people for international negotiations and confers international credibility on the country. At the same time, in an effective democracy, the role of the people is not just to legitimize options already set in motion by the state, nor to simply accept the agenda of the country's foreign policy establishment. Public opinion has its own agenda. Recent examples are the cases of Brazilian dentists in Portugal or miners in Venezuela, situations that will by repeated as Brazilians migrate to different corners of the world. This phenomenon is not explained just by current economic circumstances but by the migratory dynamic that characterizes today's world.

Democracy provides indispensable legitimacy at a moment when this political value is attaining near universal acceptance. This reality was dramatized in 1989 by the stunning conversion to democracy of the former Socialist bloc. It is still more vivid in the Latin American region, where, in addition to sharing Western values inherited from Europe, those values are enshrined as the fundamental principle in the regional organization, the Organization of American States. It is worth underscoring the active role of the OAS in trying to restore democratic processes in Haiti, Suriname, and Peru.

Democracy as a form for ordering the life of a society defines affinities and differences. It is natural that democracies have easier relations with other democracies. Political theorists since Immanuel Kant have identified a strong relation between the democratic form of government and the peaceful vocation of states, as well as an opposite connection between authoritarian or totalitarian forms and a greater disposition to belligerence. Democracy's inherent values—pluralism, tolerance, the quest for consensus, and the primacy of law—extend to the state's external action, making the spread and consolidation of democracy a factor in international stability.

This is a special benefit for Latin America in the emerging world order because its history, culture, and values bring it close to the vibrant and prosperous democracies of North America and Europe. The border between Latin America and the United States does not mark the kind of cultural discontinuity that exists between Europe and North Africa, a clash that has been the source of reciprocal incomprehension. In the Americas, it was this common cultural base that made possible what is, by now, the old expression of Pan-Americanism known as the OAS, one of the few groupings that brought together a superpower with weaker nations on the basis of juridical equality and legal recognition of the principle of nonintervention (although that principle has been controversial in practice).

More broadly, democracy has value as the organizing principle of international order, through reinforcing multilateralism in all its manifestations. In addition to its general role in peace and security, the UN has made concrete contributions in settling local conflicts in Namibia and Cambodia and with Iraq's aggression into Kuwait.

The natural corollary of this democratic impulse, from the point of view of countries like Brazil, would be a reform of the UN Charter in order to let the organization's structure better reflect the actual distribution of international power. This would especially be true for the Security Council, which would surely gain in representativeness with a new category of permanent members such as Japan, Germany, India, and Brazil. This broadening of the Security Council, reinforcing its legitimacy, would make it still more relevant to the regionalization of conflict, which now results from local causes, not East-West confrontation.

The process of multilateralizing international relations, which contrasts with the concentration of decisive international power not only in the UN but also in the Group of 7, has yet another link to democracy—the codification of many aspects of international life. The great themes of international relations—ocean, environment, human rights, disarmament (both nuclear and now chemical)—are being codified in conventions with universal aspirations, thus diminishing the scope of the political and increasing that of the juridical among nations. However, this tendency frequently encounters the resistance of an important state that believes its interests are contravened by a convention produced by a majority, as happened with the United States and the Law of the Sea or Brazil, India, and Argentina with the Non-Proliferation Treaty (NPT). This judicial process put great pressure on those states that wanted to remain at the margin of the international regime in question, inducing them to seek alternative ways of moving in the same general direction.

### "Relegitimization" from the South's Perspective

All of this occurs in a world in motion. During the Cold War, the East-West conflict structured and conditioned, to a certain extent, the North-South issue. Thus, the nonaligned movement, in the realm of politics, and the Group of 77, in the economic field, derived much of their relevance from their character as a third force, distinct from both the so-called First World and the Second World of Socialist countries. The three-cornered relations made possible by the existence of these three groupings are now seen to be reduced, perhaps too simply, to a bilateral structure—a North, which is reconciling its own East and West, confronting a poor South, which is disparate and menacing.

As a result, the North-South issue ceased being just a kind of levy by the South on the North, Socialist as well as capitalist, for financial and technological resources and more cooperation in development. Now, there is also a levy raised by the North on the South, for more respect of human rights, for preservation of the environment, and for commitments to the nonproliferation of weapons of mass destruction and extending to the war on drugs, and to free markets. This paradoxical inversion of levies works to delegitimize the South's perspective in world affairs.

Using the language of Thomas Kuhn, the North American historian of science, we live in a time of "paradigm shift." In international relations, it is not the genius of scientists but rather the democratic creativity of peoples that challenges our categories. The order that is now passing, for all its deficiencies, had the virtue of stability; indeed, it was characterized by its durability—forty years for the East-West dimension, a little less for the North-South, which could be dated from the beginning of the 1950s. This rigidity in international structures contrasts with the twenty years between the two world wars. It created mental habits that are difficult to adjust quickly but that must be transformed if we are to understand the present and frame the future.

One of the principal tasks ahead is seeking to "relegitimize" the South's perspective on international order in new forms. Doing so is vital to guarantee a vision of the future. This task derives from the recognition that a North-South gap exists, one that will continue to be problematic as long as the less developed nations are not fully and satisfactorily incorporated in the dynamism of the global economy. Their incorporation is a basic ingredient of a stable world order.

### Centripetal and Centrifugal Forces

One final and perhaps most decisive consequence flows from the end of the East-West conflict. This is the possible creation of a single global economic space and the merger of the different multilateral bodies dealing with politics (including peace and security) and economics—the system constituted by the GATT, the IMF, and the World Bank. After World War II, it was possible to create a universal political order based on the Charter of San Francisco, including intense Soviet participation. But it was not possible to form a universal economic order for the Soviet Union and its allies were absent from Bretton Woods.

In an important sense, the Uruguay Round has been the "constituent assembly" of a global economic space as the disappearance of socialism has opened, for the first time in history, a virtual consensus on economic principles. This metaphor of constituent assembly must, however, be qualified because the Uruguay Round does not cover the entire economic agenda; in addition to IMF issues, the relation between commerce and environment is outside the agenda.

Economics is a centripetal force, as much in universal forums like the Uruguay Round as in the diverse processes of regional integration. The latter not only demonstrate the impulse toward larger economic units but also require, as a precondition, that countries have passed through phases of conflict, territorial dispute, and ethnic and religious hatreds. It is, in its nature, the unemotional realm of the logic of interests, in which the game is not seen as a "zero sum" contest between enemies.

Alongside these centripetal forces of cooperation and integration coexist centrifugal forces of ethnicity, nationalism, and religion. By removing the East-West conflict as the focus of the international system, the end of the Cold War provoked the spread of tension. These tensions are more evident in Eastern Europe, in the former Yugoslavia, and in the territory of the former Soviet Union, but they also exist in other areas. They seem to fill the ideological vacuum left by the fall of the great projects for the transformation of society as represented by Marxism and other less radical theories. They suggest the impossibility of reducing human behavior to the rationality of economic logic and indicate, on the contrary, the unsuspected force of solidarity based on language, religion, and race.

The different fundamentalisms represent the most extreme case of subordinating economics to ideology, and almost always, they reflect a reaction to the secularization of society set in motion by the modernization of production and consumption and by the integration of the world economy.

## The New Geometries of Power

In this context, it is necessary to examine the role of the United States, which seeks to inspire a new order but seems to lack the necessary material resources to be the sole organizer, or hegemon. The United States lives with the dilemma of having won the ideological battle while seeing that some of those who have followed its values—democracy and, above all, markets—are more efficient in implementing them. Indeed, it is worth asking to what extent the same form of market economy is at work in the United States, the Common Market, and Japan.

Distinct geometries of power thus arise. The United States organizes different coalitions for different issues. The operation against Iraq had one composition, but another project might have a different one. In other cases, such as shaping post–Cold War Eastern and Central Europe, leadership will fall to the EC.

Different geometries operate beyond the level of major powers, as well. Brazil, for instance, stands at the side of developed countries like the United States and Australia in GATT negotiations over agriculture with the EC, but closer to other countries on questions like access to markets for manufactured goods or the treatment of services. Other alliances that would not be obvious in advance are the closeness of most of the Group of 77 and the Nordic countries in regard to environmental issues.

This multiplicity of possible tactical alliances, facilitated by the end of the rigidity imposed by the Cold War, also derives from the predominance of economics on the post–Cold War agenda. Alliances are defined by interests, not by politicomilitary or ideological loyalties, which are necessarily more stable.

In this connection, it is worth mentioning that how the concept of power will evolve is uncertain. In a world that is more and more marked by economic competition, not by politico-military-ideological confrontation, power can assume new forms. For instance, although the United States is now the only state that is equally relevant in the two spheres—economics and strategy—there is no doubt that it is more and more challenged by the advance of Japan and Europe, especially Germany, in the economic realm. This is true despite the fact that these nations remain militarily dependent on the United States, no longer in response to the Soviet threat but in relation to what might be perceived as threats, such as those related to their oil supplies.

All this had led some observers to unwisely discount the military factors of power and to imagine a fully peaceful world under the rule of the United Nations and international law, one in which competition is limited to a pragmatic search for more efficiency and prosperity. This view seems unrealistic, especially in view of the first post–Cold War events, like the Gulf War or the crisis in Yugoslavia, not to mention the tensions in the former Soviet Union.

That said, the new definition of power is, in a certain sense, still more punitive for developing countries. It devalues some traditional attributes of power in the international hierarchy, like territory, population, and national resources, emphasizing instead education, scientific capacity, and productivity. Moreover, it is easier and quicker for a country to acquire status as a military power than to substantially improve its economic or, especially, social indexes in the short run—the only ones that make for a positive international profile today, including for their indirect effects on human rights, environmental preservation, and attractiveness for foreign investment.

Moreover, another feature of the Cold War's end has been the reduced amount of space available for potentially destabilizing projects to accumulate national power at the margins of the international system. For the central countries, the watchword for the international system is order or its corollary in the realm of security, stability. The doctrine of nonproliferation, which already united the USSR and the United States at the end of the 1960s through the Non-Proliferation Treaty for nuclear weapons, acquired even more force with the end of the Cold War; it has since been extended into new areas, like chemical or biological weapons and their delivery vehicles. The allied campaign against Iraq—particularly its legal basis in UN Security Council Resolution 687—sought, in large measure, to serve as an example to deter any temptation by a developing country to acquire weapons of mass destruction.

The implications of this development are especially relevant for Brazil, a country whose peacefulness was proven during its republican history and for which the consolidation of its physical integrity ended its use of military power. But the consensus among the countries of the North regarding international control of the transfer of technologies with possible military uses includes those with dual use, both military and nonmilitary. This consensus is a preoccupation to the extent that the controls put in place actually impede Brazil's legitimate access to scientific and technological advances for peaceful purposes, the basis of contemporary economies.

Brazil will not accept the idea of a monopoly of sensitive technology implicitly defended by some countries. Its diplomacy seeks to assure that international controls over sensitive technology are based on the principles of non-discrimination, transparency, and predictability. To that end, control should be progressively multilateralized and embodied in international conventions, instead of remaining the prerogatives of closed and informal supplier clubs (for example, the Missile Control Transfer Regime, or COCOM), which proved ineffective in the case of Iraq.

In light of this double preoccupation with international peace and security as well as access to technology, Brazil participated actively in the negotiation of the Convention to Prohibit Chemical Arms. It also negotiated and signed, with Argentina, an agreement with the International Atomic Energy Agency (IAEA) to assure the international community of its peaceful intentions in the nuclear area. In addition to these efforts, as well as those made in conjunction with Argentina and Chile that brought the Treaty of Tlatelolco into effect (with improvements Brazil suggested), Brazil's leaders expect to be assured access to the technologies they require; they will not sign agreements traditionally considered discriminatory.

## A Vision of the Future

These considerations suggest the magnitude of the challenge Brazil faces in reinserting itself in international affairs—a challenge made all the more difficult by the profound and surprising transformations of the contemporary world. Moreover, it is necessary to try to correlate internal needs with external possibilities. Society's demands, based on objective and agreed upon criteria, must be satisfied by taking advantage of the opportunities inherent in the international reality.

This process develops, in my view, in two distinct areas. The first comprises foreign policy initiatives at the level of the international system's structure and its rules, both general and specific; it requires, as conceptual guidelines, what I call creative adaptation and a vision of the future. The second area of diplomatic action has to do with Brazil's relations to different regions and key countries in its foreign policy; in this context, I identify operational partnerships and niches of opportunity.

Examples of creative adaptation include the Rio Conference and the new Brazilian attitude toward the control of sensitive technologies. With regard to a vision of the future, the task is to work for an international system that would be more compatible with Brazilian values and aspirations, one in which ideas of peace and democracy would not just coexist with efforts at development but would, in practice, reinforce them through establishing cooperative structures of commerce, investment, and technology transfer.

As at the Rio Conference, it is necessary to harmonize the two distinct planes of foreign policy: to think of the universal—the collective interest— while bearing in mind the specific—the regional or national interest. Brazil's vision of the future was reflected in its advocacy of a serious debate over the reform of the Security Council, a key point in the process of democratizing international relations.

Brazil must strengthen its participation in the decisionmaking processes of global intercourse, including those that bear on so-called transnational themes. Humanitarian or ecological concerns give rise to conceptions, like the *devoir d'ingerence* ("the duty to intervene"), that collide with principles of international law, like respect for the sovereignty of states. The decision of the U.S. Supreme Court about the kidnapping of a Mexican citizen in his own country by U.S. police officials underscores this preoccupation.

In the Brazilian foreign policy vision, relations between states are—and should continue to be—conditioned by incentives to cooperation, not by impositions or prohibitions. The agenda of international relations should be positive, not negative. On that basis, Brazilians deplore the idea of a duty to intervene as contrary to an egalitarian structure of world order. For the same reason, though, they defend as a matter of basic human solidarity the duty of the international community—through the United Nations, the Red Cross, or other entities—to send assistance to men, women, and children in crisis situations. This is the case now in Bosnia and Somalia, where grave problems require international action to lessen hunger, misery, and hopelessness.

The same process of resolving regional conflicts endorses international peacekeeping forces and mechanisms for verifying agreements on security and disarmament. Both the UN and the OAS have reinvigorated their functions in this field, as has been demonstrated in the former Yugoslavia, in Cambodia, and in Angola. Brazil's armed forces have taken part in these international efforts, a reflection of the convergence between the nations's actions in the diplomatic and the military spheres. At the invitation of the UN secretary general, Brazil sent military observers on peacekeeping operations in Central America and Yugoslavia; at the invitation of the OAS secretary general, it sent military observers to Suriname to oversee demobilization efforts.

At this point, I turn to competition. The fundamental objective of current foreign policy—seeking Brazil's competitive insertion in the world—should take place through operational partnerships. These are predominantly economic, but they do have political content in some cases. They are complementary and coherent in taking advantage of the possibilities of Brazil's international role.

For Brazil there is space for bilateral, multilateral, regional, subregional, and continental agreements. Proximity and the thickness of historical relations matter, as in the Mercosur. The priority of the Mercosur, however, does not imply that other partnerships are excluded. For Brazil, creating operational partnerships presupposes a legal structure to regulate international commerce, and that, in turn, depends on the success of the Uruguay Round of GATT. The existing impasse increases the risk of regional blocs and of rivalry among them that could threaten the entire system of international commerce. For instance, NAFTA might come to divert existing flows of commerce, investment, and technology, as well as affect Mexico's commitments to Latin America.

Assuming that, despite the pessimists, GATT does not fail, it is possible to visualize the opportunities that might open for Brazil within the criteria of "operational partnerships" and Mercosur. The United States, as its largest single trading partner, is a natural attraction in the process of reinserting Brazil in the competitive modern economy. In the international context of the time, both nations will have an interest in creating the basis for a new partnership, one that will overcome commercial frictions and produce a more confident, mature cooperation.

That said, Brazilians are global traders, and so a diversification of options is necessary because their pattern of exports is not concentrated in a few products or a few markets. Moreover, Brazil only stands to gain through the different modalities that market economies are assuming around the globe, both in adjustment policies and in degree of openness.

Indeed, it is plain that there are different forms of market economy today. The model of the European Community has, for example, different ingredients than the North American model. The community process is preoccupied with ameliorating regional differences and the necessity to transfer resources. The EC also puts a high value on the social question, to the point that it does not talk simply of a market economy but rather of a "social market economy."

Japan, for its part, enriches capitalist practice in two ways. First, it has made innovations in production process. It substituted "Fordism"—that is, assembly lines—with a new concept of integrated production, with emphasis on innovative technology and cost reduction. Japan also incorporated the notion of strategic planning, both in government and in the private sector, developing a common policy that produced significant gains in competitiveness. The idea of industrial policy, over both the medium and the long term, reinforces the considerable advantages of the Japanese economy and distinguishes it in many ways from the North American model.

Japanese experience suggests, as well, useful lessons for Brazil's future development, and it demonstrates the priority of an operational partnership with an Asian industrial power. At the same time and despite its existing level of protectionism, the EC opens other visions of the market economy and new horizons for Brazilian operational partnerships. In this area, the Agreement on a Third Generation multiplies the potential areas of cooperation with the Europeans.

This analysis underscores the point that foreign policy cannot follow a fixed or predetermined course. To remain dynamic and seek innovative adaptations to a constantly changing international reality, it must seek what I call "niches of opportunity." These niches do not imply abandoning multilateralism; they can be identified in politics as well as economics. Countries like Iran, Turkey, the United Arab Emirates, South Korea, and Israel offer possibilities to be explored in terms of services, technical cooperation, and technology interchange.

What Brazil must seek, then, is to put in place a policy of "multilateralism with differentiated niches of opportunity." This means paying attention to strategic objectives while exploring the economic opportunities on the various fronts of its foreign policy. On the political plane, there are also many niches of opportunity in the wake of the Cold War. One of them, offered by the community of Ibero-American nations, is to contribute to projecting values dear to Brazilian foreign policy, such as democracy, pluralism, and respect for human rights. But the utility of such an approach is not diminished if it also offers possibilities for diplomacy to defend concrete short- and medium-term interests—the concept of sustainable development, the opening of international commerce, and access to technological and financial resources.

## Confronting a New World
### *Jesús Silva Herzog*

The profound changes that have occurred in the world in recent years have caught us by surprise. In fact, today's world is very different from the one that existed barely an instant ago. The new economic order (or disorder) is in motion; indeed, it is in ferment. The process of transformation has begun, but we do not know what its final result will be.

Amid all this change, several tendencies have special relevance for Latin America.

- The formation of regional blocs. In spite of the European Community's current travails, the impulse to integration will persist in Europe and will, moreover, give rise to the gradual and sometimes halting incorporation of other European members. The problems of Europe's east— enormous financial requirements and pressures for migration—will confront the Continent for a long time.

  Japan and the countries of Southeast Asia form a zone—the most dynamic in the world—without a formal association but with growing connections of every sort. China, with its extraordinary economic growth of recent years, begins to be a presence in the region and in the wider world, as well.

The United States, Canada, and now Mexico, with the North American Free Trade Area, comprise an important zone, one that seeks to recover the predominant place that it occupied in the global economy.

The world's course in the next few years will be profoundly influenced both by how these three blocs act internally and by how they interact with each other. The commitment to multilateralism, always proclaimed, is not, in fact, so clear at present; a number of looming questions need to be resolved.

- The concentration by the industrialized countries on their own relations, to a greater extent than in the past. Relations among these states will intensify and so will the North-North dialogue. The developing countries—the nations of the South—will occupy second place. This is hardly new, but it is possible that their secondary status will be sharper still in the future than it has been in the past. Moreover, what attention is paid to the developing countries will be selective—that is, only some nations will be the objects of attention from the great centers of decision.

- The world's relative lack of savings. Savings have been reduced by the recent slowing of global economic growth and by elevated levels of consumption. It is very possible that the 1990s will be a decade of capital shortage. At the same time, there is the difficulty of correcting the huge U.S. budget deficit, the financial requirements of German unification, and the enormous internal demands of Japan. Together, these constitute an immense sum of funds whose destination is predetermined. That means that the external capital available to the developing world will be especially scarce, and only some countries—those recognized as particularly attractive—will be possible receivers of transfers.

For its part, Latin America has registered a profound transition over the last decade. It has been said, with reason, that the 1980s were a "lost decade" economically. But that decade was accompanied by substantial advances in the process of democratization, even if there is a lingering uncertainty about democracy's consolidation over the longer term.

Similarly, the 1980s saw a "silent revolution" in the political economy of most Latin American countries. The fundamental features of that transformation were, on one hand, the redefinition of the role of the state—including the privatizing of public enterprises—greater prominence for the private sector, and a new attitude toward deficits in public finance; on the other, there was an opening of commerce, the reduction of protectionism, and a search for a greater presence in the international markets of the future.

To these profound changes in Latin America should be added the striking renewal of regional integration. After thirty years of failure, there is a new attitude toward integration, among enterprises as well as among governments. The concept of integration itself has changed: Not only has regional integration received, for the first time, the support of the United States, but Latin America now seeks integration—it is no longer looking inward but facing outward, encouraging efficiency and international competitiveness. Now, too, there are advances in subregional integration—Mercosur, the Andean Pact, the Central American area—as steps toward an eventual integration across the continent. And there is also the prospect of extending integration to the United States and Canada within a focus that is explicitly Pan-American.

Regional integration is, today, a necessity, given the global setting of the years ahead. Not to undertake it would be to remain passive spectators to world events—a conviction that is held ever more widely and deeply in the Latin American community.

In the last several years, the Latin American region has begun to shake the lethargy of the previous decade, renewing growth, reducing inflationary pressures, managing to service the external debt, and registering net inflows of capital. That said, however, differences among countries have sharpened. Brazil, for example, which accounts for two-fifths of the region's GNP, has not found a solution to its fundamental problems.

There is no doubt that the new economic policies adopted by most states of the region have borne fruit. Latin America today is more efficient and competitive. It has reduced or eliminated distortions in the allocations of resources, and it is more open to international competition. State intervention has receded, and private enterprise has been given a more important role. Latin America has, in short, been a faithful follower of prevailing free market economic orthodoxy.

Yet in the process, questions of a social character have arisen, ones that will merit more attention in the years ahead. Old deficiencies have been sharpened by the crises of the 1980s, as well as by the inevitable consequences of the economic reforms that have been adopted. The deterioration of basic social indicators is all too apparent—and irreversible, in some cases.

Thus, economic policy in the years ahead will have to pay more attention to these social problems. This will imply a shift in the attitudes that now reign supreme, even if that shift leads to slower growth. Not to make that shift could bring huge political costs.

In these circumstances, the region will require strong governments. State intervention is necessary not only to counteract the limited development and weakness of markets themselves but also to compensate for the limited maturity of the private sector. The effectiveness of the state in intervening in the economy does not depend on its size but rather on the quality of its action. Perhaps the 1992 electoral results in the United States and the platform on which President Clinton was elected will serve to produce a more reasonable consensus on these issues. The swing of the pendulum toward free markets must be somewhat less severe and more in accord with the reality of Latin circumstances—historic, political, economic, and social.

Still, there can be no doubt that the import-substitution model—with its high levels of commercial protection—has exhausted its possibilities. It served Latin America well for many years, permitting substantial advances in industry, employment levels, and development. But it was also excessive, too prolonged, and too generalized in its application.

A good number of Latin American countries do, in fact, have markets that are open to international competition. Indeed, that has been one of the most important changes in the basic orientation of the region's economies. Yet Latin America's economic opening has coincided with the slowing of economic activity in the industrial countries, which then, logically, reduces Latin possibilities for exporting while it encourages the placement of the industrial world's exports in Latin markets.

The result has produced a paradox: Some champions of free trade now impose various restrictions on external commerce, while some old defenders of protectionism now introduce bold measures of liberalization. In a good number of cases, it may be that the economic opening, like the previous approach it sought to correct, has occurred too fast and been too generalized and too far-reaching.

The further north a nation is in Latin America, the more its trade is concentrated with the United States—ranging from 20 percent for Chile to 70 percent for Mexico. And relations with the United States always have been complex and trying. The new U.S. administration has clear priorities for its internal economy, and the role for Latin America, aside from Mexico, is not clear, especially in the longer run.

Diversifying its commerce should be, no doubt, a fundamental component of Latin America's strategy for redefining its position in the global political economy. Japan and its area of influence offer an attractive alternative. The European Community also should be a center of attention, despite its current inward preoccupation. In both cases, however, various subtle protectionist barriers, ones difficult to bring down, reduce the possibilities for access to their markets. Still, in the global economy in which we live, it is more and more important to have windows open in all directions.

For long decades, it was common in Latin America to attribute all ills to external causes. Now this has changed. Although no one would deny the importance of external circumstances, there is a growing willingness to recognize Latin America's own responsibility for the facts of the past and, above all, for the possibilities of the future. It is a great step forward. To paraphrase the great Mexican Benito Juárez: "No one will do for us what we do not do for ourselves."

# 13

# Latin America and the United States in a New World: Prospects for Partnership

## *Abraham F. Lowenthal*

Although the perspectives included in the foregoing chapters are not uniform, the dominant thrust of most of the essays suggests that the prospects for Western Hemisphere partnerships are more promising in the mid-1990s than they have been for decades—at least since the Alliance for Progress of the early 1960s.[1]

The movement toward Western Hemisphere cooperation was crystallized in former President George Bush's soaring vision of a "system that links all of the Americas—North, Central, and South—as regional partners in a free trade zone stretching from the Port of Anchorage to Tierra del Fuego."[2] What Bush in 1990 called the Enterprise for the Americas Initiative has not yet been implemented in reality, but the goals he expressed have been widely endorsed and embraced, and they have shaped most recent discourse on inter-American relations. In a period of inter-American "convergence and community," most contemporary debate centers on how to build inter-American partnerships, not on whether they should or can be forged.[3]

Three regional trends, widely seen as important and mutually reinforcing, are highlighted in the previous chapters and elsewhere to explain the origins and appeal of this turn toward Western Hemisphere cooperation. There is greater political and economic homogeneity in the Americas than ever before, Latin American leaders are more disposed than formerly toward harmonious relations with Washington, and the United States has greater reasons than heretofore to invest in building a regional community. Never before have so many Latin Americans and North Americans, especially elite leaders, understood so clearly that they have shared values and common interests, made both more obvious and more important by the shifting geopolitical and geoeconomic realities of the post–Cold War world.

There is much truth in these widely repeated affirmations, but each of them is also often overstated. The cumulative effect of these exaggerations is an illusion of probability, even of inevitability, about the chances for hemispheric partnership. It is by no means clear, in fact, that cooperation will replace conflict as the dominant mode of inter-American relations in the new world of the 1990s. Renewed tensions, albeit over different issues, may well occur.

## Latin America's Transformations

Three shifts have unquestionably been taking place in Latin America during the past few years: an emerging consensus among economic policymakers on the main tenets of sound policy, the even more universal embrace of constitutional democracy as an ideal, and the growing disposition toward pragmatic cooperation with the United States.

By the late 1980s, most Latin American economic policymakers came to agree on a diagnosis of the region's fundamental maladies and a set of prescriptions for restoring its health. Throughout Latin America and the Caribbean, it became clear that the fiscal crisis of the state had to be confronted and that it would be essential to bring inflation under control, even if that meant drastically reducing public expenditures. It became accepted, as well, that the import-substitution approach to economic growth—however successful it was in some countries during the 1950s and 1960s—was exhausted everywhere and that the region's recovery depended primarily on boosting exports, which, in turn, necessitated competitive exchange rates and an end to various subsidies and other forms of protection. It was also agreed that Latin America must sharply prune the state's industrial and regulatory activities, privatize public enterprises, facilitate competitive markets, stimulate the private sector, and attract foreign investment. The emergence of this regionwide consensus is a paradigm shift of historic dimensions.

Equally striking has been the gathering accord on the desirability of constitutional democratic politics. Just twenty-five years ago, self-proclaimed "vanguards" on the Left and "guardians" on the Right openly expressed disdain for democratic procedures, and both claimed significant followings. Since the mid-1970s, however, a wide spectrum of Latin American opinion has come to recognize the value of democratic governance: military officers and former guerrillas, intellectuals and religious leaders, corporate executives and labor organizers. Year by year, it has become clear that most Latin American elites, as well as the public at large, agree that government authority must derive from the uncoerced consent of the majority, tested regularly through fair, competitive, and broadly participatory elections. Latin America's commitment to electoral democracy has thus far survived even the hyperinflations in Argentina, Bolivia, and Brazil; democratic institutions in many European nations crumbled under similar conditions during the 1920s and 1930s.

The broad regional turn toward harmonious relations with the United States has also been unmistakable. For years, many Latin Americans defined their foreign policies primarily in opposition to Washington. They denounced U.S. interventionism and exploitation, bemoaned Latin American "dependence," and blamed the United States for many of their frustrations. Restrictive policies on foreign investment, reserved markets, high tariff barriers, movements toward regional economic integration and diplomatic *concertación* ("consultation and coordination") were all forged, in part, as responses to U.S. power. Only in the "banana republics" could a Latin American leader advocate close collaboration with Washington without political risk.

All this has changed. Most Latin American governments and many opposition movements in Latin America today want stronger links with the United States. Mexico made the most dramatic move toward U.S.–Latin American cooperation when President Carlos Salinas de Gortari and his team began to pursue the North American Free Trade Agreement with the United States and Canada in 1990. In Buenos Aires, Carlos Menem has gone to great lengths to build close ties with the United States. Chile under Patricio Aylwin has pushed hard for a free trade agreement with Washington, and most other Latin American countries actively seek to improve their ties with the United States. Only Fidel Castro's Cuba holds on to its anti-Americanism, and even Cuba might well be open to rapprochement if only Washington were willing.

The turns toward free market economics, democratic politics, and inter-American cooperation result from the widely perceived failure of Latin America's course in the 1970s and 1980s. Statist economics proved to be a dead end. So did authoritarian governments, which lost legitimacy everywhere—in some cases, because prosperity made their high political costs seem unnecessary and in most others, because they were ineffective even in economic terms. Confrontation with the United States proved to be a losing proposition as well, particularly as brave Third World talk of a new international economic order dissolved into mere palaver.

All these shifts were also accelerated by the dramatic international changes discussed in earlier chapters: the collapse of the perceived Soviet threat and then of the Soviet Union itself, the end of the Cold War, the widespread validation of open markets and politics, and especially the fundamental restructuring of the world economy, driven by technological change. These global transformations, together with Latin America's internal experience, help account for developments in the Western Hemisphere that were unexpected just a few years ago: not only Mexico's embrace of NAFTA but the Sandinista's acceptance of electoral defeat in Nicaragua; the historic compromises for peace made by both the government and the insurgent Left in El Salvador; the switch in many countries, even by old-time leaders, to economic policies diametrically opposed to those of the 1970s; the coming to power of rank outsiders in some countries; and the adoption of neoliberal economic recipes throughout the region.

Latin America's recent changes, in short, are not accidental or unconnected, nor are they merely cyclical. They are responses to profound regional experiences and to a transformed global context.

## The Fragility of Change

Yet these important shifts are still at grave risk. The regionwide promulgation of neoliberal economic reforms was deceptively easy. It was stunning that such similar measures would be announced in short order in extremely different countries, often by presidents who had campaigned against such reforms. But this convergence owed much more, in most cases to the lack of credible alternatives than to broad-based national consensus or to the unshakable convictions of political leaders. Except in Chile, where accord on the core national economic programs was built over many years as part of the tacitly negotiated gradual transition away from the Pinochet regime, the political base for the economic reforms is still tentative, firmly supported only by leading technocrats and some segments of the private sector.

Unless Latin America's economic reforms generate demonstrable results soon, they may not become solidly entrenched. Centrally planned economies linked to a world Socialist system are obviously no longer relevant, but the commitments to all-out privatization, extremely liberal foreign investment regimes, truly open economies, and full regional integration are likely to be modified in the coming years unless the current approaches promptly yield tangible benefits.

Changes in policy are all the more probable as it becomes generally perceived that income concentration is worsening and that social, economic, and, in some cases, ethnic divisions are widening. It is difficult, if not impossible, for governments to sustain popular backing for reforms that enrich a privileged few without providing a credible promise of broad prosperity. Strong social safety nets and improved public services might help, but they are hard to achieve while the neoliberal economic reforms are being put in place, for these reforms tend to cut back the state. It is probably not accidental, in fact, that the two countries that have advanced most toward combining economic reforms with effective social programs—Chile and Mexico—both have the major earners of foreign exchange in government hands, as well as the strongest states.

Weakening support for the neoliberal programs is evident throughout much of Latin America: in the electoral gains registered by the Workers Party

(PT) and the Social Democratic Party (PSDB) in Brazil, the Movement Toward Socialism (MAS) and the Radical Cause (Causa R) in Venezuela, and the Broad Front (Frente Amplio) in Uruguay, as well as the mounting criticism in Colombia and Argentina. Particularly striking was the resounding rejection by 70 percent of Uruguay's voters of President Luis Alberto Lacalle's privatization program in a December 1992 plebiscite. Bolivia's privatization program, too, was sidetracked because of strong labor union opposition.

It is much too early to be confident that Latin America as a whole can recapture the economic dynamism of the 1960s and 1970s or achieve gains comparable to that of today's East Asian "tigers." Chile has managed several consecutive years of impressive growth, to be sure, after long years of painful structural reform. But growth is not yet occurring in Brazil or Peru, and it has not yet proved sustainable at high levels in Mexico, Venezuela, Colombia, Ecuador, Bolivia, Uruguay, Paraguay, or the Central American and Caribbean countries. The best growth records during the past few years have been achieved by Argentina, Mexico, Chile, Panama, and Venezuela—but the latter two countries have been rebounding from very deep recessions and have still not fully recovered their prior levels, and the first two are facing mounting difficulties.

The flow of voluntary capital into several Latin American countries since 1990 has been encouraging by contrast with the lean years from 1982 through 1989. But much of the capital entering Latin America has been portfolio rather than direct investment, and most of it is selectively concentrated in a few large, low-risk firms. A good deal of it appears, moreover, to be flight capital—originally taken out of Latin America by elites and likely to leave again at the first sign of trouble. Recent foreign investment in Latin America has been drawn to the region, in part, by high interest rates and by quick stock market spurts, as well as by the relatively low interest rates prevalent in industrial countries. It could leave as rapidly as it has entered if any of these conditions change for the worse.

Latin America's economies have made strides, but they are not yet out of the woods. Fiscal deficits have been reduced, and inflation has largely been tamed in most countries, but pressure continues on both counts. The ratio of interest payments to exports has been sharply reduced, but the stock of debt is still dangerously high. Export surpluses have been impressive, but even the modest recoveries now occurring are quickly pushing imports upward again.

On the positive side, some of the obstacles to growth have been eliminated or reduced, many of the bases of sustainable development are now in place, and the gains made by Chile and Mexico suggest that success can be achieved. This surely is notable progress against the disastrous background of the 1980s. If Latin America's external environment is supportive—that is, if growth rates in the industrial countries rebound, if international protectionism is avoided, if interest rates stay low, and/or if further debt relief is achieved—there is good reason to hope that most Latin American economies can continue to advance. But these propitious international circumstances are far from assured, given the persistent sluggishness in the U.S. economy and the signs of a global economic slowdown.

The regional turn toward democracy is also highly vulnerable. Indeed, effective democratic governance in Latin America is unchallenged only in those very few countries—Chile, Costa Rica, Uruguay, and the Commonwealth Caribbean—where democratic traditions were already well implanted thirty-five years ago.

In country after country, polls show that most people still favor democracy as a form of government but are increasingly skeptical of all democratic political institutions. The hard truth is that representative democracy is not being successfully consolidated in most of Latin America. What is often being entrenched instead is what has been called "democracy by default," "delegative democracy," or "low-intensity democracy."[4] Governments that derive their initial mandate from popular elections are tempted to govern "above" parties, legislatures, courts, interest groups, or the organizations of civil society. To the extent that they do, weak institutions are further undermined, accountability is thwarted, public cynicism and apathy grows, and legitimacy is eroded. This syndrome poses the danger, in several countries, of a slide toward renewed authoritarian rule, although of a different stripe from the anti-Communist military regimes of the 1970s.

The apparent Latin American enthusiasm for cooperation with the United States may also signify something less than meets the eye. In a post–Cold War world, where Europe and East Asia seem to be building economic communities, it is obvious why some Latin Americans want regional integration with North America. But Mexico's avidly pursued goal of a free trade agreement with the United States and Canada has been far from easy to assure. Many South American nations may still conclude that what they can secure in the 1990s from possible accession to NAFTA is not worth the uncertainty and the costs. For several South American nations, it is not at all clear how best to relate to the United States: whether through closer integration or through greater autonomy and more diversified relationships. The choice is especially difficult and important for Brazil—a country twice as large as Mexico, with six times the population of Argentina and twelve times that of Chile, yet with no generally accepted national sense of direction. Although Latin Americans are talking more about regional integration than they have in many years, their very different ways of fitting into the global economy make it unlikely that rapid progress will be made toward a meaningful hemisphere-wide accord.

There is greater convergence in the Americas, North and South, on political values and economic fundamentals than ever before, but a hemispheric political community is still far from being achieved. Agreement in principle within the OAS on collective measures to protect democracy, although a notable accomplishment, has been hard to put in practice in the cases of Haiti and Peru, amid disagreement about whether, how, and how long to impose sanctions. Although talk of dependency is no longer fashionable, resentment in Latin America about the stance and style of the United States lurks not far below the surface. The recalcitrant U.S. role at the Rio environmental summit in 1992, the Supreme Court's decision to let stand the U.S. government's seizure of a Mexican citizen in his own country, and the extraterritorial application of the Cuban trade embargo approved by Congress in the midst of the 1992 U.S. presidential campaign have all brought this resentment to the fore. In much of Latin America, there is continuing wariness about possible U.S. interventionism—now no longer justified by anticommunism but motivated instead by human rights, democracy, drugs, environmental degradation, or the proliferation of deadly weapons. The election of President Clinton and the Democrats, moreover, accentuated concerns in some quarters about the prospect of rising U.S. protectionism and deeper conflict on economic issues.

## Is the United States Ready for Partnership?

President Bush's Enterprise for the Americas Initiative—promising a reduction of Latin America's official debt owed to U.S. government agencies, offering aid to facilitate investment in the region's economic recovery, and holding out the prospect of free trade agreements—provided a positive, if sketchy, vision of how inter-American relations should evolve in the 1990s. It reflected the Bush administration's inchoate recognition that Western Hemisphere partnerships would be helpful to the United States now that the Cold War competition is over, old alliances are breaking up, new international rivalries are intensifying, and global challenges to the environment, health, arms control, and governance are taking center stage.

The Bush administration began to translate its vision into policy, but it did not get very far. It succeeded in getting a NAFTA text negotiated with Mexico and Canada and in submitting it for congressional approval on a "fast-track" basis, but it did not adequately consider environmental and labor issues, nor did it successfully persuade the U.S. public of NAFTA's benefits. Moreover, congressional appropriations for the proposed multilateral investment fund and authorization of debt-reduction agreements were slow to materialize. Latin America's interest in prospective regional partnerships was aroused, but the United States under Bush was not able to deliver much.

The main reason for this shortfall was the domestic difficulties facing the United States. Proposals to reduce Latin America's debt, facilitate U.S. investment in the region, or open U.S. markets cannot be implemented unless they are part and parcel of an overall strategy for restoring dynamism to the U.S. economy. Domestic U.S. interests—small business, organized labor, and particularly affected firms and communities—understandably oppose proposals to aid Latin America's development if they think that the region's prosperity will come at their own expense. They will reject Western Hemisphere partnerships unless they understand clearly why it is in the interest of the United States for Latin America to succeed.

There are, indeed, reasons to believe that Latin American prosperity is, objectively, of considerable importance to the United States, more so than has been subjectively recognized until recently. Although some observers predicted at the end of the Cold War that Latin America would disappear from Washington's map, the region has actually grown in real significance for the U.S. policy community during the 1990s.

Latin America's first value for the United States is economic. As the region's countries emerge from recession, Latin America has once again become the fastest-growing market for U.S. exports, as it was in the 1970s. Latin American countries are buying more than $65 billion of U.S. exports a year, more than Japan or Germany, and the rate of increase in U.S. exports to Latin America recently has been three times as great as that for all other regions. Latin America's importance as an export market is all the greater at a time when U.S. dependence on trade has increased and when regaining export competitiveness is a central U.S. aim. Investment opportunities for U.S. firms are also expanding, as prospects for recovery and enlarged markets make Latin America attractive and as investors realize that the region's combination of resources, infrastructure, an educated work force, and long experience with market economies make it a better bet than the former Communist countries. Latin America also remains the source for nearly 30 percent of U.S. petroleum imports, and several U.S. money-center banks still make a significant share of their income there.

Latin America's second significance is related to its effect on major problems facing U.S. society. The most dramatic example is narcotics. Latin American countries supply almost all the cocaine, most of the marijuana, and an increasing share of the heroin that enters the United States. Although the drug curse can ultimately only be reduced by cutting internal demand, an effective antinarcotics campaign will also require enduring cooperation by the Latin American nations where narcotics are cultivated, processed, and trafficked. Another illustration is the environment. As the site of some of the world's largest rain forests and as leading destroyers of them during the past few years, Latin American countries are also central actors on ecological issues and crucial test cases of the prospects for sustainable development policies.

A third significance of Latin America is as a prime arena, together with the former Soviet Union and the countries of Eastern and Central Europe, for the core U.S. values of democratic governance and free market economics. As both democracy and capitalism are severely challenged in the former Communist countries, the worldwide appeal and credibility of these ideas may depend importantly on whether the nearest U.S. neighbors can make them work.

Perhaps most important, the burgeoning Latin American pressures for emigration create additional links between the sending countries and the United States and enlarge the U.S. stake in the region's social, economic, and political conditions. Almost half of all legal immigrants to the United States during the 1980s came from Latin America and the Caribbean, together with many more than half of all undocumented entrants. Some 10 percent of the U.S. population today are Latin American immigrants or their descendants, and Latinos are the fastest-growing population group in the United States. Latin Americans no longer come to the United States in isolated or temporary waves but in a sustained flow, blurring the borders between Latin and Anglo America, especially in Florida, Texas, and Southern California. Half the babies born in Los Angeles County in the 1980s were of Latino descent, for instance, as were 63 percent of the students in the county's public schools. The line between "domestic" policy and "Latin American" policy is thus becoming harder to define as the regions of the hemisphere become ever more interconnected. Instead of falling off Washington's map, Latin Americans are helping to redraw it.

If Latin America's advances of the past few years can be fortified and if cooperative inter-American programs can be built, the United States stands to benefit through expanded exports and other economic opportunities, some alleviation of immigration pressures, improved international programs to resolve key problems, and a better chance for the success of core U.S. values. Latin America's potential for partnerships with the United States is now greater than ever, as its politics stabilize and its market-oriented economies shape up.

The United States, in turn, will have a better prospect for success in solving some of its domestic problems (especially creating jobs and managing the rate and impact of immigration) if Latin America can become more prosperous and if inter-American cooperation can be made more effective.

The chances for positive U.S. policies to reinforce Latin American progress and thereby advance U.S. aims depend fundamentally, however, on revitalizing the U.S. economy. The United States cannot successfully implement NAFTA or help build a wider hemispheric economic community if it does not, at the same time, rejuvenate its decaying infrastructure, upgrade its technology, enhance the skills of its work force, retrain displaced workers, and assist uncompetitive industries and their communities to adjust to change. The U.S. public will not support closer economic ties with Mexico or the rest of Latin America if the United States fails to confront its accumulated domestic agenda.

A key question for the 1990s, in effect, is whether the United States itself is ready for inter-American partnerships. President Bill Clinton came to office at a critical juncture. Most Latin American countries were more ready than ever for close cooperation with the United States, and the United States stood to gain from inter-American approaches. But there was also rising skepticism within the United States about liberal internationalist policies.

Unless Clinton can persuade the people of the United States that they have a strong self-interest in Latin America's growth and in hemispheric cooperation, the next few years will likely see, instead, a great deal of inter-American strife over trade and protectionism, commodity prices, advanced technology, arms sales, population growth, immigration, narcotics, and the environment. These frictions will surely intensify if the U.S. public, frustrated by its domestic difficulties, turns to approaches that are protectionist, restrictionist, punitive, and interventionist. The followings generated in the 1992 presidential campaign by Jerry Brown, Pat Buchanan, and Ross Perot revealed a large potential constituency for such approaches, one that Perot has been expanding ever since with his attacks on NAFTA.

It is too early to be sure which way the United States will turn in the rest of the 1990s and into the next century. What is clear and strongly underlined by the chapters of this book is that Latin American nations have responded to the new world by looking north and that much now depends on how the United States behaves. Congressional approval of NAFTA, after a long and difficult fight, is one important step forward, and the successful GATT negotiations comprise another. But the future of inter-American relations will not clarify until the United States is more truly set on a decided course, after a decade of drift.

## Notes

1. Part of this essay is adapted with permission from Abraham F. Lowenthal, "Latin America: Ready for Partnership?" *Foreign Affairs,* 72, no. 1 (1993).

2. George Bush, "Remarks Announcing the Enterprise for the Americas Initiative," White House press release.

3. See Inter-American Dialogue, *Convergence and Community: The Americas in 1993: A Report of the Inter-American Dialogue* (Washington, D.C.: The Aspen Institute, 1992).

4. The quoted phrases are from Giorgio Alberti, an Italian scholar; Guillermo O'Donnell, an Argentine; and Edelberto Torres Rivas, a Guatemalan.

# *Acronyms*

ASEAN    Association of Southeast Asian Nations

BIS    Bank for International Settlements

CACM    Central American Common Market
CAP    Common Agricultural Policy
CECON    Special Commission on Consultation and Negotiation
CEPAL    UN Economic Commission for Latin America
CICAD    Inter-American Drug Abuse Control Commission
COCOM    Missile Control Transfer Regime
CPC    Chinese Communist Party
CPSU    Communist Party of the Soviet Union
CSBM    confidence- and security-building measures
CSCE    Conference on Security and Cooperation

DEA    Drug Enforcement Agency
DFI    direct foreign investment

EBRD    European Bank for Reconstruction and Development
EC    European Community
ECLA    UN Economic Commission for Latin America
ECLAC    UN Economic Commission for Latin America and the Caribbean
EEA    European Economic Area
EFTA    European Free Trade Area

FTA    free trade agreement or free trade area

GATT    General Agreement on Tariffs and Trade
GDP    gross domestic product
GNP    gross national product
GSP    General System of Preferences

IADB    Inter-American Defense Board
IADC    Inter-American Defense College
IAEA    International Atomic Energy Agency

| | |
|---|---|
| IDB | Inter-American Development Bank |
| IEPES | Instituto de Estudos Politicos e Sociais |
| IFI | international financial institutions |
| IMF | International Monetary Fund |
| ISI | import substitution industrialization |
| | |
| LDC | less developed country |
| LDP | Liberal Democratic Party |
| | |
| MAS | Movement Toward Socialism |
| MFN | most favored nation |
| | |
| NAFTA | North American Free Trade Agreement or North American Free Trade Area |
| NATO | North Atlantic Treaty Organization |
| NGO | nongovernmental organization |
| NPT | Non-Proliferation Treaty |
| | |
| OAS | Organization of American States |
| ODA | official development assistance |
| OECD | Organization for Economic Cooperation and Development |
| OECF | Overseas Economic Cooperation Fund |
| | |
| PSDB | Social Democratic Party |
| PT | Workers Party |
| | |
| UNCED | UN Conference on Environment and Development |
| UNEP | UN Environment Program |
| USAID | U.S. Agency for International Development |
| | |
| WHFTA | Western Hemisphere Free Trade Association |

# About the Contributors

José Octavio Bordón, a member of the Argentine Senate (Justicialista party), is the former governor of Mendoza. He is a member of the Inter-American Dialogue.

Jorge G. Castañeda is graduate professor of political science at the National Autonomy University of Mexico (UNAM) and contributes frequently on Mexican and Latin American affairs in the international press. His most recent book is *Utopia Unarmed* (1993).

Jorge I. Domínguez is a professor of government and chairman of the Latin America Program at Harvard University, and he is a member and visiting fellow of the Inter-American Dialogue. His most recent book is *Democracy in the Caribbean* (1993).

Albert Fishlow is the former Dean of International and Area Studies at the University of California, Berkeley, and is a leading authority both on international financial issues and on Brazil. He served in 1975–1976 as deputy assistant secretary of state for inter-American affairs and is a member of the Inter-American Dialogue.

Jesús Silva Herzog, the former finance minister of Mexico, is now Mexico's minister of tourism. He is a member of the Inter-American Dialogue, on leave while he serves as minister.

Kotaro Horisaka is a professor of political science at Sophia University in Tokyo and one of his country's leading specialists on Latin America.

Andrew Hurrell is a university lecturer in international relations and fellow of Nuffield College, University of Oxford. His most recent book is *The International Politics of the Environment*, edited with Benedict Kingsbury.

Osvaldo Hurtado, the former president of Ecuador, directs CORDES, a social science research center in Quito. He is a member of the Inter-American Dialogue.

Helio Jaguaribe, Brazil's former minister of science and technology, directs the Institute for Political and Social Studies in Rio de Janeiro. One of Latin America's foremost social scientists, Jaguaribe's most recent book is *Crisis in the Republic* (1993).

**Celso Lafer,** the former foreign minister of Brazil, is both an industrial executive and a professor of international law at the University of São Paulo. He is a member of the Inter-American Dialogue.

**Abraham F. Lowenthal** directs the Center for International Studies at the University of Southern California. The founding director of the Inter-American Dialogue, he is now a member on its board of directors.

**Sergo A. Mikoyan** was the editor in chief of the academic journal *América Latina* in Moscow for twenty years, after which he became a chief researcher at the Institute of Peace at the Russian Academy of Sciences. Currently, he is a visiting fellow at Georgetown University in Washington, D.C.

**Heraldo Muñoz** is Chile's ambassador to the Organization of American States and president of the Foro Interamericano, a Chile-based effort to promote inter-American exchange on hemispheric issues. A leading scholar on Latin America's international relations, Ambassador Muñoz's most recent book (coauthored with Carlos Portales) is *Elusive Friendship: A Survey of U.S.-Chilean Relations* (1991).

**Barbara Stallings** is director of the Global Studies Program at the University of Wisconsin (Madison) and chair of the Joint Committee on Latin American Studies of the Social Science Research Council and the American Council of Learned Societies.

**Gregory F. Treverton** is vice chairman of the National Intelligence Council of the U.S. government. During the preparation of this volume, he was a senior fellow at the Council on Foreign Relations.

**Richard H. Ullman** is the David K.E. Bruce Professor of International Affairs at Princeton University. His most recent book is *Securing Europe* (1991).

**Alberto van Klaveren,** a Chilean authority on international issues, is research director of Spain's Asociación de Investigación y Especialización Sobre Temas Iberoamericanos (AIETI). He is currently serving as special adviser to the director general of Chile's foreign ministry.

**Feng Xu** is a Ph.D. candidate in international relations at the University of Southern California. A specialist in Latin America, he has studied and taught at Fudan University in Shanghai.

# About the Book

In this book, distinguished international authors offer the first comprehensive analysis of the ways in which Latin America and its role in the global arena are being reshaped by the stunning international changes of the past few years: the end of the Cold War and the breakup of the former Soviet Union; the European Community's expansion and its progress toward enhanced integration; the widespread validation of democratic governance and market economies; the revision of global trade and financial regimes; the tendency toward regional economic blocs; and the underlying changes in the world economy, driven by technological advances.

Coedited by two senior analysts of inter-American relations, *Latin America in a New World* examines the region's international relationships, providing timely, in-depth discussions of the North American Free Trade Agreement, the Mercosur Pact involving Argentina and Brazil, the changing relationship between Cuba and Russia, expanded Chinese involvement in the Americas, and the evolving roles in the Americas of Japan, Russia, and Europe. The essays are complemented by analysis from experienced policymakers from the region, including the former president of Ecuador, the former foreign minister of Brazil, Mexico's minister of tourism, and Chile's ambassador to the Organization of American States.

# Index

253